AMERICAN

LITERARY CRITICISM

SELECTED AND EDITED, WITH AN
INTRODUCTORY ESSAY

BY

WILLIAM MORTON PAYNE, LL.D.

Essay Index Reprint Series

 BOOKS FOR LIBRARIES PRESS
FREEPORT, NEW YORK

First Published 1904
Reprinted 1968

LIBRARY OF CONGRESS CATALOG CARD NUMBER:

68-26465

PRINTED IN THE UNITED STATES OF AMERICA

To get rid of provinciality is a certain stage of culture; a stage the positive result of which we must not make of too much importance, but which is nevertheless indispensable, for it brings us on to the platform where alone the best and highest intellectual work can be said fairly to begin. — MATTHEW ARNOLD.

GENERAL EDITOR'S NOTE

THE Wampum Library of American Literature has been planned to include a series of uniform volumes, each of which shall deal with the development of a single literary species, tracing the evolution of this definite form here in the United States, and presenting in chronological sequence typical examples chosen from the writings of American authors. The editors of the several volumes provide critical introductions, in which they outline the history of the form as it has been evolved in the literature of the world.

Every volume is complete in itself, and wholly independent of its fellows. It contains a large variety of carefully chosen selections taken chiefly from the works of writers now no longer living; and although it has been found advisable sometimes to draw on writings of authors born in the first half of the nineteenth century, no selection has been made from any living American writer whose birth has occurred since December 31st, 1850.

B. M.

PREFACE

THE purpose of this volume is to give an outline of the history of American literary criticism, accompanied by a number of representative examples sufficient to illustrate the chief phases of the development of this department of American literature. The twelve authors from whom selections have been made all belong to the nineteenth century, for within that term is included all the writing having any critical significance thus far produced in this country. The number would be greater had it not been decided to exclude writers born after the middle of the century. In each case the selection made is of a character which seems to illustrate in the most typical manner the critical ideas, methods, and interests of its author. In the mechanical matters of spelling, punctuation, and the like, all the peculiarities of the original texts have been scrupulously preserved. The chronological order of the selections is determined by the birth-dates of their respective authors, rather than by the publication-dates of the essays reproduced.

For permission to reprint the copyright matter included in this volume the following acknowledgments are due: to Messrs. Houghton, Mifflin & Co. for Lowell's "Thoreau," Whipple's "Thackeray," and Stedman's "The Faculty Divine"; to Messrs. Charles Scribner's Sons for Lanier's "The English Novel"; and to Messrs. Harper & Brothers for Howells's "The Art of the Novelist" and "Tolstoy." Both Mr. Stedman and Mr. Howells have joined with their publishers in granting the above permission; and Mr. James has made a special revision of his "Sainte-Beuve" (first published in *The North American Review*) for the purposes of the present volume.

W. M. P.

CHICAGO, August, 1904.

CONTENTS

AMERICAN
LITERARY CRITICISM

INTRODUCTION

THE literature of a nation or a race, in its normal development, is first creative, and then critical. In the creative stage, there is a natural process of growth from instinctive or *naïve* beginnings to the perfection of self-conscious art. The crude folk-song becomes the finished lyric; the popular ballad or tale of legendary heroism becomes the formal epic; and the puppet-show or religious pageant becomes the play, comic or tragic according as it has for its burden the follies of mankind or the deep issues of human fate. Similarly the philosophical historian finds the beginnings of his art in the saga, or the monkish chronicle, or the personal memoirs of the garrulous man of action; and the founder of the metaphysical system derives from those who, in the childhood of the race, first questioned the world with open-eyed wonder, and indulged in fanciful speculations concerning the real, as distinguished from the apparent nature of things. Throughout all this process of development, while there is much criticism implied in the gradual perfecting of the several literary forms, there is practically none in the explicit

sense. But the time comes to every people when,
finding itself in the possession of a considerable body
of works, the bequest of many generations, it turns to
the examination of its inheritance, seeking to account
to itself for the various kinds of excellence in literature, to analyze, to classify, and to formulate the
underlying laws of literary composition. It produces
an Aristotle to expound the philosophy of the drama
and the epic, a Quintilian to penetrate the secrets of
oratorical power, a Boileau to set forth the principles
of the art of poetry, a Lessing to differentiate the
province of poetry from that of sculpture and painting, a Coleridge to view literature in the light of the
eternal verities of the spirit. In a word, the creative
impulse slackens and formal criticism supervenes.
Henceforth, the literature of this people may no
longer be the spontaneous thing that it has been; it
may never again be the product of "that first fine
careless rapture" of the morning of the race.

Through some such development as this the literature of every people must pass — of every people,
that is, which grows up from infancy upon its own
soil. But while the process thus outlined is typically
illustrated by English literature, it is not, of course,
to be looked for in the history of American literature,
which is nothing more than that part of English literature produced in the new world during three centuries
of English occupation. The question here is not of
beginning, but of going on under the conditions of
the new environment. The biological analogy is to
be sought, not in the growth of the tree from the
seedling, but rather in the modifications which the
tree undergoes when, full-grown, it is transplanted to
new soil. Now the invariable consequence of trans-
planting a tree is that all the processes of growth are

retarded. It takes time to recover from the shock of uprooting and then it takes more time to strike root in the new earth and test its powers of sustenance. For a while, it is a question of keeping alive at all; such matters as growth and the putting forth of flowers and fruit must wait until existence has been made secure. This analogy offers a precise explanation of what happened, as far as the production of literature is concerned, when, in the seventeenth century, the civilization of England was transplanted to the eastern coast of North America. The common speech of the time bears witness to the truthfulness of this comparison; the colonies were "planted," and more frequently than anything else were called "plantations."

Bringing with them to the new world, as they did, the inherited culture of centuries, and being, as they were, not men of average ability and enterprise, but the picked men of the race, the English settlers in America might easily enough, as far as we can see, have carried on the literary tradition of the mother country. But the peculiar mixture of religious and political motives which impelled these men to seek new homes in the wilderness operated to select a class of colonists that were not predisposed toward the cultivation of the literary graces. These men, "flying from the depravations of Europe to the American strand," had a more serious task than that of writing poems and plays. In fact, they held literature, in its noblest Elizabethan manifestations, to be chief among those depravations that they were seeking to escape. In sheer intellectual power, Cotton Mather is a fair match for Samuel Johnson, and the contrast between these two autocrats is typical of the contrast between the two societies over which they respectively held sway.   The lives of our New England forbears were strenuous indeed, not in the cheap physical sense, but in the sense of straining for ideal goals, and waging constant battle with the adversaries of the spirit.

It is small wonder, then, that the colonial period of American history produced little literature of the sort that men cherish for its intrinsic worth.   For nearly two centuries our annals are barren in this respect save for an occasional gleam of fancy or imagination, such as could hardly fail to occur in so voluminous and earnest a mass of writing as that which was left us by our early politicians and theologians.   If there were no poems or plays or novels worthy of the name, still less was there anything that might be called literary criticism, during these two centuries of the slow upbuilding of the commonwealth.   Men read books, no doubt, and had opinions concerning them, but these opinions found no published expression of the kind that arrests attention and interests the readers of a later day.   It would be possible to glean from the books and other publications of the seventeenth and eighteenth centuries a considerable collection of haphazard views about literature, but it would not be profitable for the purposes of the present cursory sketch.

Not until early in the nineteenth century did literature in America become what we commonly understand by the term — a product in which artistic considerations prevail over all others.   The preceding centuries had shown much industry in the recording of historical facts, more or less quaintly colored, and in the promulgation of theological and political doctrines, more or less passionately urged.   They had produced a great metaphysician in Jonathan Edwards, and a shrewd commentator upon nature and human affairs in Benjamin Franklin. They had even made an approach to literature proper in the belletristic trifling of the "Hartford Wits," Barlow, Trumbull, and Dwight. But of writing that is attractive by virtue of its literary quality, irrespective of any interest in its historical background or its basis of abstract ideas, we had practically nothing before the romances of Brown and Cooper, the miscellaneous prose of Paulding and Irving, and the poems of the youthful Bryant and his contemporaries. It was at the time when these men were gaining a wide hearing for their work, and giving evidence that America was at last ready to make a distinctive contribution to the common literature of the English people, that our first serious attempt was made to cultivate the hitherto untouched field of literary criticism.

Criticism as a department of literary production presupposes a certain degree of liberal cultivation among readers, and the existence, if not exactly of a leisure class, at least of a class sufficiently detached from the grosser cares of life to be able to take a serious and sustained interest in literature. It also presupposes the existence of suitable vehicles for its publication. Such a class of readers had for the first time appeared during the early decades of the nineteenth century, and such vehicles were provided by the magazines which were then springing up in astonishing profusion. With the exception of perhaps half a dozen, the very names of these periodicals are now forgotten, but they performed an important service for the cultivation of literary interests. Nor must the lecturer be forgotten in this outline of the conditions by which the growth of literary intelligence was stimulated during the earlier part of the century. The Lyceum system played an important part in the development of our national culture, and enlisted the services of many of our best men. Some of these lecture-courses found their way into print and thus appealed to still larger audiences. The lectures of Samuel Lorenzo Knapp (1829), for example, elicited the following comment from an enthusiastic reviewer:

"Long after the puny revilers of American genius shall have supplied the grocer with wrappings and the book-worm with food, the Lectures on American Literature will have a place in the library of the American scholar and minister to the instruction of American youth."

If the fame of Knapp has belied this forecast, the memory of Henry Reed has not wholly lapsed, and his lectures on "English Literature" and on the "British Poets" still find occasional readers. Even John Quincy Adams, who was a man of letters before he became a statesman, was numbered among the lecturers on literary themes, discoursing with no little eloquence and acumen upon rhetoric and oratory, and upon the plays of Shakespeare.

In a letter written by George Ripley a few years before his death to a young and over-zealous admirer who had styled him "the father of literary criticism in the American press," the following passage occurs:

"When I have the pleasure of seeing you again, I will enlighten your youthful mind on the history of American criticism, and you will hide your head in remorse. At present think of Bryant, Verplanck, Cogswell, Henry, God-win, Greeley, Raymond, in New York; Dana, Channing, Tudor, Willard, Sparks, Everett, Palfrey, Willard Phillips, in Boston, — all of whom were distinguished reviewers and critics before my name was ever heard of."

John Nichol, in his "American Literature," adds to this list such names as those of Prescott, Hillard,

Tuckerman, Halleck, and Griswold among our early critics, besides paying tribute to Longfellow, Lowell, and Poe. This array of names is imposing, but it is lacking in discrimination. Some of the names do not count at all in a serious survey of the subject; others of them count only in a minor and secondary way; but a few of them must be reckoned with. Aside from Poe and Lowell, who will be considered later, even a summary review of our earlier critical endeavor should find space to mention Verplanck for his "Discourses on American History, Art, and Literature" as well as for his edition of Shakespeare, Griswold for his several compilations of American poetry, Prescott for his miscellaneous studies in American and European literature, Tuckerman for his "Thoughts on the Poets," and many other volumes of graceful writing, Channing for his "Essay on National Literature" and his "Remarks on Milton," Longfellow for his "Poets and Poetry of Europe," Bryant for his review of Solyman Brown's "Essay on American Poetry," and Dana for his lectures on Shakespeare and his elaborate critical reviews.

It would be invidious to single out any one of these writers as "the father of literary criticism" in America. Perhaps Bryant would come as near as any to deserving that title, by virtue of the article above mentioned, which appeared in "The North American Review" for 1818. But Bryant's critical writing was merely incidental to a career that achieved distinction in other fields, and too inconsiderable in amount to call for much attention. A better case is made out for Richard Henry Dana (1787–1879), who in the years 1817–19 contributed to that Review a number of lengthy critical studies. It is not an

American critic, but one from the other side of the Atlantic, John Nichol, who speaks of certain of these studies as "the most appreciative and subtle criticisms of the English Lake poets that had, up to that date, anywhere appeared." The most important of these studies is a review, filling something like a hundred pages, of Hazlitt's "Lectures on the English Poets," and is a really admirable piece of critical writing done in the approved eighteenth-century manner. It may be noted also that the series of miscellaneous writings of a few years later, which Dana collectively styled "The Idle Man," includes a penetrating critique of "Kean's Acting" — perhaps the most important early example of dramatic criticism in American literature.

The suggestion of a belated eighteenth-century manner in Dana's criticism is not merely accidental. American literature has always, until very recently, shown a tendency to hark back to the English models of an earlier age. This tendency, which seems to have been a consequence of the arrested development resulting from transplantation, was very marked during the seventeenth and eighteenth centuries, and continued to be manifest well down into the nineteenth. Professor Barrett Wendell, who has brought out and illustrated this principle more clearly than any other writer, has made of it, so to speak, the essential formula of American literary development. It falls in, then, with the general character of contemporary writing in this country that our early reviewers should have clothed their opinions in the ponderous garb of the eighteenth-century essayists, and made their pronouncements with a sort of pontifical emphasis. At the very time when British criticism was being refashioned in freer and more flexible forms by such men as Coleridge, Lamb, and Hazlitt, American criticism was still proceeding upon the assumption that literature was a matter of fixed and rigid laws, which it was the duty of the critic to apply to the case in hand with Rhadamanthine sternness.

The seething literary ambitions of the twenties and thirties were by no means confined to Boston, New York, and Philadelphia, the three recognized centres of intellectual activity. Would-be literary centres in various other parts of the country were asserting their claims, and giving them embodiment in new periodical enterprises. In the South, Baltimore had not unfounded pretensions of this sort, and in the West, Lexington and Cincinnati were rivals for recognition. New magazines and reviews were started in the most unexpected places — in Knoxville, Tennessee, in Oxford, Ohio, and in Vandalia, Illinois. In 1849, Oquaqua, Illinois, had aspirations for literary prestige, and tried to persuade Edgar Allan Poe to migrate thither for the purpose of editing a magazine. Dr. W. B. Cairns, in his valuable study of American literature from 1815 to 1833, enumerates over one hundred and fifty periodicals, more or less literary in character, established during that period. Pitiful enough most of them were, no doubt, but they have their place in the history of American culture. A natural consequence of this dispersion of energy was an excessive display of the provincial spirit. Small local rivalries and petty personal jealousies had a more prominent place in criticism than the discussion of principles. Even Poe, the foremost critic of this period, could not always rise above partisanship and sectional prejudice, and his work is frequently marred by the exhibition of an unworthy petulance directed toward the New England writers.

This provincialism had its natural result in the production of a great deal of writing in the form of criticism which was in reality not critical at all. It was mere boastfulness, and its purpose was to make claims in behalf of the writers of this or that section rather than to arrive at disinterested conclusions. It was utterly ephemeral, no doubt, and it seems particularly amusing when we consider that the entire nation which included all these aspiring literary centres was only just beginning to produce books that belonged to literature. Even when this vaunting of the domestic product took the form of an appeal to national pride rather than to a narrowly local self-esteem it was equally amusing in its vainglorious pretensions. The final word upon this tendency was said in " A Fable for Critics."

" But what 's that ? a mass-meeting ? No, there come in lots
    The American Bulwers, Disraelis, and Scotts,
    And in short the American everything elses,
    Each charging the other with envies and jealousies; —
    By the way, 't is a fact that displays what profusions
    Of all kinds of greatness bless free institutions,
    That while the Old World has produced barely eight
    Of such poets as all men agree to call great,
    And of other great characters hardly a score
    (One might safely say less than that rather than more),
    With you every year a whole crop is begotten,
    They 're as much of a staple as corn is, or cotton ;
    Why, there 's scarcely a huddle of log-huts and shanties
    That has not brought forth its own Miltons and Dantes ;
    I myself know ten Byrons, one Coleridge, three Shelleys,
    Two Raphaels, six Titians, (I think) one Apelles,
    Leonardos and Rubenses plenty as lichens,
    One (but that one is plenty) American Dickens,

A whole flock of Lambs, any number of Tennysons, —
In short, if a man have the luck to have any sons
He may feel pretty certain that one out of twain
Will be some very great person over again."

It is to be feared that the tendency thus satirized has not even yet altogether disappeared from American criticism. We are still occasionally bidden to behold in Bryant a poet of the true Wordsworthian stamp, and to discover serious parallelisms between the graceful workmanship of Longfellow and the divine art of Tennyson, while more than one writer of dialect doggerel has been dubbed an American Burns by innocent critics quite devoid of any sense of absolute literary values.

Lowell could afford to say the sharp things that he put into " A Fable for Critics," because he was himself over-zealous, if anything, as a champion of American ideas. His indignation at the condescension of foreigners is familiar to us all, and his aggressive way of resenting their real or fancied slights is sufficiently pronounced to satisfy our most ardent patriots. His sense of humor, however, made him see clearly that much of our early criticism was the result of a determination " to find swans in birds of quite another species." But if, on the one hand, he made good-natured sport of this exaggerated Americanism, on the other, he had no patience whatever with our weak imitation of British models or with our obsequious deference to British opinion. That these qualities were characteristic of our early nineteenth-century literature is evident upon a very cursory inspection. In Bryant's "North American Review" article, already mentioned, the writer finds American poetry " tinged with a sickly and affected imitation of the peculiar manner of some of the late popular poets of

England." And Professor Lounsbury, speaking of
the other matter, says that " it requires a painful and
penitential examination of the reviews of the period
to comprehend the utter abasement of mind with
which the men of that day accepted the foreign estimate upon works written here, which had been read
by themselves, but which it was clear had not been
read by the critics whose opinions they echoed."   In
Lowell's satire, we find this form of subserviency
illustrated by the minor poet, who frankly confesses
that

> " In private we 're always embracing the knees
>   Of some twopenny editor over the seas,
>   And licking his critical shoes, for you know 't is
>   The whole aim of our lives to get one English notice."

At first sight, the attitude thus neatly described may
seem to be the exact opposite of the swaggering
Americanism with which it was frequently associated,
but the paradox is easily explained away.   Bragging,
whether it is done by a man on his own account, or
impersonally in the name of his fellows, usually
results from the sense of inferiority, and an uneasy
feeling that this inferiority is in danger of discovery.
In the defiant inquiry that has so frequently been
made by excited Americans, " What have we to do
with abroad ? " there has nearly always been implied
a tacit recognition of the importance of foreign opinion, and the very vehemence of the demand marks the
anxiety that is felt lest our literary product should not
be taken at our own declared valuation.

Although a considerable part of the American critical writing done before 1840 was characterized by
the faults above set forth, it would be unfair to discuss the subject without saying, in behalf of critics of

the better class, the few words that bare justice demands. Dr. Cairns, in the monograph already mentioned, takes exception both to Lowell's off-hand statement that of " criticism there was none," and to Professor Lounsbury's theory of " abasement of mind." He says:

" There was produced a considerable body of critical writings of which no nation need have been ashamed. The reader is continually surprised to find American criticisms which pronounce verdicts almost identical with those which have been given by the subsequent judgment of seventy-five years — verdicts not alone on the right of books to hold a place in literature, but on the nature of their merits and defects. This is especially true in the case of English works, where, as has already been said, distance gave a chance for a fair view. Such comparisons are always dangerous : but it is probably not rash to say that the judgment of to-day upon Byron, Wordsworth, Scott, and others, was more accurately expressed by the best American criticism than in any reviews of their works that appeared in Great Britain during the same time."

Specific instances of this recognition of British authors by American criticism in advance of their recognition at home are to be found in abundance. Shelley had a more appreciative early following in America than in England. Henry Reed anticipated Matthew Arnold as a devout Wordsworthian. No British critic of the first half of the century quite dared to say about Tennyson what Poe said about him in all sincerity. While upon this subject it may be added that later illustrations of the quick critical receptivity of this country are afforded by men as diverse as Carlyle and Clough, Edward FitzGerald and Herbert Spencer, all of whom found for a time their most serious appreciation on this side of the Atlantic. FitzGerald, indeed, used to refer to himself playfully as "the great American poet," in view of the cordial reception early accorded in this country to his famous Persian paraphrase.

Having thus sketched in brief outline the American critical environment of the first forty years of the century, we are prepared to record the advent of a more important critic than had hitherto appeared. With the entrance into the arena of Edgar Allan Poe (1809–1849) — the *enfant terrible* of American criticism — a new era is opened in this department of our literature. Poe had a fashion of plain speaking that was rather startling, and that was sometimes animated by personal feeling or narrow prejudice, but that illustrated, when viewed as a whole, the application to literature of definite critical principles, and that cleared the air wonderfully. In sheer intellectual power, Poe's critical writing was so much superior to the best of what had preceded it that one might almost be pardoned for saying that this department of our literature began when, in 1835, the "Southern Literary Messenger" engaged his services, first as contributor, and almost immediately thereafter as editor. Poe was a good deal more than a critic, as his friends still occasionally with a certain emphasis remind us, but had he written neither poems nor tales he would occupy an important position in American literature by virtue of his critical writings. These writings are very considerable in amount. How considerable was not fully realized by the public until the appearance (1902) of the "Virginia" edition of Poe under the editorial supervision of Professor James A. Harrison. Of the sixteen volumes of his writings comprised in that edition,

six contain literary criticism only, while still other
volumes give us the important essays on "The Ra-
tionale of Verse" and "The Poetic Principle," the
thirty-eight thumb-nail sketches of "The Literati of
New York City," and the fragmentary "Marginalia."
Nearly one-half of Poe's writings are thus seen to
take the form of literary criticism. While it is true
that a great deal of this work is concerned with men
and books of ephemeral importance, and that much
of it is also disfigured by the introduction of petulant
personalities, it constitutes, nevertheless, a body of
critical writing that has many elements of permanent
value, and that is vastly more important than anything antedating it in American literature.

One of the many prospectuses that Poe at different
times prepared, outlining his projected ventures in
periodical literature, is dated 1841, and yields the
following statement of principles:

"It shall be a leading object to assert in precept, and
to maintain in practice, the rights, while in effect it dem-
onstrates the advantages, of an absolutely independent
criticism; — a criticism self-sustained; guiding itself only
by the purest rules of Art; analyzing and urging these
rules as it applies them; holding itself aloof from all
personal bias; acknowledging no fear save that of outrag-
ing the right; yielding no point either to the vanity of the
author, or to the assumptions of antique prejudice, or to
the involute and anonymous Cant of the Quarterlies, or to
the arrogance of those organized *cliques* which, hanging on
like nightmares upon American literature, manufacture, at
the nod of our principal book-sellers, a pseudo-public-
opinion by wholesale."

Writing just a year later, Poe embodied in the following terms the kernel of his critical doctrine:

" Following the highest authority, we would wish, in a word, to limit literary criticism to comment upon *Art*. A book is written — and it is only *as the book* that we subject it to review. With the opinions of the work, considered otherwise than in their relation to the work itself, the critic has really nothing to do. It is his part simply to decide upon *the mode* in which these opinions are brought to bear. Criticism is thus no ' test of opinion.' For this test, the work, divested of its pretensions as an *art-product*, is turned over for discussion to the world at large — and first, to that class which it especially addresses — if a history, to the historian — if a metaphysical treatise, to the moralist."

The two statements just quoted belong to the author's fullest intellectual maturity, and illustrate at once the fearlessness and the narrowness of his critical practice. He did not always live up to his own principles, but for that the personal equation and the exigencies of hand-to-mouth journalism must be held responsible. His own master in criticism, as far as he recognized one, was Coleridge, and he proved himself a not unworthy disciple. If we adopt from Symonds the classification of critics which distinguishes three types — the judge, the showman, and the natural historian of literature — we shall have to assign Poe to the first class. He was too dogmatic by disposition to be a mere showman, and he lived a full generation too early to be a natural historian. As a pronouncer of judgments, he bears well the most searching of tests. As far as his judgments concern contemporary writers who are worth remembering at all, they have with only an occasional exception been sustained. His instinct for the recognition of new genius was almost unerring, and the writers of his time who had already won recognition were appraised by him at about what posterity has held to be their real worth. He did American criticism the service of lifting it out of provincialism, of bringing into it impersonal standards based upon a well-defined, if a narrow, æsthetic philosophy. It remained for his successors to broaden the basis thus for the first time established upon this side of the Atlantic.

The unscrupulous treatment which Poe's work and memory suffered at the hands of his biographer and literary executor has so darkened the reputation of Rufus Wilmot Griswold (1815–1857) that we are hardly apt to do justice to the services of that industrious editor and anthologist. Although his critical ability was anything but brilliant, and although his compilations — "Poets and Poetry of America," "Prose Writers of America," and "Female Poets of America" (1842–1849) — have long since outlived their usefulness, he was a person of importance in his day, and must not go unmentioned. An even more useful work than Griswold's was that done in the next decade by Evert Augustus Duyckinck, whose " Cyclopedia of American Literature " (1855), the first comprehensive work of its kind produced in this country, had a certain critical value, and remains a useful work of reference for the earlier period. Had Henry Wadsworth Longfellow chosen the vocation of critic rather than of poet, his taste and scholarship would have assured him a high rank; his chief claim upon our attention in the present connection comes from his " Poets and Poetry of Europe " (1845), which considerably widened the horizon of American readers, and foreshadowed the marked interest which was to be taken in foreign literature during the coming years. Among other critical writings of the thirties and forties we may mention Timothy Flint's articles on " Literature in the United States" contributed to the London "Athenæum" (1835), William Hickling Prescott's "Biographical and Critical Miscellanies" (1845), William Gilmore Simms's "Views and Reviews in American Literature, History, and Fiction" (1846), Henry Norman Hudson's "Lectures on Shakespeare" (1848), and George Ticknor's monumental "History of Spanish Literature" (1849). Meanwhile, a literary movement that was both critical and creative, and that was destined to play an important part in American literature, had acquired headway in New England, and to this we must now direct our attention.

New England transcendentalism eludes anything like exact definition. It was not so much a movement as a tendency of thought, not even so much a tendency of thought as an intellectual atmosphere created by a number of concurring influences, — the liberalizing of the old religious dogmatism, the widening of the spiritual outlook, the newly-made acquaintance with the masterpieces of Continental literature, the dallyings with strange philosophies, ancient and modern, and the eager experiments in new modes of living, which ranged all the way from the community life of the Brook Farmers to Thoreau's attempted personal repudiation of the social bond which most of us tacitly acknowledge. We are here concerned with transcendentalism only in its bearings upon the critical appreciation of literature, which practically restricts our attention to "The Dial" of 1840–44, and to the influence of Ralph Waldo Emerson, Margaret Fuller, and George Ripley, the three persons chiefly responsible for that short-lived but significant periodical venture. We should probably regard the period of the forties as the meridian term of transcendentalism, although its influence remained

evident for many years afterward, and made of New
England, down to the time of the Civil War and even
later, one of the most interesting places in the world
to live in. This region, at this time, became the scene
of a sort of provincial Renaissance, curiously match-
ing, on its narrow scale, the lofty thought, the fresh
enthusiasm, the spiritual enterprise, the ardor of intellectual discovery, and also the confused sense of
values, which characterized the great rebirth of the
modern world from its mediæval torpor. An intelligent observer in the mid-year of the nineteenth
century must have seen in the writings of Poe and in
those of the New England transcendentalists the two
leading directive influences in recent criticism. If
unusually intelligent, he would also have seen that,
despite their outward lack of mutual sympathy, these
two influences had been working toward a common
end. Poe made sport of the transcendentalists upon
many occasions, but as a professed Coleridgian, he
may properly be classified as one of their number.

The importance of "The Dial" is out of all proportion to its modest appearance and its brief career.
From our vantage-point of the twentieth century,
looking back upon its contents and their contributors,
we can see how much of the subsequent development
of our culture was potential in its pages. It served as
the forum in which a group of singularly enlightened
and far-seeing spirits gave vent to their opinions upon
all sorts of subjects. It was the vehicle of their
idealism, their impatience of tradition, their zeal for
intellectual discovery, and their passion for political
and social reform. Unlike its namesake of forty years
later, it was not primarily concerned with literature,
although criticism had a large share of its attention.
In its relation to literature, it stood for untrammelled

thought, for the freest individual expression, and for
the advocacy of that theory of culture which Matthew
Arnold long afterwards defined as "getting to know,
on all the matters which most concern us, the best
which has been thought and said in the world." During the first two years of its publication, "The Dial"
was edited by Margaret Fuller. After she had joined
the forces of the New York "Tribune" in 1842,
Emerson succeeded her in the editorship, and piloted
the frail and ill-ballasted periodical craft through the
two remaining years of its existence. Ripley was
identified with the management throughout, and his
sagacity in practical affairs doubtless served to keep
it afloat longer than would have been possible without
his support.

The most cursory sketch of literary criticism in
America must say something about Ralph Waldo
Emerson (1803–1882), and yet we do not often think
of him in the character of a critic of literature. Every
reader of his essays knows how richly they are furnished with allusions to works of literature and illustrations taken from its domain, but these matters are
by the way, as it were, and we are as baffled in our
search for any body of critical doctrine as in our
endeavor to reduce to a system the philosophical
teaching of the essays. There are about seventy-five
of these essays and addresses altogether, and not more
than half a dozen of them have literature in the more
specific sense for their subject-matter. In the essays
on "The Poet" and "Books," and in two or three of
the lectures on "Representative Men," Emerson keeps
closer to literature than elsewhere, but even in these
works his purpose seems to be the inculcation of general ideas rather than the intensive examination of
any phase or section of literary production. When

he takes literature for the text of his discourse, it seems to be for the express purpose of leading us away from it into some region of abstract thought which belongs to religion, to ethics, or to general æsthetics quite as much as it belongs to literature. With him, literature is always subordinated to life, and life itself, if not exactly subordinated to thought, is held to receive its chief significance from the light cast upon it by the reflective mind. It is, then, only in a very broad sense that we are to look to Emerson for literary criticism; he teaches that books "are for nothing but to inspire," and that every reader should be his own critic. He would have been the last man in the world to call a book good or bad because of its agreement or disagreement with some canon of Aristotle or Lessing; for him the true test of literary virtue is to be found in the direct personal appeal of the book to its reader. Does it say "that which lies close to my own soul, that which I also had wellnigh thought and said?" If so, it is a good book — for me. Does it "pin me down, does it impede the free action of my spirit?" Then it is a bad book — for me — however high it may rank in the history of culture. Emerson's critical method, as far as he had such a thing, is thus seen to be clearly subjective; for him all objective standards have little or no meaning, and the attempt to enforce them upon literary production is sure to be mischievous.

We have already noted the intimate association with "The Dial" of Miss Fuller and Dr. Ripley. These two writers claim attention as the first of our professional critics, for Poe, in spite of the amount of his critical writing, hardly deserves that title. Sarah Margaret Fuller (1810–1850) has the further distinction of being the most important American woman of letters before the middle of the nineteenth century. A forced education and a somewhat morbid childhood, followed by some years of teaching, prepared her for the position of leadership that she occupied for a time among the transcendentalists and in the literary society of Boston. After she had done with " The Dial " and Brook Farm, she went to New York, where she lived in the home of Horace Greeley, and was for two years the literary critic of the " Tribune." Her scattered critical writings, although the best of them were afterwards collected into volumes, have slight permanent value, and their interest for us is mainly historical. She did much to extend our acquaintance with the masterpieces of European literature, and especially with the works of Goethe, acting as both commentator and translator.

" It has been [she says] one great object of my life to introduce here the works of those great geniuses, the flower and fruit of a higher state of development, which might give the young who are soon to constitute the state, a higher standard in thought and action than would be demanded of them by their own time. I feel with satisfaction that I have done a good deal to extend the influence of the great minds of Germany and Italy among my compatriots."

It was characteristic of Margaret Fuller's mind to view " with satisfaction " her own achievements. Self-consciousness and the Sibylline pose are everywhere manifest in her writings, and prevent them from being exactly charming. She took herself very seriously, and was without the saving grace of humor. Her expression, moreover, was stilted and marked by mannerisms, her style was rhapsodical and inorganic. But she took a broader view of the critical function than had hitherto obtained in this country, and was

notably prescient when she urged the claims of that
mode of criticism

" which enters into the natural history of everything that
breathes and lives, which believes no impulse to be entirely
in vain, which scrutinizes circumstances, motive and object
before it condemns, and believes there is a beauty in each
natural form, if its law and purpose be understood."

With a certain resemblance to Mrs. Browning in her
education and interests, she is also suggestive of
Mme. de Staël in her pioneer work for extending
the acquaintance of her countrymen with foreign
literature.

" A Socinian Minister, who left his pulpit to reform
the world by cultivating onions " — this is Carlyle's
characterization of Dr. George Ripley (1802–1880),
whose career as a Unitarian preacher and as a pillar
of the Brook Farm community need not further concern us. But Ripley had begun to write articles as
early as 1830, and he was actively associated with
" The Dial" during the whole period of its existence.
Two years after the Brook Farm experiment ended
in 1847, he began the connection with the New York
" Tribune" which lasted until his death. For this
period of over thirty years he was an untiring literary worker, and great quantities of criticism flowed
from his facile pen. At the height of his activity we
find him writing at the rate of six columns a week
for the " Tribune," besides doing much outside work
for " Harper's Magazine" and other periodicals, and
editing, with C. A. Dana, the " New American Cy-
clopædia." He was a critic of wide range, optimistic
in temperament and kindly in disposition, concerned
more with ideas than with the form of their expression, and, as the natural consequence of his early

training and occupation, largely occupied with religious and philosophical subjects. In one respect he is almost unique among American authors. An early volume of sermons and a controversial pamphlet were his only independent publications. The two volumes of essays, to be called "Books and Men," which he projected in 1862, were never printed, probably never even selected. Practically the entire mass of his writing was of the ephemeral sort, and yet he was one of the most influential writers of his country and generation, and fairly deserved the recognition accorded him when, two years after his death, a volume in the series of "American Men of Letters" was devoted to his life and work.

Also a professional critic in the stricter sense of the term, Edwin Percy Whipple (1819–1886) next claims our attention. He was a highly cultivated Bostonian, most of whose critical essays were prepared for the Lyceum platform, and addressed to hundreds of audiences in many parts of the country. These essays, collected into a series of nine volumes, occupy an honorable place in our prose literature, although they no longer have anything like their former constituency of readers. Their publication covered a period of forty years, during the greater part of which time Whipple devoted his entire activity to their preparation and delivery. He enjoyed much popularity, and was extravagantly praised by a public not given to nice discrimination. His style was earnest, vigorous, and at the same time polished; his essays were enriched by apt quotations, and made attractive by a liberal use of illustration and anecdote. In point of æsthetic appreciation he lacked delicacy, and did little more than repeat the conventional judgments of his predecessors. His insistence upon the ethical aspects of literature was an important element in his popular success. He was a critic of the expository type, aiming to interpret the inner experience of the writers whom he studied rather than the outward forms of their utterance, and always to represent literature in its relation to life. Conservative in temperament, he faced the past rather than the future, and had little sense of the significance of new modes of thought and methods of expression. Most of his nine volumes are miscellaneous collections; his "Literature of the Age of Elizabeth," which is perhaps the best of them, is his only work dealing with a single subject in an extended way. His influence has not proved enduring, but it was on the whole stimulating and helpful to the reading public of the last generation.

The Elizabethan poets (and Chaucer) also inspired the first critical venture of the writer whose rank as the foremost of American critics is beyond dispute. James Russell Lowell (1819–1891) published in 1845 the "Conversations on Some of the Old Poets," his first prose book. Three years later appeared his satire in verse, "A Fable for Critics." For the first thirty years of his literary activity, the poet overshadowed the critic, but with the publication of "Among My Books" (1870) and "My Study Windows" (1871), it became evident that with the poet was combined a critical writer superior in both knowledge and insight to any who had preceded him. A second series of "Among My Books" (1876) deepened the impression made by the first. These three volumes of essays, chiefly made up from the author's contributions to "The Atlantic Monthly" and "The North American Review," both of which periodicals he had for a time edited, are mainly studies in literary criticism, although a few of the essays lie outside that field. Their subjects include, to mention only the writers of enduring reputation, Chaucer, Spenser, Shakespeare, Milton, Dryden, Pope, Wordsworth, Keats, Carlyle, and Swinburne, in British literature, Emerson and Thoreau in American literature, and Dante, Lessing, and Rousseau in Continental literature. A later volume (1886) added Fielding, Wordsworth, and Coleridge to this list. Of two posthumous volumes, the one gave us Gray, Walton, and Landor, and the other an unrevised reprint of the Lowell Institute lectures of 1887, in which the author had recurred to the first subject to occupy his critical attention, and discussed, in the ripeness of his powers, the most important of the Elizabethan dramatists. This long series of critical essays, continued through a period of more than forty years, clearly outweighs the production of any other American critic. It constitutes a body of writing informed by sound scholarship, penetrated by deep sympathy, illuminated by coruscating wit and lambent imagination. It is the expression of a mind so richly stored and so quick in its response to the stimulus of literature that the average reader becomes breathless in his endeavor to keep pace with it. Its very faults are a part of its charm, and what Professor Wendell calls its " paradoxical conflict between purity of taste and mischievous extravagance of temper," if not commendable upon high æsthetic grounds, at least saves it from the soporific character that not infrequently attaches to serious criticism. Yet it must be admitted that our delight in Lowell's essays springs in large measure from their revelation of the workings of his own genial intellect. If we could imagine them divested of that element of personality which

keeps them so intensely alive, and reduced to a series
of reasoned arguments and abstract judgments, we
should often be made painfully aware that the arguments were defective and the judgments unsound;
that neither, in a word, resulted from the logical application of a consistent body of critical principles to
the work under discussion. Taking the essays as they
actually are, we are also forced to confess that they
are rambling in structure, and abound in indefensible
vagaries of detail. Such adverse comments must be
made in Lowell's case, when we refrain from making
them in the case of lesser critics, for the very reason
that his work is richer and finer than that of his
fellows, and consequently demands measurement by
standards that we would not think of applying to the
work of men like Whipple and Ripley, or even to
the product of the pronounced but narrow genius of
Poe. But when all these reservations have been
made, the final verdict must probably be registered
in some such terms as these of Professor Charles
Eliot Norton:

" There are no literary studies in the language more instinct with the true spirit of critical appreciation, none
which may serve better as an introduction not merely to
the work of special poets, but to English poetry in general."

During the last half-century literary criticism, the
world over, has undergone a marked transformation
of method and aim. No longer content, as in the
past, with the analysis, exposition, and judgment of
literary productions, it has come to realize that its
business is also to account for them. That is, it
must do what it can to explain the conditions under
which a work is produced, show how it has been
moulded by the form and pressure of the time and

place in which it has appeared, and seek also to bring it into its proper historical relations with what has gone before. A powerful impetus toward this new trend of criticism was given by the publication of Taine's masterly account of the history of English literature, which minimized the importance of personality in literary production, and insisted upon the all-important influence of environment and racial characteristics. Although this influence was over-emphasized by Taine and his followers, his work in pointing it out was salutary, and permanently enlarged the scope of criticism. At the same time that the doctrine of Taine was making itself felt, the philosophy of evolution was finding its way into men's minds, and gradually working a vast transformation in their outlook upon nature, society, and art. Once fixed in the consciousness, the evolutionary doctrine acted as a universal solvent upon the artificial distinctions and classifications of the past; all fixity of natural type was seen to be illusive, and the rigid definitions of science came to be viewed in their true character as ideal constructions serving a provisional purpose. No department of thought has remained unmodified by the evolutionary organon, and literary criticism has come quite noticeably under its influence. It has been applied consciously and systematically to the study of literature by such men as Symonds and Brunetière, and it is traceable, at least as a semi-conscious influence, in the work of the newer schools of criticism everywhere.

In this country, which thus far has not made of criticism the serious business that has been made of it in France, Germany, and England, we cannot point to many deliberate and thoroughgoing applications to literature of the evolutionary principle.

Nevertheless, we may find it clearly at work, by implication rather than by direct expression, in many quarters. Poe died long before it was in the air, but Emerson had prophetic glimpses of it, and his later essays show some traces of its direct influence. Whipple and Lowell remained until the end almost untouched by it, but Walt Whitman (1819–1892), born in the same year with them, felt the ferment in his receptive but unregulated mind, and many passages crop out in his writings to prove him a sort of inchoate evolutionist. From a professional rhapsode we do not expect formal criticism, and we certainly do not get it from Whitman, but his prefaces to the several editions of " Leaves of Grass " are documents that cannot be ignored, and there is much pregnant critical suggestion in his " Democratic Vistas," his essay on " Poetry To-day in America," and his random comment on Burns and Carlyle, on Shakespeare and Tennyson. If we do not distinctly gather the meaning of his pleas for democratic poetry and his diatribes against the feudal spirit in literature, our study of his prose is far from going unrewarded, for it brings us into contact with a rugged and interesting personality, and convinces us that genuine ideas are struggling for expression in his uncouth and formless paragraphs.

After Poe, the most important critic (as well as poet) produced by Southern influences was Sidney Lanier (1842–1881), whose life, like that of his chief predecessor, was cut too short for the full realization of its powers. Poetry and music were Lanier's leading interests, but in his later years he turned more and more to criticism, convinced that it needed to be re-established upon a scientific basis, and persuaded that he had the power to be helpful in such a reconstruction. How strongly he felt on this subject appears in his complaint embodied in a letter to E. C. Stedman, that, "in all directions the poetic art is suffering from the shameful circumstance that criticism is without a scientific basis for even the most elementary of its judgments." His critical writing is contained in "The Science of English Verse," "The English Novel and the Principles of Its Development," "Shakespeare and His Forerunners," and the volume of essays entitled "Music and Poetry." These works suffer under a twofold disadvantage. They were (except the last) prepared as courses of lectures, and their publication (except in the case of the first) was posthumous, and consequently without revision. Both in his verse and his criticism Lanier rather forced the relation between poetry and music, and his scholarly equipment was inadequate to the ambitious tasks which he set himself in these lecture-courses that were afterwards made into books. But he brought to his discourses upon literary art the insight of a poet and the sympathies of a richly-endowed nature, and these qualities are sometimes better worth while than a gift for abstract theory. In Lanier's case, they go far to make up for technical limitations, and to outweigh his defects.

New York journalism has already been brought into this sketch through the connection of Margaret Fuller and George Ripley with the literary editorship of the "Tribune." With that newspaper the labors of James Bayard Taylor (1825–1878) are also associated, and with other newspapers the names of Richard Grant White (1821–1885) and Richard Henry Stoddard (1825–1903). Taylor wrote a good deal of criticism of scholarly character, but his chief service to literature, aside from his creative work, was done in his translation of "Faust," with its rich accompaniment of apparatus. Apart from this, two posthumous volumes, "Studies in German Literature" and "Critical Essays and Literary Notes," must stand for the more lasting part of his work. White is chiefly to be remembered for his Shakespearian work and his discussions of verbal usage rather than for critical writing pure and simple. Stoddard industriously wrote criticism for newspapers and periodicals during a long term of years, but it was mostly fragmentary and ephemeral. A lengthy essay on Poe, prefaced to an edition of that writer's works, is probably his most important critical study, although an interesting collection of other essays might doubtless be made from the newspaper and periodical files of the past fifty years.

Connected also for a time with New York journalism, and intimately associated with the men just mentioned, Edmund Clarence Stedman (1833–) claims far more serious consideration in his critical capacity. Himself a poet of no mean achievement, he has chosen poetry for the special field of his studies, which are embodied in a series of three volumes, — "Victorian Poets," "Poets of America," and "The Nature and Elements of Poetry." The first two volumes give us the most complete discussion in existence of the main body of later nineteenth-century poetry in the English language, while the third is a general treatise which serves as their "natural complement," and was prepared for delivery in 1891 as the first course of Turnbull lectures to be given at the Johns Hopkins University. The three volumes together are of such weight and authority that they make Stedman second only to Lowell among American critics. Their author even has the advantage

over Lowell in certain respects; he has a consistent
foundation of principle, and he occupies the stand-
point of modern thought. How consciously he takes
this position may be illustrated by his own words :

" Nor can any work henceforth be an addition to the
literature of the subject, which fails to recognize the obligation of treating it upon scientific lines. For no one feels
the steadfast energy of science more than do the poets
themselves, and they realize that, if at first it caused a dis-
enchantment, it now gives promise of an avatar."

It is the distinguishing quality of Stedman's work
that, while abreast of the modern world, its sensibility
has not become blunted by too much knowledge, and
that it is no less keenly receptive than the best older
criticism to the appeal of pure beauty. It is the product of an eager and finely-organized intellect, which
makes the best of the old and the new alike, which
is both generous in its sympathies and contagious in
its enthusiasms. It recognizes the fact that literary
art must have its underlying laws, and goes far to
reduce them to their philosophical statement; but it
also recognizes the other fact that the workings of
genius evade exact calculation, and its manifestations
are almost infinite in their variety. While Stedman's
criticism is fundamentally objective and scientific, it
is at the same time the expression of a rich and
interesting personality, intensely alive, felicitous in
its use of " wise saws and modern instances," and saturated with the subject of its discourse. It is criticism which satisfies the ideal expressed in the author's
own words :

"which applies both knowledge and self-knowledge to
the test; which is penetrative and dexterous, but probes

only to cure ; which enters into the soul and purpose of a work, and considers every factor that makes it what it is."

The poet turned critic has been illustrated by Stedman, Lanier, Whitman, Lowell, and Poe. The novelist also becomes the critic on occasion, and our chief illustrations of this particular versatility are found in Howells and James. William Dean Howells (1837–) has done a great deal of discursive writing about books, and done it in so genial a fashion as to disarm the opposition even of those who are farthest from sharing in his opinions. His unaffected enjoyment of good literature, and his *naïve* assumption that all the literature he likes must be good, are made evident in the very personal confession which he calls " My Literary Passions." The title of the book exemplifies the spirit in which all his literary comment is made ; he is frankly subjective, and his criticism hardly pretends to be an act of reasoned judgment. It seems to be written without much regard to standards, and exhibits strange personal vagaries. A passage which has aroused much sarcastic discussion may be given by way of illustrating the lengths to which the subjective method may take a critic :

" The art of fiction has, in fact, become a finer art in our day than it was with Dickens and Thackeray. We could not suffer the confidential attitude of the latter, nor the mannerism of the former, any more than we could endure the prolixity of Richardson or the coarseness of Fielding."

The grain of truth embodied in this dictum is obvious, but the expression of opinion is unfortunate. Henry James (1843–) is a critic of far more serious quality, for he applies ideas to the literature about which he writes, and the marvellous subtlety which he has acquired in many years of novel-writing stands him in good stead when he comes to analyze the work of his fellow-craftsmen. His own temperament, indeed, colors his criticism everywhere, and is chiefly accountable for the charm of the writing, but beneath the exhibition of the author's personality there is a basis of sound principles, which show an excellent balance of the intellectual, artistic, and ethical elements. Nothing, for example, could be truer and finer than this remark about the moral element in literature:

"It is in reality simply a part of the essential richness of inspiration — it has nothing to do with the artistic process and it has everything to do with the artistic effect."

His judgments are rarely at fault, and are expressed with a delicacy of shading such as few, if any, other American critics have equalled. His overwrought style assuredly finds justification in his critical essays, however we may complain of its use in the author's fiction.

Of essayists who have incidentally been critics, some have already been named, and others, with a certain hesitation, omitted. Such of the earlier essayists as Irving, Paulding, Willis, and Thoreau, although they occasionally touched upon literature, have not seemed to call for discussion in the present connection, and for similar reasons we must be content with the mere mention of such later essayists as George William Curtis, Charles Dudley Warner, Donald Grant Mitchell, and John Burroughs. The work of Horace Elisha Scudder (1838–1902) comes more distinctly within our purview, for it includes the volume of essays entitled "Men and Letters,"

and the important memoirs of Taylor and Lowell.
Thomas Wentworth Higginson (1823–) has been
many things besides — preacher, soldier, historian,
and poet — but he has been a discerning critic at the
same time, and we could ill spare his intimate discussions of his New England contemporaries. Ham-
ilton Wright Mabie (1845–) has written gracefully,
and even with eloquence, upon literature both past
and present; he has realized more fully than most
writers do the deep significance that the great spirits
of the ages have for our modern lives, and has been
unwearying in exhorting as to keep in touch with our
Homer and Plato, with our Dante and Shakespeare
and Goethe. He is a critic of ideas rather than of
forms, an apostle of ideals rather than of literary
methods.

The men mentioned in the preceding paragraph
have done their work outside the institutions of higher
learning. Another important group must be made up
of the men who have worked in and from the univer-
sities. Any sketch of our subject would be painfully incomplete that did not mention Charles Eliot
Norton (1827–), and yet no list of his publications
can give an adequate notion of his far-reaching and inspiring influence upon the whole modern generation
of writers, both in America and England. Something similar must be said of Francis James Child
(1825–1896), although his was an influence mainly
exerted in one special field of scholarship. In the
case of Thomas Raynesford Lounsbury (1838–) we
find the more tangible evidences of critical activity that
are represented by his masterly studies in Chaucer
and Shakespeare. Henry Augustin Beers (1847–)
has done valuable service to criticism, especially in
the two volumes of his history of " English Roman-

ticism." Hjalmar Hjorth Boyesen (1848–1895), whom we may fairly claim as an American critic, since all his manhood was spent in this country and all his work written in English, has left us many interesting studies of German and Scandinavian literature. And it is to Moses Coit Tyler (1835–1901) that we owe the most thoroughgoing treatment, both critical and historical, that has thus far been given to our early American literature. This survey of the work in literary criticism done by men who are engaged in university teaching might be extended much further were it not for the time-limit which has been set for the present series of volumes. Men born later than 1850 are excluded from the scope of the series, and this arbitrary demarcation cuts off a great number of praiseworthy writers, most of whom are teachers as well as critics. Our closing word shall violate the injunction for a moment, in order to name Charles Francis Richardson (1851–), Barrett Wendell (1855–) and William Peterfield Trent (1862–), who deserve this distinction as the authors of the three most important continuous histories of American literature that have thus far been written. All three are admirable books, and are genuine contributions to the literature of criticism in the United States.

RICHARD HENRY DANA

1787 – 1879

ALEXANDER POPE

[*From a review of Hazlitt's " Lectures on the English Poets."
Published in " The North American Review," 1819. Reprinted in
"Poems and Prose Writings," by Richard Henry Dana. 2 vols.
N. Y. 1850.*]

IT is somewhat puzzling to ascertain what our author's
notions of poetry really are. At one time neither
mere descriptions of natural objects, nor mere delineations
of natural feelings, constitute poetry; but there must be
imagination and passion, and an uneasy, restless sense of
beauty, which is only to be relieved by connecting itself
with images of beauty and grandeur, to be thrown off from
the mind, and then to come floating before us accompanied
by modulated sounds harmonizing with them.   Words, too,
must be as pictures to our minds. — But presently he overtakes one who has few or none of these qualities, all of a
sudden becomes extremely intimate with him, and straightway turns round, contradicts all he has said before, and
falls to abusing those who had gone peaceably along with
him from his starting.   He has now a new matter in hand,
and without a very clear notion what he is to do with it.
Of course, it is worked into a variety of odd forms, and
put to as odd uses.   He is a very Gonzalo in matters of
poetry; and the latter part of his commonwealth is continually forgetting the beginning.

Thus, when he comes upon Pope, doors are straight
shut, curtains dropped, and chandeliers lighted up.   How
brilliant and fascinating every thing and every body appear !
The essence of roses, my Lady, is surely a finer perfume
than the rose unexpressed !   And those perennial flowers,

too, that give such dazzling brightness to the eye, blooming in a light where nothing withers, but all is warmed, — how much happier in their lot than those that perish under the oppressive sun! Yes, so that he can talk of them in taffeta phrases, silken terms precise, he neither sees nor cares that they are paint and rags. Quite natural, too, upon my word! — Yes, the crackling, ill-savoured things, very like to honest out-of-door flowers, and as fragrant of the fields as Pope himself!

It is not merely because Pope wrote so much upon manners and fashions, — upon what we term the artificial, — so many now-a-days deny, that, in the strictest and highest sense of the term, he is a poet; although it is true that a prevailing disposition for such subjects indicates a defective poetic temperament and genius. Without dwelling upon this point, it may be said, that, let the subject be what it may, a poetic mind will permeate it with its own poetic character. Shakspeare is the poet everywhere and in all companies. Whether he argues or moralizes, is witty or sentimental, he dwells in a poetical atmosphere, and whatever he has to do with takes its tone from it. The same may be said of most of his contemporaries, and, with some qualification, of a few of the poets yet living, and of others who not long ago died. But rarely indeed does Pope touch the heart, or awaken our associations with those things to which the mind naturally goes in its poetic moods. And when does he fire the passions, or burst as with a glory over our heads?

No one questions his wit, his keenness, or good common-sense, or denies him the merit of expressing his moral sentiments with plainness and vigor, — although the best apology that is made for the scheme of his Essay on Man is, that he did not understand himself. But these qualifications do not of themselves constitute poetry; and to partake of it at all, they must have had their life in a poetic temperament, must have been moulded by poetic thought, and have been associated with poetic images. Nor will

their having been measured into verse make them poetry,
— for measured verse is not always the poetic voice.

Among the English satirists, Pope has been generally
placed next to Dryden, by some ranked as his equal.
Upon the difference between them Mr. Hazlitt remarks : —

"His Satires are not in general so good as his Epistles.
His enmity is effeminate and petulant from a sense of weakness, as his friendship was tender from a sense of gratitude. I
do not like for instance, his character of Chartres, or his characters of women. His delicacy often borders upon sickliness ;
his fastidiousness makes others fastidious."

And again, speaking of Dryden : —

"Mac Flecknoe is the origin of the idea of the Dunciad ;
but it is less elaborately constructed, less feeble, and less heavy.
The difference between Pope's satirical portraits and Dryden's
appears to be this in a good measure, — that Dryden seems to
grapple with his antagonists, and to describe real persons ;
Pope seems to refine upon them in his own mind, and to make
them out just what he pleases, till they are not real characters, but the mere drivelling effusions of his spleen and malice.
Pope describes the thing, and then goes on describing his own
description till he loses himself in verbal repetitions. Dryden
recurs to the object often, takes fresh sittings of nature, and
gives us new strokes of character as well as of his pencil."

Aside from the philosophy of Pope's views respecting
man, — if philosophy it must be called, — his Epistles, but
more especially the Prologue to his Satires, and his Imitations of Horace, are the most satisfactory to us of all his
writings. Beside their fine wit, they are full of capital
remark growing out of the observation of a sensible man
who had been long conversant with society. To be sure,
there is no attempt in them to rise above the world, and
this is well ; for besides that it would have ill sorted with
their general character, it would have been but an attempt,
as Pope had not the eagle's wing for such ascents. Subjects like these, when treated in such a form, tend to

sententiousness and to plainness of speech; so that here
Pope is more compact and logical in his use of words than
he is elsewhere. Where all, too, is on a level, that balance
and monotony of versification, which so wearies us in his
other writings, is less noticed from its falling in better with
the general character of the work. How far this compact-
ness, plainness, and logic of words was the result of the
paraphrastic and imitative character of these writings, and
placed them, in this particular, above his other works, we
cannot now stop to consider. That it was somewhat a
consequence there can be little doubt, and as little that
just so far it detracts from his merit.

As Pope has been denied to possess imagination, Mr.
Hazlitt claims for him fancy, — a claim which is immediately allowed, for up starts before us the Rape of the
Lock, with its fairy creatures. It would be as unnecessary
as difficult to show that these beings are original creations
of our poet. It is enough that they are not mere copies
of any particular writer, that they are self-congruous, and
adapted to their new offices and circumstances.

But allowing its full merit to this extraordinary work of
the fancy, we must remember that fancy has its modifications, being sometimes tinged with the ingenious, conceited,
and curious; and, again, glowing with the solely and highly
poetical, and even so blending with that higher faculty, the
imagination, as to be hardly distinguished from it.

Now, with all the lively talents shown in the Rape of the
Lock, and sprightly and delicate as its supernatural beings are,
its fancy seems to us to be modified by the former qualities
of mind, rather than by the latter and higher faculty. Indeed, where the fancy is called out in sprightly satire, it is
more likely to partake of the ingenious than of the poetic,
though this is not the tendency of graver satire. And in
whatever approaches to parody, travesty, or any form of the
mock character, still more likely is this to be the case, and
fancy to be merged in cleverness and a certain species of
wit. Parody, travesty, or the like, however near it may

seem to come to poetry, and however generally it may be taken for it, gives no assurance, but rather the contrary, of the writer's success in works of an opposite and strictly poetic kind : it is the product of talents rather than of genius, — poetic genius we mean. Now the Rape of the Lock does partake somewhat of this character ; and though we do not intend to dispute its possessing poetic fancy, yet in so far as it savours of the other character will the principle spoken of more or less apply.

The poem is full of life ; and it is animating to see how briskly at work the author is, how gay upon fashionable follies, and dexterous in setting out a toilet ; how well arranged things are ; and what a show there is of beaux and belles, powdered heads, craped cushions, fans and furbelows, ruffs, cards, and tea-cups, with all sorts of washes, and essences too, till the senses nigh ache at it.

This taking of supernatural poetic beings from poetic scenes and relations, and shutting them up in a drawingroom, and associating them with the most anti-poetic form of artificial society, is primarily the work of wit rather than of fancy ; and while we would not, for a moment, question the predominance of fancy in the poem, yet is it fancy quickened by the former faculty, wit, and working in its service and wearing its badge : it is fancy owing much of its activity to wit. It is the very reverse of the fairy parts of Midsummer Night's Dream, where what there may be of wit is salient from and subordinated to poetic fancy, — poetic fancy in its amusive mood.

And how do Shakspeare's little creatures divert themselves with honest Bottom ? Why, with fanning the moonbeams from his sleeping eyes with the wings of painted butterflies, caught in their airy chases. Some kill cankers in the musk-rose buds ; some war with rearmice, and others keep back the clamorous owl ; — all their duties and all their language bring before you poetic beings of substance as delicate as the soft air they play in, and doing the offices of poetry. They are not tied up to the leading object, —

a comic one,— as in Pope, but are seen coursing among flowers and silver dew-drops, or just coming into sight through the moonlight, with some trophy of their skill and spirit; yet the main purpose is not neglected. Drayton's Nymphidia, too, partakes of the ludicrous, — but how subordinated to the poetical! Considered in reference to its *poetical* character solely, is it inferior to Pope's work?— While we would not detract a jot from the really great merit of Pope's poem, we would make what we think to be a well-grounded distinction respecting it.

But the English moralist, as he has been styled, has produced one work — at least so says Mr. Hazlitt — in which "the tears shed are drops gushing from the heart: the words are burning sighs breathed from the soul of love." And can Mr. Hazlitt come away from reading the old poets, or the better poets of this day, and take up the Epistle of Eloisa to Abelard, and feel his eyes moisten and heart move? We doubt whether even Mr. Hazlitt is so tenderly constituted as ever to have shed a tear on the occasion.

We quarrel with no one on the point of taste; but it is something more serious when a man can come directly before the lady and gentlemen auditors of the Surrey Lectures, with an intimation of a certain sort, and in language so warm, upon a poem on so gross a subject as this. Yet how can we speak thus, when we find the Rev. Joseph Warton saying of the most offensive line in this licentious poem, — "And then follows a line exquisitely passionate, and worthy the sensibility [sensibility!] of Sappho or Eloisa." — And so they wrap it up, and call the *furor* of appetite passion and sensibility in these dear creatures!

The truth is, Pope's frequent allusions of a certain kind, in his works, show that his mind was tainted; and this, together with the disgusting nature of his subject and his lack of truly poetic sentiment and passion, has made the poem what it is. Fuzeli has well termed it "hot ice." For, with the exception of a few lines of simple passion, — and we must remember that most of these are gathered from the original prose, — it is hot with lust, and cold with false sentiment, vague generalities, sought antitheses, forced apostrophes, and all sorts of artificialities, in the place of natural feeling and plain truth.

But we must leave Eloisa ; for the lamps are dying around, a voice from the shrine summons her to prepare for death, and she bursts away in the following rhapsody : —

> "I come, I come! prepare your roseate bowers,
> Celestial palms, and ever-blooming flowers."

We have spoken of Pope's general closeness and correctness of language in the imitative, satirical, and didactic portions of his works.   With that same want of discrimination which has been shown in other points, he has been praised for these qualities, as if his writings at large partook of them.   On the contrary, few poets of high rank have been so defective in this respect as Pope, when he left satire and moral teaching, for nature and subjects strictly poetical. Here he felt less vividly and saw and thought less distinctly, and, of course, uttered himself too often in generalities, less logically, with less life, definiteness, and adaptedness of terms ; for words are the manifestations of the spirit within. In what commonplace tawdriness is the couplet just now quoted dressed, with its "roseate bowers," and "ever-blooming flowers," — which, we suppose, mean pretty much the same thing.   And here, again, we have "bowery mazes," and "sequestered scenes," and "surrounding greens" : —

> "Ye sacred Nine! that all my soul possess,
> Whose raptures fire me, and whose visions bless,
> Bear me, O, bear me to sequestered scenes,
> The bowery mazes, and surrounding greens."

Not so talked the veritable Eloisa !

> "But e'en those clouds at last adorn its way,
> Reflect new glories, and augment the day."

Whoever talks of clouds *augmenting* the day? or of any

thing else doing so? Nor is *elevates* a fitting term in the
following connection : —

> "It is for thee the lark ascends and sings?
> Joy tunes his voice, joy elevates his wings."

And of a piece with it, or worse, —

> "Or under southern skies exalt their sails."

Exalt a *sail!*

> "Come, with one glance of those deluding eyes
> Blot out each bright idea of the skies."

Beside the illogical combination of words, we ask whether
any small compounder of amatory or complimentary verses
could be guilty of the manufacture of flimsier tinsel? —
"deluding eyes," "glances," and "bright ideas." But this
is called Eloisa and passion. And so, we suppose, is this : —

> "And waft a sigh from Indus to the pole."

And this : —

> "Yet here for ever, ever, must I stay;
> Sad proof how well a lover can obey."

> "Unequal task a passion to resign."

Resign a *passion !* But not only so ; flames, too, must be
resigned : —

> "Here all its frailties, all its flames resign."

> "The transient landscape now in clouds decays."

Better still, we have *decays* as a noun plural, which we
hold to be singular, and which we would hardly have found
here, but for the rhyme's sake : —

> "These ever new, nor subject to decays,
> Spread and grow brighter with the length of days."

Mr. Hazlitt has noticed the frequent recurrence of *sense*
as a rhyming word. There are a few others quite as great
favorites with our poet, coming in full as often, and rather

more inappropriately; such as *display*, *survey*. Then we have *greens* in abundance.

We wish that some one had the patience and curiosity to ascertain the number of times these words occur! For, poor things, they seem to have been kept like a family drudge, to do the service of all or any who happened not to be at hand. We have already quoted lines, for another purpose, in which *scenes* and *greens* occur as rhymes; and here are more : —

> " To paint anew the flowery sylvan scenes,
>   To crown the forests with immortal greens,"

> "Call forth the greens, and wake the rising flowers."

How is one to wake flowers that are already *rising*, unless they get up in their sleep?

> " Her gloomy presence saddens all the scene,
>   Shades every flower, and darkens every green."

Here we have " gloomy," " saddens," " darkness," all in the space of a couplet. And this, too, is called " close writing," we suppose!

And now for a *display*.

> " New graces yearly like thy works display,
>   Soft without weakness, without glaring gay."

> " Beneath the shade a spreading beech displays
>   Hylas and Ægon sung their rural lays."

> " Here waving groves a chequered scene display,
>   And part admit, and part exclude the day."

And, next, for a *survey* of other couplets.

> " The face of nature we no more survey,
>   All glares alike, without distinction gay."

> " There at one passage oft you might survey,
>   A lie and truth contending for the way."

> "Stretched on the lawn his second hope survey,
>   At once the chaser, and at once the prey."

> " Methinks already I your tears survey,
>   Already hear the horrid things they say."

How would a lad, who had written such lines, have fared, had he fallen into the hands of some old master Bowyer? — Helicon and the Pump! But enough of such instances.

Much has been said of the melody of Pope's verse; and, if the term be taken in its most limited sense, as implying the smoothness of single lines, we will not question it. But what can be more wearisomely monotonous (to say nothing of the closes of every line) than the ceaselessly regular return of the cæsural pause? We remember meeting somewhere with examples of this from Pope, in which lines were drawn by the side of the cæsura through long passages, and almost without a bend. But is there not a melody better than this, and with more of rhythm and varying flow? Surely, he had never prayed, or had prayed in vain, —

> " Lend me your song, ye nightingales! O, pour
> The mazy-running soul of melody
> Into my varied verse."

As to " linked harmonies," he was incapable of perceiving them in music, — much less could his spirit utter them in verse. Bowles has said of his Pastorals, what he might have applied to his other poems, — " Warton does not seem sufficiently to discriminate between the softness of individual lines, . . . and the general harmony of poetic numbers." And again, — in too limited a way, however, — " His nice precision of every line prevented, in a few instances, a more musical flow of modulated passages." We may well apply to his versification his own lines, —

> " In wit, as nature, what affects our hearts
> Is not the exactness of peculiar parts;
> 'T is not a lip, or eye, we beauty call,
> But the joint force and full result of all."

It is not this mechanical meting out of the lines alone which wearies you. The effect is increased by the over-frequently inverted form in which the lines are made to terminate in verbs, for the sake of rhyme.

> " Meanly they seek the blessing to confine,
>   And force the sun but on a part to shine,
>   Which not alone the southern wit sublimes,
>   But ripens spirits in cold northern climes."

> " 'T is not enough your counsel still be true;
>   Blunt truths more mischief than nice falsehoods do."

A sufficiently clumsy inversion this last, yet in some degree emulated by the following : —

> " With his own tongue still edifies his ears,
>   And always listening to himself appears."

> " Made for his use all creatures if he call,
>   Say what their use, had he the powers of all."

> " (Her guide now lost) no more attempts to rise,
>   But in low numbers short excursions tries:
>   Content, if hence the unlearned their wants may view,
>   The learned reflect on what before they knew."

Another defect in his versification is the nearness to each other of couplets terminating in the same rhyme. Yet, notwithstanding this fault and that of the very frequent endings in verbs, his rhymes are, after all, allowed by Mr. Hazlitt to be frequently imperfect, and rather to the eye than for the ear.

> " Who now reads Cowley ? If he pleases yet,
>   His moral pleases, not his pointed wit ;
>   Forgot his Elic, nay, Pindaric art,
>   But still I love the language of his heart.
>   Yet surely, surely, they were famous men !
>   What boy but hears the sayings of old Ben ?
>   In all debates where critics bear a part,
>   Not one but nods, and talks of Jonson's art,
>   Of Shakspeare's nature, and of Cowley's wit :
>   How Beaumont's judgement checked what Fletcher writ."

And again : —

> " F.   See libels, Satires, — here you have it, — read.
>   P.   Libels and Satires ! lawless things indeed !
>   But grave Epistles, bringing vice to light,
>   Such as a King might read, a Bishop write,

> Such as Sir Robert would approve —
> > > > F. Indeed ?
> The case is altered, — you may then proceed."

> "Where towering oaks their growing honours rear,
> And future navies on thy shores appear,
> Not Neptune's self from all her streams receives
> A wealthier tribute than to thine he gives.
> No seas so rich, so gay no banks appear,
> No lake so gentle, and no spring so clear."

In this latter extract we have again an instance of the terminations in verbs.

> "Think what an equipage thou hast in air,
> And view with scorn two pages and a chair.
> As now your own, our beings were of old,
> And once inclosed in Woman's beauteous mould;
> Thence, by soft transition, we repair
> From earthly vehicles to these of air."

> "And I not strip the gilding off a knave,
> Unplaced, unpensioned, no man's heir, or slave?
> I will, or perish in the generous cause :
> Hear this, and tremble, you who 'scape the laws.
> Yes, while I live, no rich or noble knave
> Shall walk the world, in credit to his grave."

It will be observed that the fault reaches to the repetition of the very words. We might go on multiplying instances, to the surprise of any who have not taken particular notice of this defect ; for no poet has sinned oftener in this way. Should any one doubt it, let him examine more strictly the poems that do not come under the head of the satirical.

This repetition may occur over-frequently in some writers, from their relucting at the labour of correction. But Pope, it is boasted, was the most patient and painstaking of men at this work. — It is apparent how much this frequent falling of similar sounds upon the ear must add to the wearisomeness of the general monotony.

While on the subject of rhymes, we may as well set down some instances of identical rhymes which we chanced upon.

> "Why not with equal ease
> Confess as well your folly, as disease ?"

> " Who sent the thief that stole the cash away,
>   And punished him that put it in his way."

> " The doubtful beam long nods from side to side;
>   At length the wits mount up, the hairs subside."

> " But this bold lord with manly strength endued,
>   She with one finger and a thumb subdued."

Pope himself would hardly have been inclined to plead some of the older English poets in justification of a practice which, if we mistake not, had nearly ceased in his own day; and which, however in conformity to French and Italian usage, is not agreeable in our own language to an English ear.

In speaking of his inverted form of bringing in his verbs, we would not be understood as laying the inverted structure of sentences under the sweeping condemnation which many pass upon it. For, undoubtedly, it is often the natural utterance of impassioned and lofty thought, and where it is so it adds force and grandeur. But where it is evident that its frequent occurrence is simply for the rhyme's sake, and in poetry, too, as unimpassioned and as far from sublimity as Pope's, its only effect is to weary us with its sameness and offend us with its artificiality.

In his Moral Essays, we meet with much exaggeration, and with perpetually recurring antithesis, that in its effect may be often called a form of exaggeration, and which young minds are apt to run into, but from which the matured mind should have freed itself so far as to use it sparingly.

> " While the gaunt mastiff, growling at the gate,
>   Affrights the beggar whom he longs to eat,"

is an instance which, however witty some may think it, is inconsistent with the general spirit of a passage that is among Pope's best descriptions.

> " But on some lucky day, (as when they found
>   A lost bank-bill, or heard their son was drowned)."

And again : —

> " Narcissa's nature, tolerably mild,
> To make a wash, would hardly stew a child."

This is a striking example, and the more so as it is a work of supererogation, not being in the Satire of which it is an Imitation, and which surely goes far enough.

> " A few gray hairs his reverend temples crowned,
> 'T was very want that sold them for two pound."

A goodly price, truly, and a part of which we should have guessed to have gone for the rhyme, had it not been for the spirit of exaggeration of which we complain, and that the verse is made to halt with the weight of " two," when it might have carried *a* pound easily enough.   Though there is not wanting authority for such a use of the noun singular as we find in the above and following couplets : —

> " Or in pure Equity (the case not clear)
> The Chancery takes your rents for twenty year," —

still it would hardly be looked for in Pope.   And we believe that, notwithstanding his sanction, good writers have nearly or quite given it up, on account of its certain air of vulgarity.

We cannot but ask, in passing, what must have been the reading of the lovers of poetry in that day, when one could think of stealing from the Comus without fearing immediate detection.

> " By grots and caverns shagged with horrid shades."

Now Pope : —

> " Ye grots and caverns shagged with horrid thorn."

And, alas ! with the " shades " fled the imaginative character of the poetry.   Again, —

> " Above the smoke and stir of this dim spot
> Which men call Earth, and with low-thoughted care
> Confined, and pestered in this pin-fold here."

And now for Pope once more : —

> " O Grace serene ! O Virtue heavenly fair ! [" O " indeed !]
> Divine oblivion of low-thoughted care."

Every one feels immediately that Pope never could have
used such an epithet but by an act of memory, — that no
length of time could have made it his own to his mind.
There were no *mento*-chemical affinities for it to combine
with there.

We have dwelt awhile on particulars which may seem to
some of small importance ; yet they are not so.   Besides,
the consummate skill of Pope, his mastery over his art, his
faultlessness as a writer, have been urged upon the world,
till those who do not class him with the few poets of highest rank have conceded to him these merits almost without
qualification, and notwithstanding such marked defects after
all his labour at finish.   Is not much in his art, for which
he has been so praised, a very little way removed from
mechanic art?   The smoothness of single lines is dearly
bought, when obtained by such monotony and inversion,
and by Latin terms ill sorting with their context, and
rendering vaguely general what should be particular, con-
founding the abstract with the concrete, and effacing the
image where there should be a distinct picture.   If such
things be, as Byron and some others would have us believe,
the consummation of Art, we can only say, give us Nature,
then, in her ruggedest form, and we will be content.   We
well remember, after having travelled on, page after page,
to one unchanging tune, with what a sense of surprise, with
what a rousing effect, the close of the following passage
from the Imitation of Horace broke upon us : —

> " Loud as the wolves, on Orca's stormy steep,
> Howl to the roarings of the Northern deep."

It calls up the sounding close of Campbell's couplet, —

> " And waft across the waves' tumultuous roar,
> The wolf's long howl from Oonalaska's shore,"

and certainly goes sounding on with a grandeur surpassing
that of the woods and waters of the original : —

"Garganum mugire putes nemus, aut mare Tuscum."

From what we have before said, our remarks, especially
where they bear upon his language, will be understood as
intended less for the satirical and didactic portions of his
works, than for those of which the subjects are of a more
strictly poetical nature. While he confines himself to
naked satire, or plain moral or critical teaching, he is, for
the most part, clear, apt, and logical in his use of words.

But as soon as he turns to a strictly poetic subject, or
would illustrate a plainer one by a passing poetic image,
clear and appropriate words seem to take their flight, and
vague and unapt ones to light in their places, as if a sudden
dimness had fallen on his mental vision, blurring the imagery, and a confusion of speech had happened to him.
He has a deal too much of what was wont to be called
poetic phraseology, for no better reason than that it would
make intolerably bad prose. He was for hanging the
inner room of the Muses' Temple in the ill-shaped imagery
of a worn and faded tapestry. He was a trained and
worthy servitor in its courts, but no Aaron to burn the
heaven-ascending incense before its shrine.

We all know on what nicety and exact truth of terms
the entire living form of poetry depends. Yet Pope's
notions about poetical language went but little beyond a
Frenchman's. Seldom are there any attachments or poetic
associations with his words; nor have they more power
over our emotions than the sing-song of his metre. They
are, as we have said, rarely pictures, but rather cold ab-
stractions, too often loosely and unphilosophically combined. Place his poetical passages by the side of our old
poets, or by the better poets since his day. Take, in his
translations, the much talked of description of Night, the
meeting of Hector and Andromache, the description of
Polypheme, or, indeed, most of the noted passages of

Homer, and put them along-side the "bald and naked" version of Cowper, as it has been called, and you see at once how wanting in the peculiar eye and tongue of a poet he is.

Says Cowper, in a letter to his friend Hill, —

"I have two French prints hanging in my study, both on Iliad subjects; and I have an English one in the parlour, on a subject from the same poem. In one of the former, Agamemnon addresses Achilles exactly in the attitude of a dancing-master turning Miss in a minuet: in the latter the figures are plain, and the attitudes plain also. This is, in some considerable measure, I believe, the difference between my translation and Pope's; and will serve as an exemplification of what I am going to lay before you and the public."

Had Coleridge applied his hand to analyzing Pope's poetic language, as he has done to analyzing that of some others, with what dust and chaff would his sifting of words have filled the air, and how small a heap of golden grain would have been left behind! The passages which we have already quoted furnish instances enough, and make it needless to encumber ourselves with more.

This mere difference of style between the treatment of his satirical and didactic subjects, and of his strictly poetical ones, is of itself something more than an indication that Bowles is not far from right in denying to Pope the character of poet, in its highest and strictest sense. Nor will Byron's clever, savage, but superficial letter alter the matter with any one who is clear of party, and has a right apprehension of the distinctive attributes of poetry.

While we think there is little in the objection, that Pope produced no one great poem approaching the epic, we do think that the light amount of his original poetry, compared with his Translations and Imitations, is presumptive of a secondary order of poetic power. When language, and verse, and all the mechanics of art are appropriated to *turning out* modified expressions and forms of the thoughts and images of other minds, we may be well assured that there are within no great multitude of living forms struggling to break forth, nor many emotions of the soul striving for relief in voice. Real poetic genius may be unproductive, through constitutional indolence, and find ease in musings and day-dreams ; or the sorrows or cares of life may weigh upon it, and the man may endeavour to forget his higher and complete self in the exercise of any faculty save this supreme one ; — he may not have the heart for it. As Coleridge once replied to a friend, — " I am too unhappy for that." But when one, to the neglect of original working, continues to busy himself about his art with manufacturing and finishing off verse for the conveyance of others' thoughts, the suspicion will arise, that he has more fondness for the use of the instruments, than he possesses substance in those attributes of the soul for whose organs of utterance the instruments were meant.

Another point is, that the pathos of the true poet is not dependent upon his personal interest in the event or individual that gives it birth. But events lying far off in place or time, hints which the formative principle in him seizes upon and gives expanse and shape to, things acting through the creative faculty, — these the true poet utters in tones of tenderness and deep passion. But Pope's heart must be first touched, not through the ideal, but by some fact or person near and tangible, something relating to himself, before he can utter the language of simple pathos : — it must be his mother, or Gay, or — for we will not here question its true and simple tenderness — the Unfortunate Lady. And this has enabled many a one, of no high poetic character of mind, to express himself in pleasing and moving verse. Unless it had its origin in the *pride* of pity, the Death of Villiers may be taken as an exception, as, so far from its being introduced from personal attachment, it was to censure and to warn that it is spoken of. It is one of the most touching things in this poet, more touching to us than Mr. Hazlitt's bewept Eloisa and Abelard, — from the line

" In these deep solitudes and awful cells,"

" He best can paint 'em who shall feel 'em most."

Rarely is Pope's thought illustrated by any thing from nature ; and when so, it is with the faultiness which we have spoken of. His early attempts in verse — his Pastorals and Windsor Forest — are drawn from books, not from fields and woods that surrounded him at his birth, and amidst which he was then living : — little of eye had he for nature, and, even then, less of heart.

We have just spoken of his pathos being dependent upon something personal to himself. And it is well worth remarking how much of his satire even, in which he was more at home, rests upon it, and owes its dexterous vivacity to a double personality, if we may so express it, — to the love of himself and his personal hatred of another. With what keen and malign glee does he seize upon the weapons of Horace, and turn them upon his own enemies ! — and they were legion ; for with him party opposition was too much personal enmity, especially towards his superiours in rank and in wealth. But the highest poetic genius, though it may sometimes make use of its near enmities, loves, and interests, as of other things, does it seldom, and never owes its life and power to these. It embodies from itself, and finds in its own world the objects of its passions, and its ideal is its real state. This habitual indulgence in personalities argues a mind limited, and dwelling more upon small particulars than upon great principles, and constitutionally wanting in lofty thought. Accordingly, passages of high moral indignation are but thinly scattered through Pope's works, — such passages, for instance, as are found in the epilogue to his Satires, and in his lines on the Unfortunate Lady, — which, from their seldomness, bring with them a certain sense of surprise.

His mind and affections wanted expansibility. He talks much about his right and duty to castigate the vices and follies of the age, but loved rather, we fear,

"To make Vice sit for purposes of strife,
And draw the hag much larger than in life."

He seems to have been moved by an unkind delight at
the failings of others, and to find more amusement in showing up the fool than the folly. His perpetual recurrence,
also, and in gross forms, to Lady Mary Wortley Montague,
indicates that spite towards her was seldom out of his mind;
and an asp-like venom seems to be infused into the pertinacity of his hate. How different the general character of
his satire from the broad view and the moral loftiness of
that of Cowper and Young, which, in the very act of making
us ashamed of our weaknesses, imparts to us strength, and
cleanses our hearts in making us feel our pollution! — We
rise from their satire with our natures not degraded, but
ennobled.

But does not all this show a lower poetic action in Pope?
He tried to deceive himself in this matter, and, with the
help of his friends, succeeded but too well, we fear; and
the darts dipped in the poison of his own gall were called
the honest weapons of an open warfare waged against vice.
So, in his eternal splenetic flings at courts and kings, like
many others, he mistook envy for scorn; and with a consistency like theirs, while seeking anxiously to make out a
pedigree from noble blood, talked loudly of owing all to
self. Among the greatest egotists, the melancholy part of it
is, that he discovered it more in his enmity towards others,
than in honest boasting of his own powers. Surely this is
not favourable to poetry in its beautiful and grander forms.
The groundwork of his Essay on Man and his Moral Epistles is not only false philosophy, but, what is the important
point here, is contrary to a deep poetic nature. The poet
of the higher order may hold to a mistaken philosophy, but
then it will be of a mystic character, with something in it
congenial with our profounder spiritual being, moving with
our more mysterious emotions and blending with our aspirations after things unseen. But Pope's adopted scheme

indicates that pathos and sublimity were not the elements of his soul.

If we have gone somewhat particularly into his defects, and have said comparatively little upon his undoubted merits, it has not been from any party feeling, — for we hope that we like whatever is good in its kind, and relish as much as others that in which he excels, — but for the purpose of pointing out how indiscriminate has been the praise bestowed upon him, and with how little propriety he has been classed, in strictly poetic qualities, in the first rank of our great poetic qualities, in the first rank of our great poetic worthies. The keen satirist and plain-sense moralist must needs be set up as the first of poets. Our poetic language, the language of Shakspeare and Milton, had not, we have been told, attained its perfectness till he spoke. And the full organ-tones of Milton, and the varying and mellifluous harmonies of Shakspeare, and Spenser, and the singers of old, must be hushed, for all the world to stand listening to the one unvarying note from the pipe of Pope.

No wonder that such notions should have prevailed in his time, and that Warburton and others should have lauded him in ludicrously bad taste. For the tide of the poetic sea had then run out, and little was to be seen or heard but the dull flats and the warm dribblings through the gullies of the shore. But now, when the channels have so far filled again with the returning waters, it is strange indeed that any should maintain there was at that day no ebbing of the tide.

Of the effect left upon a thoughtful mind after a long continued reading of Pope, we fear we must say that it is by no means a grateful one. We pass by his choice of such subjects as Eloisa to Abelard, the loose character of his selections from Chaucer, his Sappho to Phaon, and his many gross allusions, — for greater minds than his have sinned more or less in this way, and something must be set down to the times. But the personalities of his satire, with all its wit and cleverness, at length make us heart-weary ; and the absence of an elevated spirit, and of a yearning after something higher than we possess and better than we are, depresses us with a sense of the littleness and poorness of the world, without quickening us into a purer life by awakening our finer emotions, or making us feel the strength of life by stirring the loftier passions which have being within us. We pity the man who can read Pope for any length of time, and not feel his need of the restoring and elevating influences of our older, yes, and of some of our later bards, — who can say to himself, " I 'm content." We have dwelt overlong on this part of our review, and yet have left much unsaid.

GEORGE RIPLEY

1802 – 1880

BENJAMIN CONSTANT

[*From the introductory notice to the translations contained in "Philosophical Miscellanies," Volume 2, Boston, 1838*]

THE name of BENJAMIN CONSTANT is so intimately associated with the great political events of his time, that we usually think of him as the strenuous and fearless advocate of constitutional freedom, rather than as a scholar, engaged in the most elaborate and profound researches, and a writer of singular originality and masterly skill, on subjects which address only the higher instincts of the soul.

It is in the latter character, however, that we apprehend he will be most favorably known to posterity. His services as a politician, though uniformly consecrated to the defence of popular rights and the prostration of hereditary abuses, will be comparatively lost sight of, in the changes of society and the progress of affairs, while his investigations in the field of abstract truth and the clear light which he has shed on many questions of paramount importance to the hopes and the happiness of man, will constantly meet with a more correct appreciation and a wider sympathy.

Various as were the pursuits of Benjamin Constant, large as was the compass of action and thought, in which he has gained a brilliant reputation and bestowed durable benefits upon his race, his character as a writer presents an example of consummate unity, that is no less rare than it is attractive. He was always the same man, always possessed with the same dominant ideas, always devoted to the same interests, always looking to the same objects, whether in the sphere of politics, of elegant literature, of historical investigation or of philosophical discussion. His opinions, of course, like those of every honest and thinking man, were not unfrequently modified; his views on some points, indeed, underwent a thorough revolution; and the practical measures, which he supported may not in every case have the appearance of perfect consistency; but still, we find the same distinct and strongly marked impression of individuality under all circumstances; we recognize in every change of costume or of position, the same peculiar mental endowments and tendencies, which were brought to our notice upon our first acquaintance with the man.

This identity may be resolved into the relation which he sustained to the excited and destructive spirit of his age. He was keenly susceptible to its influence, but was never overcome by its power. He rejoiced in the demolition of every ancient prejudice; his taste and his reason were alike offended by the abuses inflicted on the present by the tyranny of the past; he had no tolerance for hallowed absurdities or venerated errors; he cherished a true and cordial sympathy with the men who began to vindicate their long neglected rights, though it brought perplexity to monarchs and terror to nations; but still he could never be satisfied with any merely negative results; he could take no pleasure in the work of destruction as such; he wished to overthrow falsehood only for the sake of establishing truth; and in the midst of the ruin, which a revolutionary age had brought over the institutions of society and the opinions of men, he could not rest contented, until the materials were gathered for the reconstruction of a better edifice, upon a broader and firmer foundation than before. Hence he was never exclusively devoted to the interests of a party. He could not bind down his free thoughts to the opinions of any sect or corporation. He was unwilling to make his own ideas the gauge of another man's intellect; or to be measured himself by any arbitrary standard which might be proposed. He valued truth above all things, and independence as the condition of obtaining truth. Accordingly, he could not be made the victim of any of the partial and limited tendencies of the day. He refused to be shackled by devotion to the favorite theories or projects which were everywhere springing up. The realization of his principles were deemed by him to be of greater consequence than the success of his plans. We therefore find that though acting with others, he always acted out himself; though a lover of sympathy, he never courted it, at the expense of his convictions. Fearful of unwise extremes, — in consequence of the soundness of his mind, and never of paltry timidity, — he exercised a healing, reconciling influence over the conflicting views, which came within his province. He accordingly holds an eminent rank among those who may be honored as the true mediators of society.

"I have always endeavored [he tells us] to speak out my whole thought, on all the subjects, to which I have directed my attention. Perhaps I shall give equal offence in what I have said concerning religion, to devotees and to infidels, at least, to those who embrace infidelity as a systematic dogma; in what concerns the history of our troubles, to the well-disposed admirers of Robespierre and Saint-Just, and to the enemies of Malesherbes and La Fayette; in what is connected with the Empire, to the enthusiastic partisans of Napoleon and to his detractors. Perhaps my aversion to the rigorous precepts which have so long fettered the progress of our literature, will bring upon me the hostility of those who assert that imitation is necessary, because they cannot attain originality. But these things do not move me. He who has no purpose but that of comprehending the great crisis, which has been approaching for the last two centuries, and which has now manifested itself for forty years, he who wishes only to forward the movement which is bringing the whole human race into a better sphere of ideas and institutions, — he can and should speak out whatever is in his mind."

Benjamin Constant was qualified to a remarkable degree for this independent course, by the circumstances of his birth and education, no less than by the natural bent of his genius and the force of his convictions. This is the idea which serves to explain the identity of his character, and to unfold the exact nature of his position and influence.

Descended from ancestors, who had removed from France to French Switzerland, about the commencement of the seventeenth century, he was born at Lausanne in 1767 ; and thus a genuine Frenchman by natural descent, by language, by early association, and by the influences which surrounded his childhood, he soon learned to regard himself as a citizen of the nation, in whose affairs he was subsequently to take such an active and efficient interest. It was a fortunate circumstance that his first impressions were received in Protestant Switzerland. They would serve, as we may suppose, to prevent him from yielding to the shallow and frivolous spirit which prevailed, to so great an extent, at that time in the metropolis of France. His early education was received at a German Seminary ; and for a considerable time, he was attached to the service of the Duke of Brunswick. In this situation, he acquired the taste for German literature, which he afterwards cultivated with uncommon success, and which exerted a salutary influence on the formation of his character and habits of thought. We perceive the effects of his familiarity with the literature of Germany throughout the whole of his subsequent career. It gave a depth to his conceptions and a vigor to his reasonings, which combined with the charming graces of French expression and the native fire and brilliancy of his wit, produced a style of composition which few continental prose writers have equalled and which none have surpassed.

He had not yet attained the age of thirty years, when he presented himself at Paris, in the midst of the Revolution ; and soon gained signal distinction by the commanding powers of his intellect, the energy of his discourse, and the burning zeal with which he espoused what he deemed the cause of humanity, and the inborn rights of the soul. His political course from that time is familiar to all who are in any degree acquainted with the public movements which agitated the commencement of the present century ; and

which were brought to a temporary crisis immediately
before his decease, which by a remarkable coincidence
took place in 1830, a short time after the Revolution of
July. By that Revolution, the great constitutional principles to which his life had been devoted, were supposed to
have gained an illustrious triumph ; he survived to witness
their victory ; and as if his mission were completed, and
there were nothing further left for him to do, he departed
from the world. He had lived long enough to stamp a
true image of himself upon his age ; and he went away to
that unseen state of being, in whose reality he had learned
to cherish a heart-felt faith.

The history of Benjamin Constant, as a literary man,
exhibits the reconciling tendency which has been pointed
out, as the peculiar characteristic of his mind. Born at a
period when the literature of France was at the summit of
its glory and seemed to fill the eye of the world, he was not
seduced into the unqualified admiration which was claimed
for it as its due ; but was impressed, from the beginning,
with the pure and lofty promise of a more substantial literature which was just rising from an opposite quarter of the
heavens. He had been accustomed to look up to Bayle,
Voltaire and Montesquieu, as the masters of his mind ; but
he was not so strongly bound by the spell of their names, as
to be indifferent to the new and glorious manifestations of
thought which were bursting forth from such men as Lessing
and Herder, Wieland and Göthe, though beyond the Rhine.

His mode of thinking accordingly betrays nothing of the
polished but cold exclusiveness which characterized the
fastidious literature of France, during the latter part of
the last century. He perceived that the violation of dainty
forms is oft-times more than atoned for, by the fresh and
gushing life which breaks through them ; and that a strict
observance of conventional canons is easily made the refuge of imitators and the shield of stupidity. He would
not withhold his sympathy from the spirit of beauty, though
appearing in an unauthorized shape ; and hence refused to

worship the reigning idols of the public taste. He scorned
to narrow his mind to the petty limits of artificial restric-
tions; and thus was enabled to enrich the literature, to
which he might have been denounced as a traitor. After
leaving, for a season, the path which was prescribed by the
prevailing taste of the day, he returned from his wanderings
through a land of fragrant wild-flowers, with noble offerings
for his native shrine. We perceive from the earliest display of his powers, a broader foundation of logical strength,
a higher degree of robust action, and a more daring bold-
ness of expression in his style, than had hitherto been
usually exhibited by the most popular writers. These characteristics gained vigor and harmony, as his experience
ripened and his sphere of action was enlarged. As he was
led, at a subsequent period of his life, to reside for different
intervals in Germany, we find the increasing effect of his
familiarity with the kindling literature of that country, in
the new paths of speculation and inquiry which he struck
out, and the fulness and variety of learning which he brought
to the illustration of all topics, on which erudition was
required.

At the same time that he refused to acknowledge the
canons of taste, by which thought was then restrained in the
reigning fashion of French Literature, he cultivated a true
classical purity of expression, free from the affectation of
foreign combinations, presenting no trace of the imitation
of favorite authors, clothing unwonted thoughts in the genuine forms of the mother tongue, and though embodying
the most profound ideas, transparent as the day. His
native clearness of mind, his inborn sense of the Beautiful
and the True, and his sharp logical acuteness, prevented
him from falling into the obscurity and extravagance which
are usually found in the first growth of a strong and luxuriant literature, and no less in the writing of those who are
so enamored of its freshness and bloom, as to lose their
self-subsistence and waste the very pith of life in foolish
imitations. If he sometimes approaches by the exceeding

fineness of his views and the airy subtilty of his distinctions, to the confines of Teutonic mysticism, he is soon drawn back by the precision of French taste and the balanced action of his own mind, to the regions of daylight and common sense. He thus presents a beautiful example of the healthful influence of one literature upon another. Combining the pointedness and rapid movement of the French writers, with the depth and solidity of the German, he exhibits the excellent effects of discarding the precise formulas of a pedantic school and indulging the mind with the freest and most varied culture, which it can gain. His wit is not unfrequently no less salient and biting than that of Voltaire, while his reverence for all that is truly venerable, his sympathy with the higher feelings and holier aspirations of our nature, indicate the spiritual and religious direction, which he was compelled by the force of light, the supremacy of thought, to adopt as the only natural and just path for a being like man.

The influence of Benjamin Constant was combined with that of August Wilhelm Schlegel and Madame de Staël to promote a better understanding between the literary men of France and Germany; and to reveal the treasures of the latter country to the students and thinkers of the former. His own translation of Schiller's Wallenstein was made with the view of adapting it for representation on the French stage; and hence, it is easy to conceive that it must have failed of doing anything like justice to the magnificent original. Of its merits or defects, however, I am unable to speak from personal knowledge. It is alluded to in terms of disparagement by the most competent English authority, that I am acquainted with,[1] who appears to intimate that ill-success could not but be the fate of such an undertaking. Benjamin Constant himself acknowledges in a singularly candid criticism on his own production, that many of the objections which had been brought against it were perfectly just, and that by a too strict adherence to the rules of the

[1] Carlyle.

French theatre, he destroyed much of its dramatic effect. But however this may be, it served to awaken attention to the masters of German poetry and to increase the general interest in a literature which has since done so much for the refreshment of France. Among the miscellaneous writings of Benjamin Constant we find the critical essay on this drama, to which I have just alluded. It presents an accurate delineation of its chief characteristics, and a true conception of its spirit, while it breathes a warm sympathy with its fine moral portraitures. The description of Thecla is scarcely surpassed by any thing that I know of in modern French prose; and I cannot but regard the whole piece as an admirable specimen of discriminating, philosophical criticism. Its concluding passage is so expressive a summary of the literary principles of the author, that I will close my remarks on that topic with introducing it here. " It is incontestable that our writers ought to throw off the yoke of superannuated rules in their new dramatic system. They need only take care that the changes be not too frequent or too abrupt. There may be some unavoidable inconveniences; but these, in literature, as in politics, will not be of long duration. Wherever liberty exists, reason will not delay to assume the sovereignty. Stationary spirits cry out in vain that innovations will corrupt the public taste; but the public taste is not thus corrupted; it approves that which is in accordance with truth and nature; it rejects that which perverts the truth and which deviates from nature by extravagance and exaggeration. The many possess an admirable instinct. This instinct has already traced, in our political emergencies, the limits necessary to reconcile order and liberty; it is laboring with success to place religion, in the position which belongs to it, between incredulity and fanaticism; and the same instinct will exercise its influence on literature and restrain our writers without hampering them."

RALPH WALDO EMERSON

1803 – 1882

SHAKSPEARE; OR, THE POET

[*From " Representative Men," 1850*]

GREAT men are more distinguished by range and extent than by originality. If we require the originality which consists in weaving, like a spider, their web from their own bowels; in finding clay and making bricks and building the house; no great men are original. Nor does valuable originality consist in unlikeness to other men. The hero is in the press of knights and the thick of events; and seeing what men want and sharing their desire, he adds the needful length of sight and of arm, to come at the desired point. The greatest genius is the most indebted man. A poet is no rattle-brain, saying what comes uppermost, and, because he says every thing, saying at last something good; but a heart in unison with his time and country. There is nothing whimsical and fantastic in his production, but sweet and sad earnest, freighted with the weightiest convictions and pointed with the most determined aim which any man or class knows of in his times.

The Genius of our life is jealous of individuals, and will not have any individual great, except through the general. There is no choice to genius. A great man does not wake up on some fine morning and say, ' I am full of life, I will go to sea and find an Antarctic continent: to-day I will square the circle: I will ransack botany and find a new food for man: I have a new architecture in my mind: I foresee a new mechanic power: ' no, but he finds himself in the river of the thoughts and events, forced onward by the ideas and necessities of his contemporaries. He stands where all the eyes of men look one way, and their hands all

73

point in the direction in which he should go. The Church has reared him amidst rites and pomps, and he carries out the advice which her music gave him, and builds a cathedral needed by her chants and processions. He finds a war raging: it educates him, by trumpet, in barracks, and he betters the instruction. He finds two counties groping to bring coal, or flour, or fish, from the place of production to the place of consumption, and he hits on a railroad. Every master has found his materials collected, and his power lay in his sympathy with his people and in his love of the materials he wrought in. What an economy of power! and what a compensation for the shortness of life! All is done to his hand. The world has brought him thus far on his way. The human race has gone out before him, sunk the hills, filled the hollows and bridged the rivers. Men, nations, poets, artisans, women, all have worked for him, and he enters into their labors. Choose any other thing, out of the line of tendency, out of the national feeling and history, and he would have all to do for himself: his powers would be expended in the first preparations. Great genial power, one would almost say, consists in not being original at all; in being altogether receptive; in letting the world do all, and suffering the spirit of the hour to pass unobstructed through the mind.

Shakspeare's youth fell in a time when the English people were importunate for dramatic entertainments. The court took offence easily at political allusions and attempted to suppress them. The Puritans, a growing and energetic party, and the religious among the Anglican church, would suppress them. But the people wanted them. Inn-yards, houses without roofs, and extemporaneous enclosures at country fairs were the ready theatres of strolling players. The people had tasted this new joy; and, as we could not hope to suppress newspapers now, — no, not by the strongest party, — neither then could king, prelate, or puritan, alone or united, suppress an organ which was ballad, epic, newspaper, caucus, lecture, Punch and library, at the same time. Probably king, prelate and puritan, all found their own account in it. It had become, by all causes, a national interest, — by no means conspicuous, so that some great scholar would have thought of treating it in an English history, — but not a whit less considerable because it was cheap and of no account, like a baker's-shop. The best proof of its vitality is the crowd of writers which suddenly broke into this field; Kyd, Marlow, Greene, Jonson, Chapman, Dekker, Webster, Heywood, Middleton, Peele, Ford, Massinger, Beaumont and Fletcher.

The secure possession, by the stage, of the public mind, is of the first importance to the poet who works for it. He loses no time in idle experiments. Here is audience and expectation prepared. In the case of Shakspeare there is much more. At the time when he left Stratford and went up to London, a great body of stage-plays of all dates and writers existed in manuscript and were in turn produced on the boards. Here is the Tale of Troy, which the audience will bear hearing some part of, every week; the Death of Julius Cæsar, and other stories out of Plutarch, which they never tire of; a shelf full of English history, from the chronicles of Brut and Arthur, down to the royal Henries, which men hear eagerly; and a string of doleful tragedies, merry Italian tales and Spanish voyages, which all the London 'prentices know. All the mass has been treated, with more or less skill, by every playwright, and the prompter has the soiled and tattered manuscripts. It is now no longer possible to say who wrote them first. They have been the property of the Theatre so long, and so many rising genuises have enlarged or altered them, inserting a speech or a whole scene, or adding a song, that no man can any longer claim copyright in this work of numbers. Happily, no man wishes to. They are not yet desired in that way. We have few readers, many spectators and hearers. They had best lie where they are.

Shakspeare, in common with his comrades, esteemed the mass of old plays waste stock, in which any experiment could be freely tried. Had the *prestige* which hedges about a modern tragedy existed, nothing could have been done. The rude warm blood of the living England circulated in the play, as in street-ballads, and gave body which he wanted to his airy and majestic fancy. The poet needs a ground in popular tradition on which he may work, and which, again, may restrain his art within the due temperance. It holds him to the people, supplies a foundation for his edifice, and in furnishing so much work done to his hand, leaves him at leisure and in full strength for the audacities of his imagination. In short, the poet owes to his legend what sculpture owed to the temple. Sculpture in Egypt and in Greece grew up in subordination to architecture. It was the ornament of the temple wall: at first a rude relief carved on pediments, then the relief became bolder and a head or arm was projected from the wall; the groups being still arranged with reference to the building, which serves also as a frame to hold the figures; and when at last the greatest freedom of style and treatment was reached, the prevailing genius of architecture still enforced a certain calmness and continence in the statue. As soon as the statue was begun for itself, and with no reference to the temple or palace, the art began to decline: freak, extravagance and exhibition took the place of the old temperance. This balance-wheel, which the sculptor found in architecture, the perilous irritability of poetic talent found in the accumulated dramatic materials to which the people were already wonted, and which had a certain excellence which no single genius, however extraordinary, could hope to create.

In point of fact it appears that Shakspeare did owe debts in all directions, and was able to use whatever he found; and the amount of indebtedness may be inferred from Malone's laborious computations in regard to the First, Second, and Third parts of Henry VI., in which, " out of 6043 lines, 1771 were written by some author preceding Shakspeare, 2373 by him, on the foundation laid by his predecessors, and 1899 were entirely his own." And the proceeding investigation hardly leaves a single drama of his absolute invention. Malone's sentence is an important piece of external history. In Henry VIII. I think I see plainly the cropping out of the original rock on which his own finer stratum was laid. The first play was written by a superior, thoughtful man, with a vicious ear. I can mark his lines, and know well their cadence. See Wolsey's soliloquy, and the following scene with Cromwell, where instead of the metre of Shakspeare, whose secret is that the thought constructs the tune, so that reading for the sense will best bring out the rhythm, — here the lines are constructed on a given tune, and the verse has even a trace of pulpit eloquence. But the play contains through all its length unmistakable traits of Shakspeare's hand, and some passages, as the account of the coronation, are like autographs. What is odd, the compliment to Queen Elizabeth is in the bad rhythm.

Shakspeare knew that tradition supplies a better fable than any invention can. If he lost any credit of design, he augmented his resources; and, at that day, our petulant demand for originality was not so much pressed. There was no literature for the million. The universal reading, the cheap press, were unknown. A great poet who appears in illiterate times, absorbs into his sphere all the light which is any where radiating. Every intellectual jewel, every flower of sentiment it is his fine office to bring to his people; and he comes to value his memory equally with his invention. He is therefore little solicitous whence his thoughts have been derived; whether through translation, whether through tradition, whether by travel in distant countries, whether by inspiration; from whatever source, they are equally welcome to his uncritical audience. Nay, he borrows very near home. Other men say wise things as well as he; only they say a good many foolish things, and do not know when they have spoken wisely. He knows the sparkle of the true stone, and puts it in

high place, wherever he finds it. Such is the happy position of Homer perhaps ; of Chaucer, of Saadi. They felt
that all wit was their wit. And they are librarians and his-
toriographers, as well as poets. Each romancer was heir
and dispenser of all the hundred tales of the world, —

> " Presenting Thebes' and Pelops' line
> And the tale of Troy divine."

The influence of Chaucer is conspicuous in all our early
literature ; and more recently not only Pope and Dryden
have been beholden to him, but, in the whole society of
English writers, a large unacknowledged debt is easily
traced. One is charmed with the opulence which feed
so many pensioners. But Chaucer is a huge borrower.
Chaucer, it seems, drew continually, through Lydgate and
Caxton, from Guido di Colonna, whose Latin romance of
the Trojan war was in turn a compilation from Dares
Phrygius, Ovid and Statius. Then Petrarch, Boccaccio
and the Provençal poets are his benefactors : the Romaunt
of the Rose is only judicious translation from William
of Lorris and John of Meung : Troilus and Creseide,
from Lollius of Urbino : The Cock and the Fox, from the
Lais of Marie : The House of Fame, from the French
or Italian : and poor Gower he uses as if he were only a
brick-kiln or stone-quarry out of which to build his house.
He steals by this apology, — that what he takes has no
worth where he finds it and the greatest where he leaves
it. It has come to be practically a sort of rule in literature,
that a man having once shown himself capable of original
writing, is entitled thenceforth to steal from the writings of
others at discretion. Thought is the property of him who
can entertain it and of him who can adequately place it.
A certain awkwardness marks the use of borrowed thoughts ;
but as soon as we have learned what to do with them they
become our own.

Thus all originality is relative. Every thinker is retro-
spective. The learned member of the legislature, at West-

minster or at Washington, speaks and votes for thousands. Show us the constituency, and the now invisible channels by which the senator is made aware of their wishes; the crowd of practical and knowing men, who, by correspondence or conversation, are feeding him with evidence, anecdotes and estimates, and it will bereave his fine attitude and resistance of something of their impressiveness. As Sir Robert Peel and Mr. Webster vote, so Locke and Rousseau think, for thousands; and so there were fountains all around Homer, Menu, Saadi, or Milton, from which they drew; friends, lovers, books, traditions, proverbs, — all perished — which, if seen, would go to reduce the wonder. Did the bard speak with authority? Did he feel himself overmatched by any companion? The appeal is to the consciousness of the writer. Is there at last in his breast a Delphi whereof to ask concerning any thought or thing, whether it be verily so, yea or nay? and to have answer, and to rely on that? All the debts which such a man could contract to other wit would never disturb his consciousness of originality; for the ministrations of books and of other minds are a whiff of smoke to that most private reality with which he has conversed.

It is easy to see that what is best written or done by genius in the world, was no man's work, but came by wide social labor, when a thousand wrought like one, sharing the same impulse. Our English Bible is a wonderful specimen of the strength and music of the English language. But it was not made by one man, or at one time; but centuries and churches brought it to perfection. There never was a time when there was not some translation existing. The Liturgy, admired for its energy and pathos, is an anthology of the piety of ages and nations, a translation of the prayers and forms of the Catholic church, — these collected, too, in long periods, from the prayers and meditations of every saint and sacred writer all over the world. Grotius makes the like remark in respect to the Lord's Prayer, that the single clauses of which it is composed were already in use

in the time of Christ, in the Rabbinical forms. He picked
out the grains of gold. The nervous language of the Common Law, the impressive forms of our courts and the precision and substantial truth of the legal distinctions, are the
contribution of all the sharp-sighted, strong-minded men
who have lived in the countries where these laws govern.
The translation of Plutarch gets its excellence by being
translation on translation. There never was a time when
there was none. All the truly idiomatic and national
phrases are kept, and all others successively picked out and
thrown away. Something like the same process had gone
on, long before, with the originals of these books. The
world takes liberties with world-books. Vedas, Æsop's
Fables, Pilpay, Arabian Nights, Cid, Iliad, Robin Hood,
Scottish Minstrelsy, are not the work of single men. In
the composition of such works the time thinks, the market
thinks, the mason, the carpenter, the merchant, the farmer,
the fop, all think for us. Every book supplies its time with
one good word; every municipal law, every trade, every
folly of the day; and the generic catholic genius who is not
afraid or ashamed to owe his originality to the originality of
all, stands with the next age as the recorder and embodiment of his own.

We have to thank the researches of antiquaries, and the
Shakspeare Society, for ascertaining the steps of the English
drama, from the Mysteries celebrated in churches and by
churchmen, and the final detachment from the church, and
the completion of secular plays, from Ferrex and Porrex,
and Gammer Gurton's Needle, down to the possession of
the stage by the very pieces which Shakspeare altered, re-
modelled and finally made his own. Elated with success
and piqued by the growing interest of the problem, they
have left no book-stall unsearched, no chest in a garret
unopened, no file of old yellow accounts to decompose in
damp and worms, so keen was the hope to discover whether
the boy Shakspeare poached or not, whether he held horses
at the theatre door, whether he kept school, and why he

left in his will only his second-best bed to Ann Hathaway, his wife.

There is somewhat touching in the madness with which the passing age mischooses the object on which all candles shine and all eyes are turned ; the care with which it registers every trifle touching Queen Elizabeth and King James, and the Essexes, Leicesters, Burleighs and Buckinghams ; and lets pass without a single valuable note the founder of another dynasty, which alone will cause the Tudor dynasty to be remembered, — the man who carries the Saxon race in him by the inspiration which feeds him, and on whose thoughts the foremost people of the world are now for some ages to be nourished, and minds to receive this and not another bias. A popular player ; — nobody suspected he was the poet of the human race ; and the secret was kept as faithfully from poets and intellectual men as from courtiers and frivolous people. Bacon, who took the inventory of the human understanding for his times, never mentioned his name. Ben Jonson, though we have strained his few words of regard and panegyric, had no suspicion of the elastic fame whose first vibrations he was attempting. He no doubt thought the praise he has conceded to him generous, and esteemed himself, out of all question, the better poet of the two.

If it need wit to know wit, according to the proverb, Shakspeare's time should be capable of recognizing it. Sir Henry Wotton was born four years after Shakspeare, and died twenty-three years after him ; and I find, among his correspondents and acquaintances, the following persons : Theodore Beza, Isaac Casaubon, Sir Philip Sidney, the Earl of Essex, Lord Bacon, Sir Walter Raleigh, John Milton, Sir Henry Vane, Isaac Walton, Dr. Donne, Abraham Cowley, Bellarmine, Charles Cotton, John Pym, John Hales, Kepler, Vieta, Albericus Gentilis, Paul Sarpi, Arminius ; with all of whom exists some token of his having communicated, without enumerating many others whom doubtless he saw, — Shakspeare, Spenser, Jonson, Beau-

mont, Massinger, the two Herberts, Marlow, Chapman and
the rest. Since the constellation of great men who appeared in Greece in the time of Pericles, there was never
any such society ; — yet their genius failed them to find out
the best head in the universe. Our poet's mask was im-
penetrable. You cannot see the mountain near. It took
a century to make it suspected ; and not until two centuries
had passed, after his death, did any criticism which we
think adequate begin to appear. It was not possible to
write the history of Shakspeare till now ; for he is the father
of German literature : it was with the introduction of Shakspeare into German, by Lessing, and the translation of his
works by Wieland and Schlegel, that the rapid burst of
German literature was most intimately connected. It was
not until the nineteenth century, whose speculative genius
is a sort of living Hamlet, that the tragedy of Hamlet could
find such wondering readers. Now, literature, philosophy
and thought, are Shakspearized. His mind is the horizon
beyond which, at present, we do not see. Our ears are
educated to music by his rhythm. Coleridge and Goethe
are the only critics who have expressed our convictions
with any adequate fidelity : but there is in all cultivated
minds a silent appreciation of his superlative power and
beauty, which, like Christianity, qualifies the period.

The Shakspeare Society have inquired in all directions,
advertised the missing facts, offered money for any information that will lead to proof, — and with what result ? Beside
some important illustration of the history of the English
stage, to which I have adverted, they have gleaned a few
facts touching the property, and dealings in regard to
property, of the poet. It appears that from year to year he
owned a larger share in the Blackfriars' Theatre : its ward-
robe and other appurtenances were his : that he bought an
estate in his native village with his earnings as writer and
shareholder ; that he lived in the best house in Stratford ;
was intrusted by his neighbors with their commissions in
London, as of borrowing money, and the like ; that he was

a veritable farmer. About the time when he was writing Macbeth, he sues Philip Rogers, in the borough-court of Stratford, for thirty-five shillings, ten pence, for corn delivered to him at different times; and in all respects appears as a good husband, with no reputation for eccentricity or excess. He was a good-natured sort of man, an actor and shareholder in the theatre, not in any striking manner distinguished from other actors and managers. I admit the importance of this information. It was well worth the pains that have been taken to procure it.

But whatever scraps of information concerning his condition these researches may have rescued, they can shed no light upon that infinite invention which is the concealed magnet of his attraction for us. We are very clumsy writers of history. We tell the chronicle of parentage, birth, birth-place, schooling, school-mates, earning of money, marriage, publication of books, celebrity, death; and when we have come to an end of this gossip, no ray of relation appears between it and the goddess-born; and it seems as if, had we dipped at random into the "Modern Plutarch," and read any other life there, it would have fitted the poems as well. It is the essence of poetry to spring, like the rainbow daughter of Wonder, from the invisible, to abolish the past and refuse all history. Malone, Warburton, Dyce and Collier, have wasted their oil. The famed theatres, Covent Garden, Drury Lane, the Park and Tremont have vainly assisted. Betterton, Garrick, Kemble, Kean and Macready dedicate their lives to this genius; him they crown, elucidate, obey and express. The genius knows them not. The recitation begins; one golden word leaps out immortal from all this painted pedantry and sweetly torments us with invitations to its own inaccessible homes. I remember I went once to see the Hamlet of a famed performer, the pride of the English stage; and all I then heard and all I now remember of the tragedian was that in which the tragedian had no part; simply Hamlet's question to the ghost: —

> " What may this mean,
> That thou, dead corse, again in complete steel
> Revisit'st thus the glimpses of the moon ? "

That imagination which dilates the closet he writes in to the world's dimension, crowds it with agents in rank and order, as quickly reduces the big reality to be the glimpses of the moon. These tricks of his magic spoil for us the illusions of the green-room. Can any biography shed light on the localities into which the Midsummer Night's Dream admits me ? Did Shakspeare confide to any notary or parish recorder, sacristan, or surrogate in Stratford, the genesis of that delicate creation ? The forest of Arden, the nimble air of Scone Castle, the moonlight of Portia's villa, " the antres vast and desarts idle " of Othello's captivity, — where is the third cousin, or grand-nephew, the chancellor's file of accounts, or private letter, that has kept one word of those transcendent secrets ? In fine, in this drama, as in all great works of art, — in the Cyclopæan architecture of Egypt and India, in the Phidian sculpture, the Gothic minsters, the Italian painting, the Ballads of Spain and Scotland, — the Genius draws up the ladder after him, when the creative age goes up to heaven, and gives way to a new age, which sees the works and asks in vain for a history.

Shakspeare is the only biographer of Shakspeare ; and even he can tell nothing, except to the Shakspeare in us, that is, to our most apprehensive and sympathetic hour. He cannot step from off his tripod and give us anecdotes of his inspirations. Read the antique documents extricated, analyzed and compared by the assiduous Dyce and Collier, and now read one of these skyey sentences, — aerolites, — which seem to have fallen out of heaven, and which not your experience but the man within the breast has accepted as words of fate, and tell me if they match ; if the former account in any manner for the latter ; or which gives the most historical insight into the man.

Hence, though our external history is so meagre, yet,

with Shakspeare for biographer, instead of Aubrey and Rowe, we have really the information which is material; that which describes character and fortune, that which, if we were about to meet the man and deal with him, would most import us to know. We have his recorded convictions on those questions which knock for answer at every heart, — on life and death, on love, on wealth and poverty, on the prizes of life and the ways whereby we come at them; on the characters of men, and the influences, occult and open, which affect their fortunes; and on those mysterious and demoniacal powers which defy our science and which yet interweave their malice and their gift in our brightest hours. Who ever read the volume of the Sonnets without finding that the poet had there revealed, under masks that are no masks to the intelligent, the lore of friendship and of love; the confusion of sentiments in the most susceptible, and, at the same time, the most intellectual of men? What trait of his private mind has he hidden in his dramas? One can discern, in his ample pictures of the gentleman and the king, what forms and humanities pleased him; his delight in troops of friends, in large hospitality, in cheerful giving. Let Timon, let Warwick, let Antonio the merchant answer for his great heart. So far from Shakspeare's being the least known, he is the one person, in all modern history, known to us. What point of morals, of manners, of economy, of philosophy, of religion, of taste, of the conduct of life, has he not settled? What mystery has he not signified his knowledge of? What office, or function, or district of man's work, has he not remembered? What king has he not taught state, as Talma taught Napoleon? What maiden has not found him finer than her delicacy? What lover has he not outloved? What sage has he not outseen? What gentleman has he not instructed in the rudeness of his behavior?

Some able and appreciating critics think no criticism on Shakspeare valuable that does not rest purely on the dramatic merit; that he is falsely judged as poet and philosopher. I think as highly as these critics of his dramatic merit, but still think it secondary. He was a full man, who liked to talk; a brain exhaling thoughts and images, which, seeking vent, found the drama next at hand. Had he been less, we should have had to consider how well he filled his place, how good a dramatist he was, — and he is the best in the world. But it turns out that what he has to say is of that weight as to withdraw some attention from the vehicle; and he is like some saint whose history is to be rendered into all languages, into verse and prose, into songs and pictures, and cut up into proverbs; so that the occasion which gave the saint's meaning the form of a conversation, or of a prayer, or of a code of laws, is immaterial compared with the universality of its application. So it fares with the wise Shakspeare and his book of life. He wrote the airs for all our modern music: he wrote the text of modern life; the text of manners: he drew the man of England and Europe; the father of the man in America; he drew the man, and described the day, and what is done in it: he read the hearts of men and women, their probity, and their second thought and wiles; the wiles of innocence, and the transitions by which virtues and vices slide into their contraries: he could divide the mother's part from the father's part in the face of the child, or draw the fine demarcations of freedom and of fate: he knew the laws of repression which make the police of nature: and all the sweets and all the terrors of human lot lay in his mind as truly but as softly as the landscape lies on the eye. And the importance of this wisdom of life sinks the form, as of Drama or Epic, out of notice. 'T is like making a question concerning the paper on which a king's message is written.

Shakspeare is as much out of the category of eminent authors, as he is out of the crowd. He is inconceivably wise; the others, conceivably. A good reader can, in a sort, nestle into Plato's brain and think from thence; but not into Shakspeare's. We are still out of doors. For executive faculty, for creation, Shakspeare is unique. No

man can imagine it better.   He was the farthest reach of
subtlety compatible with an individual self, — the subtilest
of authors, and only just within the possibility of author-
ship.   With this wisdom of life is the equal endowment of
imaginative and of lyric power.   He clothed the creatures of
his legend with form and sentiments as if they were people
who had lived under his roof; and few real men have left
such distinct characters as these fictions.   And they spoke
in language as sweet as it was fit.   Yet his talents never
seduced him into an ostentation, nor did he harp on one
string.   An omnipresent humanity co-ordinates all his
faculties.   Give a man of talents a story to tell, and his
partiality will presently appear.   He has certain observa-
tions, opinions, topics, which have some accidental prominence, and which he disposes all to exhibit.   He crams
this part and starves that other part, consulting not the fitness of the thing, but his fitness and strength.   But Shakspeare has no peculiarity, no importunate topic ; but all is
duly given ; no veins, no curiosities ; no cow-painter, no
bird-fancier, no mannerist is he : he has no discoverable
egotism : the great he tells greatly ; the small subordinately.
He is wise without emphasis or assertion ; he is strong, as
nature is strong, who lifts the land into mountain slopes
without effort and by the same rule as she floats a bubble
in the air, and likes as well to do the one as the other.
This makes that equality of power in farce, tragedy, narrative and love-songs ; a merit so incessant that each reader
is incredulous of the perception of other readers.

This power of expression, or of transferring the inmost
truth of things into music and verse, makes him the type of
the poet and has added a new problem to metaphysics.
This is that which throws him into natural history, as a main
production of the globe, and as announcing new eras and
ameliorations.   Things were mirrored in his poetry without
loss or blur : he could paint the fine with precision, the
great with compass, the tragic and the comic indifferently
and without any distortion or favor.   He carried his power-

ful execution into minute details, to a hair point; finishes an eyelash or a dimple as firmly as he draws a mountain; and yet these, like nature's, will bear the scrutiny of the solar microscope.

In short, he is the chief example to prove that more or less of production, more or fewer pictures, is a thing indifferent. He had the power to make one picture. Daguerre learned how to let one flower etch its image on his plate of iodine, and then proceeds at leisure to etch a million. There are always objects; but there was never representation. Here is perfect representation, at last; and now let the world of figures sit for their portraits. No recipe can be given for the making of a Shakspeare; but the possibility of the translation of things into song is demonstrated.

His lyric power lies in the genius of the piece. The sonnets, though their excellence is lost in the splendor of the dramas, are as inimitable as they; and it is not a merit of lines, but a total merit of the piece; like the tone of voice of some incomparable person, so is this a speech of poetic beings, and any clause as unproducible now as a whole poem.

Though the speeches in the plays, and single lines, have a beauty which tempts the ear to pause on them for their euphuism, yet the sentence is so loaded with meaning and so linked with its foregoers and followers, that the logician is satisfied. His means are as admirable as his ends; every subordinate invention, by which he helps himself to connect some irreconcilable opposites, is a poem too. He is not reduced to dismount and walk because his horses are running off with him in some distant direction: he always rides.

The finest poetry was first experience; but the thought has suffered a transformation since it was an experience. Cultivated men often attain a good degree of skill in writing verses; but it is easy to read, through their poems, their personal history: any one acquainted with the parties can name every figure; this is Andrew and that is Rachel.

The sense thus remains prosaic. It is a caterpillar with wings, and not yet a butterfly. In the poet's mind the fact has gone quite over into the new element of thought, and has lost all that is exuvial. This generosity abides with Shakspeare. We say, from the truth and closeness of his pictures, that he knows the lesson by heart. Yet there is not a trace of egotism.

One more royal trait properly belongs to the poet. I mean his cheerfulness, without which no man can be a poet, — for beauty is his aim. He loves virtue, not for its obligation but for its grace: he delights in the world, in man, in woman, for the lovely light that sparkles from them. Beauty, the spirit of joy and hilarity, he sheds over the universe. Epicurus relates that poetry hath such charms that a lover might forsake his mistress to partake of them. And the true bards have been noted for their firm and cheerful temper. Homer lies in sunshine; Chaucer is glad and erect; and Saadi says, "It was rumored abroad that I was penitent; but what had I to do with repentance?" Not less sovereign and cheerful, — much more sovereign and cheerful, is the tone of Shakspeare. His name suggests joy and emancipation to the heart of men. If he should appear in any company of human souls, who would not march in his troop? He touches nothing that does not borrow health and longevity from his festal style.

And now, how stands the account of man with this bard and benefactor, when, in solitude, shutting our ears to the reverberations of his fame, we seek to strike the balance? Solitude has austere lessons; it can teach us to spare both heroes and poets; and it weighs Shakspeare also, and finds him to share the halfness and imperfection of humanity.

Shakspeare, Homer, Dante, Chaucer, saw the splendor of meaning that plays over the visible world; knew that a tree had another use than for apples, and corn another than for meal, and the ball of the earth, than for tillage and roads: that these things bore a second and finer harvest to the

mind, being emblems of its thoughts, and conveying in all
their natural history a certain mute commentary on human
life. Shakspeare employed them as colors to compose his
picture. He rested in their beauty; and never took the
step which seemed inevitable to such genius, namely to
explore the virtue which resides in these symbols and
imparts this power: — what is that which they themselves say? He converted the elements which waited on
his command, into entertainments. He was master of the
revels to mankind. Is it not as if one should have, through
majestic powers of science, the comets given into his hand,
or the planets and their moons, and should draw them from
their orbits to glare with the municipal fireworks on a holiday night, and advertise in all towns, "Very superior pyro-
techny this evening"? Are the agents of nature, and the
power to understand them, worth no more than a street
serenade, or the breath of a cigar? One remembers again
the trumpet-text in the Koran, — "The heavens and the
earth and all that is between them, think ye we have
created them in jest?" As long as the question is of
talent and mental power, the world of men has not his
equal to show. But when the question is, to life and its
materials and its auxiliaries, how does he profit me? What
does it signify? It is but a Twelfth Night, or Midsummer-
Night's Dream, or Winter Evening's Tale: what signifies
another picture more or less? The Egyptian verdict of the
Shakspeare Societies comes to mind; that he was a jovial
actor and manager. I can not marry this fact to his verse.
Other admirable men have led lives in some sort of keeping
with their thought; but this man, in wide contrast. Had
he been less, had he reached only the common measure of
great authors, of Bacon, Milton, Tasso, Cervantes, we might
leave the fact in the twilight of human fate: but that this
man of men, he who gave to the science of mind a new
and larger subject than had ever existed, and planted the
standard of humanity some furlongs forward into Chaos, —
that he should not be wise for himself; — it must even go

into the world's history that the best poet led an obscure and profane life, using his genius for the public amusement.

Well, other men, priest and prophet, Israelite, German and Swede, beheld the same objects : they also saw through them that which was contained. And to what purpose? The beauty straightway vanished ; they read commandments, all-excluding mountainous duty ; an obligation, a sadness, as of piled mountains, fell on them, and life became ghastly, joyless, a pilgrim's progress, a probation, beleaguered round with doleful histories of Adam's fall and curse behind us ; with doomsdays and purgatorial and penal fires before us ; and the heart of the seer and the heart of the listener sank in them.

It must be conceded that these are half-views of half-men. The world still wants its poet-priest, a reconciler, who shall not trifle, with Shakspeare the player, nor shall grope in graves, with Swedenborg the mourner ; but who shall see, speak, and act, with equal inspiration. For knowledge will brighten the sunshine ; right is more beautiful than private affection ; and love is compatible with universal wisdom.

EDGAR ALLAN POE

1809 – 1849

EXORDIUM

[*From " Graham's Magazine," 1842*]

IN commencing, with the New Year, a New Volume, we shall be permitted to say a very few words by way of *exordium* to our usual chapter of Reviews, or, as we should prefer calling them, of Critical Notices. Yet we speak *not* for the sake of *exordium*, but because we have really something to say, and know not when or where better to say it.

That the public attention, in America, has, of late days, been more than usually directed to the matter of literary criticism, is plainly apparent. Our periodicals are beginning to acknowledge the importance of the science (shall we so term it?), and to disdain the flippant *opinion* which so long has been made its substitute.

Time was when we imported our critical decisions from the mother country. For many years we enacted a perfect farce of subserviency to the *dicta* of Great Britain. At last a revulsion of feeling, with self-disgust, necessarily ensued. Urged by these, we plunged into the opposite extreme. In throwing *totally* off that "authority," whose voice had so long been so sacred, we even surpassed, and by much, our original folly. But the watchword now was, "A national literature ! " — as if any true literature *could be* "national" — as if the world at large were not the only proper stage for the literary *histrio*. We became, suddenly, the merest and maddest *partizans* in letters. Our papers spoke of "tariffs" and "protection." Our Magazines had habitual passages about that "truly native novelist, Mr. Cooper,"

or that " staunch American genius, Mr. Paulding." Un-
mindful of the spirit of the axioms that " a prophet has no
honor in his own land " and that " a hero is never a hero
to his *valet-de-chambre*" — axioms founded in reason and
in truth — our reviews urged the propriety — our book-
sellers the necessity, of strictly " American " themes. A
foreign subject, at this epoch, was a weight more than
enough to drag down into the very depths of critical dam-
nation the finest writer owning nativity in the States ; while,
on the reverse, we found ourselves daily in the paradoxical
dilemma of liking, or pretending to like, a stupid book the
better because (sure enough) its stupidity was of our own
growth, and discussed our own affairs.

It is, in fact, but very lately that this anomalous state
of feeling has shown any signs of subsidence. Still it *is*
subsiding. Our views of literature in general having ex-
panded, we begin to demand the use — to inquire into
the offices and provinces of criticism — to regard it more
as an art based immoveably in nature, less as a mere system
of fluctuating and conventional dogmas. And, with the
prevalence of these ideas, has arrived a distaste even to the
home-dictation of the bookseller-*coteries*. If our editors
are not as yet *all* independent of the will of a publisher,
a majority of them scruple, at least, *to confess* a subservi-
ence, and enter into no positive combinations against the
minority who despise and discard it. And this is a *very*
great improvement of exceedingly late date.

Escaping these quicksands, our criticism is nevertheless
in some danger — some very little danger — of falling into
the pit of a most detestable species of cant — the cant of
generality. This tendency has been given it, in the first
instance, by the onward and tumultuous spirit of the age.
With the increase of the thinking-material comes the desire,
if not the necessity, of abandoning particulars for masses.
Yet in our individual case, as a nation, we seem merely to
have adopted this bias from the British Quarterly Reviews,
upon which our own Quarterlies have been slavishly and

pertinaciously modelled. In the foreign journal, the review or criticism properly so termed has gradually yet steadily degenerated into what we see it at present — that is to say, into anything but criticism. Originally a " review " was not so called as *lucus a non lucendo*. Its name conveyed a just idea of its design. It reviewed, or surveyed the book whose title formed its text, and, giving an analysis of its contents, passed judgment upon its merits or defects. But, through the system of anonymous contribution, this natural process lost ground from day to day. The name of a writer being known only to a few, it became to him an object not so much to write well, as to write fluently, at so many guineas per sheet. The analysis of a book is a matter of time and of mental exertion. For many classes of composition there is required a deliberate perusal, with notes, and subsequent generalization. An easy substitute for this labor was found in a digest or compendium of the work noticed, with copious extracts — or a still easier, in random comments upon such passages as accidentally met the eye of the critic, with the passages themselves copied at full length. The mode of reviewing most in favor, however, because carrying with it the greatest *semblance* of care, was that of diffuse essay upon the subject matter of the publication, the reviewer (?) using the facts alone which the publication supplied, and using them as material for some theory, the sole concern, bearing, and intention of which, was mere difference of opinion with the author. These came at length to be understood and habitually practised as the customary or conventional *fashions* of review ; and although the nobler order of intellects did not fall into the full heresy of these fashions — we may still assert that even Macaulay's nearest approach to criticism in its legitimate sense, is to be found in his article upon Ranke's " History of the Popes " — an article in which the whole strength of the reviewer is put forth *to account* for a single fact — the progress of Romanism — which the book under discussion has established.

Now, while we do not mean to deny that a good essay is a good thing, we yet assert that these papers on general topics have nothing whatever to do with that *criticism* which their evil example has nevertheless infected *in se*. Because these dogmatising pamphlets, which *were once* "Reviews," have lapsed from their original faith, it does not follow that the faith itself is extinct — that "there shall be no more cakes and ale" — that criticism, in its old acceptation, does not exist. But we complain of a growing inclination on the part of our lighter journals to believe, on such grounds, that such is the fact — that because the British Quarterlies, through supineness, and our own, through a degrading imitation, have come to merge all varieties of vague generalization in the one title of "Review," it therefore results that criticism, being everything in the universe, is, consequently, nothing whatever in fact. For to this end, and to none other conceivable, is the tendency of such propositions, for example, as we find in a late number of that very clever monthly magazine, Arcturus.

"But *now*" (the emphasis on the *now* is our own) — "But *now*" says Mr. Matthews in the preface to the first volume of his journal, "criticism has a wider scope and a universal interest. It dismisses errors of grammar, and hands over an imperfect rhyme or a false quantity to the proof-reader ; it looks *now* to the heart of the subject and the author's design. It is a test of opinion. Its acuteness is not pedantic, but philosophical ; it unravels the web of the author's mystery to interpret his meaning to others ; it detects his sophistry, because sophistry is injurious to the heart and life ; it promulgates his beauties with liberal, generous praise, because this is its true duty as the servant of truth. Good criticism may be well asked for, since it is the type of the literature of the day. It gives method to the universal inquisitiveness on every topic relating to life or action. A criticism, *now*, includes every form of literature, except perhaps the imaginative and the strictly dramatic. It is an essay, a sermon, an oration, a chapter in history, a philosophical speculation, a prose-poem, an art-novel, a dialogue ; it admits of humor, pathos, the personal feelings of auto-biography, the broadest views of statesmanship. As the ballad and the epic were the productions of the age of Homer, the review is the native characteristic growth of the nineteenth century."

We respect the talent of Mr. Mathews, but must dissent from nearly all that he here says. The species of "review" which he designates as the "characteristic growth of the nineteenth century" is only the growth of the last twenty or thirty years *in Great Britain*. The French Reviews, for example, which are *not* anonymous, are very different things, and preserve the *unique* spirit of true criticism. And what need we say of the Germans? — what of Winckelmann, of Novalis, of Schelling, of Goethe, of Augustus William, and of Frederick Schlegel? — that their magnificent *critiques raisonnées* differ from those of Kames, of Johnson, and of Blair, in principle not at all, (for the principles of these artists will not fail until Nature herself expires,) but solely in their more careful elaboration, their greater thoroughness, their more profound analysis and application of the principles themselves. That a criticism "*now*" should be different in spirit, as Mr. Mathews supposes, from a criticism at any previous period, is to insinuate a charge of variability in laws that cannot vary — the laws of man's heart and intellect — for these are the sole basis upon which the true critical art is established. And this art "*now*" no more than in the days of the "Dunciad," can, without neglect of its duty, "dismiss errors of grammar," or "hand over an imperfect rhyme or a false quantity to the proof-reader." What is meant by a "test of opinion" in the connexion here given the words by Mr. M., we do not comprehend as clearly as we could desire. By this phrase we are as completely enveloped in doubt as was Mirabeau in the castle of *If*. To our imperfect appreciation it seems to form a portion of that general vagueness which is the *tone* of the whole philosophy at this point : — but all that which our journalist describes a criticism to be, is all that which we sturdily maintain it *is not*. Criticism is *not*, we think, an essay, nor a sermon, nor an oration, nor a chapter in history, nor a philosophical speculation, nor a prose-poem, nor an art novel, nor a dialogue. In fact, it *can be* nothing in the world but — a criticism. But if it were all that Arcturus imagines, it is not very clear why it might not be equally "imaginative" or "dramatic" — a romance or a melodrama, or both. That it would be a farce cannot be doubted.

It is against this frantic spirit of *generalization* that we protest. We have a word, "criticism," whose import is sufficiently distinct, through long usage, at least; and we have an art of high importance and clearly-ascertained limit, which this word is quite well enough understood to represent. Of that conglomerate science to which Mr. Mathews so eloquently alludes, and of which we are instructed that it is anything and everything at once — of this science we know nothing, and really wish to know less; but we object to our contemporary's appropriation in its behalf, of a term to which we, in common with a large majority of mankind, have been accustomed to attach a certain and very definite idea. Is there no word but "criticism" which may be made to serve the purposes of "Arcturus?" Has it any objection to Orphicism, or Dialism, or Emersonism, or any other pregnant compound indicative of confusion worse confounded?

Still, we must not pretend a total misapprehension of the idea of Mr. Mathews, and we should be sorry that he misunderstood *us*. It may be granted that we differ only in terms — although the difference will yet be found not unimportant in effect. Following the highest authority, we would wish, in a word, to limit literary criticism to comment upon *Art*. A book is written — and it is only *as the book* that we subject it to review. With the opinions of the work, considered otherwise than in their relation to the work itself, the critic has really nothing to do. It is his part simply to decide upon *the mode* in which these opinions are brought to bear. Criticism is thus no " test of opinion." For this test, the work, divested of its pretensions as an *art-product*, is turned over for discussion to the world at large — and first, to that class which it especially addresses — if a history, to the historian — if a metaphysical treatise, to the moralist. In this, the only true and intelligible sense, it will be seen that criticism, the test or analysis of *Art*, (*not* of opinion,) is only properly employed upon productions which have their basis in art itself, and although the journalist (whose duties and objects are multiform) may turn aside, at pleasure, from the *mode* or vehicle of opinion to discussion of the opinion conveyed — it is still clear that he is "*critical*" only in so much as he deviates from his true province not at all.

And of the critic himself what shall we say? — for as yet we have spoken only the *proem* to the true *epopea*. What *can* we better say of him than, with Bulwer, that "he must have courage to blame boldly, magnanimity to eschew envy, genius to appreciate, learning to compare, an eye for beauty, an ear for music, and a heart for feeling." Let us add, a talent for analysis and a solemn indifference to abuse.

THE POETIC PRINCIPLE

[*From " Sartain's Union Magazine," 1850*]

IN speaking of the Poetic Principle, I have no design to be either thorough or profound. While discussing, very much at random, the essentiality of what we call Poetry, my principal purpose will be to cite for consideration, some few of those minor English or American poems which best suit my own taste, or which, upon my own fancy, have left the most definite impression. By "minor poems" I mean, of course, poems of little length. And here, in the beginning, permit me to say a few words in regard to a somewhat peculiar principle, which, whether rightfully or wrongfully, has always had its influence in my own critical estimate of the poem. I hold that a long poem does not exist. I maintain that the phrase, "a long poem," is simply a flat contradiction in terms.

I need scarcely observe that a poem deserves its title only inasmuch as it excites, by elevating the soul. The value of the poem is in the ratio of this elevating excitement. But all excitements are, through a psychal necessity, transient. That degree of excitement which would entitle a poem to be so called at all, cannot be sustained throughout a composition of any great length. After the lapse of half an hour, at the very utmost, it flags — fails — a revulsion ensues — and then the poem is, in effect, and in fact, no longer such.

There are, no doubt, many who have found difficulty in reconciling the critical dictum that the " Paradise Lost " is to be devoutly admired throughout, with the absolute impossibility of maintaining for it, during perusal, the amount of enthusiasm which that critical dictum would demand. This great work, in fact, is to be regarded as poetical, only when, losing sight of that vital requisite in all works of Art, Unity, we view it merely as a series of minor poems. If, to preserve its Unity — its totality of effect or impression — we read it (as would be necessary) at a single sitting, the result is but a constant alternation of excitement and depression. After a passage of what we feel to be true poetry, there follows, inevitably, a passage of platitude which no critical pre-judgment can force us to admire; but if, upon completing the work, we read it again; omitting the first book — that is to say, commencing with the second — we shall be surprised at now finding that admirable which we before condemned — that damnable which we had previously so much admired. It follows from all this that the ultimate, aggregate, or absolute effect of even the best epic under the sun, is a nullity : — and this is precisely the fact.

In regard to the Iliad, we have, if not positive proof, at least very good reason, for believing it intended as a series of lyrics; but, granting the epic intention, I can say only that the work is based in an imperfect sense of art. The modern epic is, of the supposititious ancient model, but an inconsiderate and blindfolded imitation. But the day of these artistic anomalies is over. If, at any time, any very long poem *were* popular in reality, which I doubt, it is at least clear that no very long poem will ever be popular again.

That the extent of a poetical work is, *ceteris paribus*, the measure of its merit, seems undoubtedly, when we thus state it, a proposition sufficiently absurd — yet we are indebted for it to the Quarterly Reviews. Surely there can be nothing in mere *size*, abstractly considered — there can be nothing in mere *bulk*, so far as a volume is concerned, which has so continuously elicited admiration from these saturnine pamphlets ! A mountain, to be sure, by the mere sentiment of physical magnitude which it conveys, *does* impress us with a sense of the sublime — but no man is impressed after *this* fashion by the material grandeur of even " The Columbiad." Even the Quarterlies have not instructed us to be so impressed by it. *As yet*, they have not *insisted* on our estimating Lamartine by the cubic foot, or Pollok by the pound — but what else are we to *infer* from their continual prating about " sustained effort ? " If, by " sustained effort," any little gentleman has accomplished an epic, let us frankly commend him for the effort — if this indeed be a thing commendable — but let us forbear praising the epic on the effort's account. It is to be hoped that common sense, in the time to come, will prefer deciding upon a work of art, rather by the impression it makes, by the effect it produces, than by the time it took to impress the effect or by the amount of " sustained effort " which had been found necessary in effecting the impression. The fact is, that perseverance is one thing, and genius quite another — nor can all the Quarterlies in Christendom confound them. By-and-by, this proposition, with many which I have been just urging, will be received as self-evident. In the meantime, by being generally condemned as falsities, they will not be essentially damaged as truths.

On the other hand, it is clear that a poem may be improperly brief. Undue brevity degenerates into mere epigrammatism. A *very* short poem, while now and then producing a brilliant or vivid, never produces a profound or enduring effect. There must be the steady pressing down of the stamp upon the wax. De Béranger has wrought innumerable things, pungent and spirit-stirring ; but, in general, they have been too imponderous to stamp themselves deeply into the public attention ; and thus, as so many feathers of fancy, have been blown aloft only to be whistled down the wind.

A remarkable instance of the effect of undue brevity in depressing a poem — in keeping it out of the popular view — is afforded by the following exquisite little Serenade :

I arise from dreams of thee
    In the first sweet sleep of night,
When the winds are breathing low,
    And the stars are shining bright;
I arise from dreams of thee,
    And a spirit in my feet
Hath led me — who knows how? —
    To thy chamber-window, sweet!

The wandering airs, they faint
    On the dark, the silent stream —
The champak odours fail
    Like sweet thoughts in a dream;
The nightingale's complaint,
    It dies upon her heart,
As I must die on thine,
    O, beloved as thou art!

O, lift me from the grass!
    I die, I faint, I fail!
Let thy love in kisses rain
    On my lips and eyelids pale.
My cheek is cold and white, alas!
    My heart beats loud and fast:
Oh! press it close to thine again,
    Where it will break at last!

Very few, perhaps, are familiar with these lines — yet no less a poet than Shelley is their author. Their warm, yet delicate and ethereal imagination will be appreciated by all — but by none so thoroughly as by him who has himself arisen from sweet dreams of one beloved to bathe in the aromatic air of a southern midsummer night.

One of the finest poems by Willis — the very best, in my opinion, which he has ever written — has, no doubt, through this same defect of undue brevity, been kept back from its proper position, not less in the critical than in the popular view.

THE shadows lay along Broadway,
    'T was near the twilight-tide —
And slowly there a lady fair
    Was walking in her pride.
Alone walk'd she; but, viewlessly,
    Walk'd spirits at her side.

Peace charm'd the street beneath her feet,
 And Honour charm'd the air;
And all astir looked kind on her,
 And call'd her good and fair —
For all God ever gave to her
 She kept with chary care.

She kept with care her beauties rare
 From lovers warm and true —
For her heart was cold to all but gold,
 And the rich came not to woo —
But honour'd well are charms to sell,
 If priests the selling do.

Now walking there was one more fair —
 A slight girl, lily-pale;
And she had unseen company
 To make the spirit quail —
'Twixt Want and Scorn she walk'd forlorn,
 And nothing could avail.

No mercy now can clear her brow
 For this world's peace to pray;
For, as love's wild prayer dissolved in air,
 Her woman's heart gave way! —
But the sin forgiven by Christ in Heaven
 By man is cursed alway!

In this composition we find it difficult to recognize the Willis who has written so many mere " verses of society." The lines are not only richly ideal, but full of energy; while they breathe an earnestness — an evident sincerity of sentiment — for which we look in vain throughout all the other works of this author.

While the epic mania — while the idea that, to merit in poetry, prolixity is indispensable — has, for some years past, been gradually dying out of the public mind, by mere dint of its own absurdity — we find it succeeded by a heresy too palpably false to be long tolerated, but one which, in the brief period it has already endured, may be said to have accomplished more in the corruption of our Poetical Literature than all its other enemies combined. I allude to the heresy of *The Didactic.* It has been assumed, tacitly and avowedly, directly and indirectly, that the ultimate object of all Poetry is Truth. Every poem, it is said, should inculcate a moral; and by this moral is the poetical merit of the work to be adjudged. We Americans especially have patronised this happy idea; and we Bostonians, very especially, have developed it in full. We have taken it into our heads that to write a poem simply for the poem's sake, and to acknowledge such to have been our design, would be to confess ourselves radically wanting in the true Poetic dignity and force : — but the simple fact is, that, would we but permit ourselves to look into our own souls, we should immediately there discover that under the sun there neither exists nor *can* exist any work more thoroughly dignified — more supremely noble than this very poem — this poem *per se* — this poem which is a poem and nothing more — this poem written solely for the poem's sake.

With as deep a reverence for the True as ever inspired the bosom of man, I would, nevertheless, limit, in some measure, its modes of inculcation. I would limit to enforce them. I would not enfeeble them by dissipation. The demands of Truth are severe. She has no sympathy with the myrtles. All *that* which is so indispensable in Song, is precisely all *that* with which *she* has nothing whatever to do. It is but making her a flaunting paradox, to wreathe her in gems and flowers. In enforcing a truth, we need severity rather than efflorescence of language. We must be simple, precise, terse. We must be cool, calm, unimpassioned. In a word, we must be in that mood which, as nearly as possible, is the exact converse of the poetical. *He* must be blind, indeed, who does not perceive the radical and chasmal differences between the truthful and the poetical modes of inculcation. He must be theory-mad beyond redemption who, in spite of these differences, shall still persist in attempting to reconcile the obstinate oils and waters of Poetry and Truth.

Dividing the world of mind into its three most immediately obvious distinctions, we have the Pure Intellect,

Taste, and the Moral Sense. I place Taste in the middle,
because it is just this position which, in the mind, it occupies. It holds intimate relations with either extreme;
but from the Moral Sense is separated by so faint a difference that Aristotle has not hesitated to place some of its
operations among the virtues themselves. Nevertheless,
we find the *offices* of the trio marked with a sufficient distinction. Just as the Intellect concerns itself with Truth,
so Taste informs us of the Beautiful while the Moral Sense
is regardful of Duty. Of this latter, while Conscience
teaches the obligation, and Reason the expediency, Taste
contents herself with displaying the charms: — waging war
upon Vice solely on the ground of her deformity — her
disproportion — her animosity to the fitting, to the appropriate, to the harmonious — in a word, to Beauty.

An immortal instinct, deep within the spirit of man, is
thus, plainly, a sense of the Beautiful. This it is which
administers to his delight in the manifold forms, and
sounds, and odours, and sentiments amid which he exists.
And just as the lily is repeated in the lake, or the eyes of
Amaryllis in the mirror, so is the mere oral or written
repetition of these forms, and sounds, and colours, and
odours, and sentiments, a duplicate source of delight. But
this mere repetition is not poetry. He who shall simply
sing, with however glowing enthusiasm, or with however
vivid a truth of description, of the sights, and sounds, and
odours, and colours, and sentiments, which greet *him* in
common with all mankind — he, I say, has yet failed to
prove his divine title. There is still a something in the
distance which he has been unable to attain. We have
still a thirst unquenchable, to allay which he has not shown
us the crystal springs. This thirst belongs to the immortality of Man. It is at once a consequence and an indication of his perennial existence. It is the desire of the
moth for the star. It is no mere appreciation of the Beauty
before us — but a wild effort to reach the Beauty above.
Inspired by an ecstatic prescience of the glories beyond

the grave, we struggle, by multiform combinations among the things and thoughts of Time, to attain a portion of that Loveliness whose very elements, perhaps, appertain to eternity alone. And thus when by Poetry — or when by Music, the most entrancing of the Poetic moods — we find ourselves melted into tears — we weep then — not as the Abbate Gravina supposes — through excess of pleasure, but through a certain petulant, impatient sorrow at our inability to grasp *now*, wholly, here on earth, at once and for ever, those divine and rapturous joys, of which *through* the poem, ·or *through* the music, we attain to but brief and indeterminate glimpses.

The struggle to apprehend the supernal Loveliness — — this struggle, on the part of souls fittingly constituted has given to the world all *that* which it (the world) has ever been enabled at once to understand and *to feel* as poetic.

The Poetic Sentiment, of course, may develope itself in various modes — in Painting, in Sculpture, in Architecture, in the Dance — very especially in Music — and very peculiarly, and with a wide field, in the composition of the Landscape Garden. Our present theme, however, has regard only to its manifestation in words. And here let me speak briefly on the topic of rhythm. Contenting myself with the certainty that Music, in its various modes of metre, rhythm, and rhyme, is of so vast a moment in Poetry as never to be wisely rejected — is so vitally important an adjunct that he is simply silly who declines its assistance, I will not now pause to maintain its absolute essentiality. It is in Music, perhaps, that the soul most nearly attains the great end for which, when inspired by the Poetic Sentiment, it struggles — the creation of supernal Beauty. It *may* be, indeed, that here this sublime end is, now and then, attained *in fact*. We are often made to feel, with a shivering delight, that from an earthly harp are stricken notes which *cannot* have been unfamiliar to the angels. And thus there can be little doubt that in the union of Poetry with Music in its popular sense, we shall find the widest field for the Poetic development. The old Bards and Minnesingers had advantages which we do not possess — and Thomas Moore, singing his own songs, was, in the most legitimate manner, perfecting them as poems.

To recapitulate, then : — I would define, in brief, the Poetry of words as *The Rhythmical Creation of Beauty*. Its sole arbiter is Taste. With the Intellect or with the Conscience, it has only collateral relations. Unless incidentally, it has no concern whatever either with Duty or with Truth.

A few words, however, in explanation. *That* pleasure which is at once the most pure, the most elevating, and the most intense, is derived, I maintain, from the contemplation of the Beautiful. In the contemplation of Beauty we alone find it possible to attain that pleasurable elevation, or excitement, *of the soul*, which we recognise as the Poetic Sentiment, and which is so easily distinguished from Truth, which is the satisfaction of the Reason, or from Passion, which is the excitement of the heart. I make Beauty, therefore — using the word as inclusive of the sublime — I make Beauty the province of the poem, simply because it is an obvious rule of Art that effects should be made to spring as directly as possible from their causes : — no one as yet having been weak enough to deny that the peculiar elevation in question is at least *most readily* attainable in the poem. It by no means follows, however, that the incitements of Passion, or the precepts of Duty, or even the lessons of Truth, may not be introduced into a poem, and with advantage ; for they may subserve, incidentally, in various ways, the general purposes of the work : — but the true artist will always contrive to tone them down in proper subjection to that *Beauty* which is the atmosphere and the real essence of the poem.

I cannot better introduce the few poems which I shall present for your consideration, than by the citation of the Proem to Mr. Longfellow's "Waif" :

The day is done, and the darkness
    Falls from the wings of Night,
As a feather is wafted downward
    From an Eagle in his flight.

I see the lights of the village
    Gleam through the rain and the mist,
And a feeling of sadness comes o'er me,
    That my soul cannot resist;

A feeling of sadness and longing,
    That is not akin to pain,
And resembles sorrow only
    As the mist resembles the rain.

Come read to me some poem,
    Some simple and heatfelt lay,
That shall soothe this restless feeling
    And banish the thoughts of day.

Not from the grand old masters,
    Not from the bards sublime,
Whose distant footsteps echo
    Through the corridors of Time.

For, like strains of martial music,
    Their mighty thoughts suggest
Life's endless toil and endeavour;
    And to-night I long for rest.

Read from some humbler poet,
    Whose songs gushed from his heart,
As showers from the clouds of summer,
    Or tears from the eyelids start;

Who through long days of labour,
    And nights devoid of ease,
Still heard in his soul the music
    Of wonderful melodies.

Such songs have power to quiet
    The restless pulse of care,
And come like the benediction
    That follows after prayer.

Then read from the treasured volume
    The poem of thy choice,
And lend to the rhyme of the poet
    The beauty of thy voice.

> And the night shall be filled with music,
>   And the cares that infest the day,
> Shall fold their tents, like the Arabs,
>   And as silently steal away.

With no great range of imagination, these lines have been justly admired for their delicacy of expression. Some of the images are very effective. Nothing can be better than —

> ———— The bards sublime,
> Whose distant footsteps echo
> Down the corridors of Time.

The idea of the last quatrain is also very effective. The poem, on the whole, however, is chiefly to be admired for the graceful *insouciance* of its metre, so well in accordance with the character of the sentiments, and especially for the *ease* of the general manner. This "ease," or naturalness, in a literary style, it has long been the fashion to regard as ease in appearance alone — as a point of really difficult attainment. But not so : — a natural manner is difficult only to him who should never meddle with it — to the unnatural. It is but the result of writing with the understanding, or with the instinct, that *the tone*, in composition, should always be that which the mass of mankind would adopt — and must perpetually vary, of course, with the occasion. The author who, after the fashion of "The North American Review," should be, upon *all* occasions, merely "quiet," must necessarily upon *many* occasions, be simply silly, or stupid ; and has no more right to be considered "easy," or "natural," than a Cockney exquisite, or than the sleeping Beauty in the wax-works.

Among the minor poems of Bryant, none has so much impressed me as the one which he entitles "June." I quote only a portion of it :

> There, through the long, long summer hours,
>   The golden light should lie,
> And thick young herbs and groups of flowers
>   Stand in their beauty by.

The oriole should build and tell
His love-tale, close beside my cell;
    The idle butterfly
Should rest him there, and there be heard
The housewife-bee and humming-bird.

And what if cheerful shouts, at noon,
    Come, from the village sent,
Or songs of maids, beneath the moon,
    With fairy laughter blent?
And what, if in the evening light,
Betrothed lovers walk in sight
    Of my low monument?
I would the lovely scene around
Might know no sadder sight nor sound.

I know, I know I should not see
    The season's glorious show,
Nor would its brightness shine for me,
    Nor its wild music flow;
But if, around my place of sleep,
The friends I love should come to weep,
    They might not haste to go.
Soft airs, and song, and light, and bloom
Should keep them lingering by my tomb.

These to their softened hearts should bear
    The thought of what has been,
And speak of one who cannot share
    The gladness of the scene;
Whose part, in all the pomp that fills
The circuit of the summer hills,
    Is — that his grave is green;
And deeply would their hearts rejoice
To hear again his living voice.

The rhythmical flow, here, is even voluptuous — nothing could be more melodious. The poem has always affected me in a remarkable manner. The intense melancholy which seems to well up, perforce, to the surface of all the poet's cheerful sayings about his grave, we find thrilling us to the soul — while there is the truest poetic elevation in the thrill. The impression left is one of a pleasurable sadness. And if, in the remaining compositions which I shall introduce to you, there be more or

less of a similar tone always apparent, let me remind you
that (how or why we know not) this certain taint of sadness
is inseparably connected with all the higher manifestations
of true Beauty.   It is, nevertheless,

> A feeling of sadness and longing
> That is not akin to pain,
> And resembles sorrow only
> As the mist resembles the rain.

The taint of which I speak is clearly perceptible even in
a poem so full of brilliancy and spirit as the "Health" of
Edward Coate Pinckney:

> I fill this cup to one made up
> Of loveliness alone,
> A woman, of her gentle sex
> The seeming paragon ;
> To whom the better elements
> And kindly stars have given
> A form so fair, that, like the air,
> 'T is less of earth than heaven.
>
> Her every tone is music's own,
> Like those of morning birds,
> And something more than melody
> Dwells ever in her words ;
> The coinage of her heart are they,
> And from her lips each flows
> As one may see the burden'd bee
> Forth issue from the rose.
>
> Affections are as thoughts to her,
> The measures of her hours ;
> Her feelings have the fragrancy,
> The freshness of young flowers,
> And lovely passions, changing oft,
> So fill her, she appears
> The image of themselves by turns, —
> The idol of past years !
>
> Of her bright face one glance will trace
> A picture on the brain,
> And of her voice in echoing hearts
> A sound must long remain ;

But memory, such as mine of her,
  So very much endears,
When death is nigh, my latest sigh
  Will not be life's but hers.

I fill this cup to one made up
  Of loveliness alone,
A woman, of her gentle sex
  The seeming paragon —
Her health! and would on earth there stood,
  Some more of such a frame,
That life might be all poetry,
  And weariness a name.

It was the misfortune of Mr. Pinckney to have been born too far south. Had he been a New Englander, it is probable that he would have been ranked as the first of American lyrists, by that magnanimous cabal which has so long controlled the destinies of American Letters, in conducting the thing called "The North American Review." The poem just cited is especially beautiful; but the poetic elevation which it induces, we must refer chiefly to our sympathy in the poet's enthusiasm. We pardon his hyperboles for the evident earnestness with which they are uttered.

It was by no means my design, however, to expatiate upon the *merits* of what I should read you. These will necessarily speak for themselves. Boccalini, in his "Advertisements from Parnassus," tells us that Zoilus once presented Apollo a very caustic criticism upon a very admirable book: — whereupon the god asked him for the beauties of the work. He replied that he only busied himself about the errors. On hearing this, Apollo, handing him a sack of unwinnowed wheat, bade him pick out *all the chaff* for his reward.

Now this fable answers very well as a hit at the critics — but I am by no means sure that the god was in the right. I am by no means certain that the true limits of the critical duty are not grossly misunderstood. Excellence, in a poem especially, may be considered in the light of an axiom, which need only be properly *put*, to become self-evident.

It is *not* excellence if it require to be demonstrated as such :
— and thus, to point out too particularly the merits of a
work of Art, is to admit that they are *not* merits altogether.

Among the " Melodies " of Thomas Moore, is one whose
distinguished character as a poem proper, seems to have
been singularly left out of view.   I allude to his lines beginning — " Come, rest in this bosom."   The intense
energy of their expression is not surpassed by anything in
Byron.   There are two of the lines in which a sentiment is
conveyed that embodies the *all in all* of the divine passion
of love — a sentiment which, perhaps, has found its echo
in more, and in more passionate, human hearts than any
other single sentiment ever embodied in words :

> Come, rest in this bosom, my own stricken deer,
> Though the herd have fled from thee, thy home is still here;
> Here still is the smile, that no cloud can o'ercast,
> And a heart and a hand all thy own to the last.
>
> Oh ! what was love made for, if 't is not the same
> Through joy and through torment, through glory and shame ?
> I know not, I ask not, if guilt 's in that heart
> I but know that I love thee, whatever thou art.
>
> Thou hast call'd me thy Angel in moments of bliss,
> And thy Angel I 'll be, 'mid the horrors of this, —
> Through the furnace, unshrinking, thy steps to pursue,
> And shield thee, and save thee, — or perish there too !

It has been the fashion, of late days, to deny Moore imagination, while granting him fancy — a distinction origi-
nating with Coleridge — than whom no man more fully
comprehended the great powers of Moore.   The fact is,
that the fancy of this poet so far predominates over all his
other faculties, and over the fancy of all other men, as to
have induced, very naturally, the idea that he is fanciful
only.   But never was there a greater mistake.   Never was
a grosser wrong done the fame of a true poet.   In the compass of the English language I can call to mind no poem
more profoundly — more weirdly *imaginative*, in the best
sense, than the lines commencing — " I would I were by

that dim lake " — which are the composition of Thomas
Moore.   I regret that I am unable to remember them.

One of the noblest — and, speaking of fancy, one of the
most singularly fanciful of modern poets, was Thomas
Hood.   His " Fair Ines " had always, for me, an inexpressible charm :

> O saw ye not fair Ines !
>   She 's gone into the West,
> To dazzle when the sun is down,
>   And rob the world of rest :
> She took our daylight with her,
>   The smiles that we love best,
> With morning blushes on her cheek,
>   And pearls upon her breast.
>
> O turn again, fair Ines,
>   Before the fall of night,
> For fear the moon should shine alone,
>   And stars unrivall'd bright ;
> And blessed will the lover be
>   That walks beneath their light,
> And breathes the love against thy cheek
>   I dare not even write !
>
> Would I had been, fair Ines,
>   That gallant cavalier,
> Who rode so gaily by thy side,
>   And whisper'd thee so near !
> Were there no bonny dames at home,
>   Or no true lovers here,
> That he should cross the seas to win
>   The dearest of the dear ?
>
> I saw thee, lovely Ines,
>   Descend along the shore,
> With bands of noble gentlemen,
>   And banners wav'd before ;
> And gentle youth and maidens gay,
>   And snowy plumes they wore ;
> It would have been a beauteous dream,
>   If it had been no more !
>
> Alas, alas, fair Ines,
>   She went away with song,
> With Music waiting on her steps,
>   And shoutings of the throng ;

But some were sad and felt no mirth,
    But only Music's wrong,
In sounds that sang farewell, farewell,
    To her you 've loved so long.

Farewell, farewell, fair Ines,
    That vessel never bore
So fair a lady on its deck,
    Nor danced so light before, —
Alas for pleasure on the sea,
    And sorrow on the shore !
The smile that blest one lover's heart
    Has broken many more !

"The Haunted House," by the same author, is one of the truest poems ever written — one of the *truest* — one of the most unexceptionable — one of the most thoroughly artistic, both in its theme and in its execution. It is, moreover, powerfully ideal — imaginative. I regret that its length renders it unsuitable for the purposes of this Lecture. In place of it, permit me to offer the universally appreciated "Bridge of Sighs."

One more Unfortunate,
Weary of breath,
Rashly importunate,
Gone to her death !

Take her up tenderly,
Lift her with care ; —
Fashion'd so slenderly,
Young, and so fair !

Look at her garments
Clinging like cerements ;
Whilst the wave constantly
Drips from her clothing ;
Take her up instantly,
Loving, not loathing. —

Touch her not scornfully ;
Think of her mournfully,
Gently and humanly ;
Not of the stains of her,
All that remains of her
Now, is pure womanly.

Make no deep scrutiny
Into her mutiny
Rash and undutiful;
Past all dishonour,
Death has left on her
Only the beautiful.

Still, for all slips of hers,
One of Eve's family —
Wipe those poor lips of hers
Oozing so clammily,
Loop up her tresses
Escaped from the comb,
Her fair auburn tresses;
Whilst wonderment guesses
Where was her home?

Who was her father?
Who was her mother?
Had she a sister?
Had she a brother?
Or was there a dearer one
Still, and a nearer one
Yet, than all other?

Alas! for the rarity
Of Christian charity
Under the sun!
Oh! it was pitiful!
Near a whole city full,
Home she had none.

Sisterly, brotherly,
Fatherly, motherly
Feelings had changed:
Love, by harsh evidence,
Thrown from its eminence,
Even God's providence
Seeming estranged.

Where the lamps quiver
So far in the river,
With many a light
From window and casement
From garret to basement,
She stood, with amazement,
Houseless by night.

The bleak wind of March
Made her tremble and shiver;
But not the dark arch,
Or the black flowing river:
Mad from life's history,
Glad to death's mystery,
Swift to be hurl'd —
Anywhere, anywhere
Out of the world!

In she plunged boldly,
No matter how coldly
The rough river ran, —
Over the brink of it,
Picture it — think of it,
Dissolute Man!
Lave in it, drink of it
Then, if you can!

Take her up tenderly,
Lift her with care;
Fashion'd so slenderly,
Young, and so fair!

Ere her limbs frigidly
Stiffen too rigidly,
Decently, — kindly, —
Smooth, and compose them;
And her eyes, close them,
Staring so blindly!

Dreadfully staring
Through muddy impurity,
As when with the daring
Last look of despairing
Fixed on futurity.

Perishing gloomily,
Spurred by contumely,
Cold inhumanity,
Burning insanity,
Into her rest, —
Cross her hands humbly,
As if praying dumbly,
Over her breast!
Owning her weakness,
Her evil behaviour,
And leaving, with meekness,
Her sins to her Saviour!

The vigour of this poem is no less remarkable than its pathos. The versification, although carrying the fanciful to the very verge of the fantastic, is nevertheless admirably adapted to the wild insanity which is the thesis of the poem.

Among the minor poems of Lord Byron, is one which has never received from the critics the praise which it undoubtedly deserves :

Though the day of my destiny 's over,
    And the star of my fate hath declined,
Thy soft heart refused to discover
    The faults which so many could find ;
Though thy soul with my grief was acquainted
    It shrunk not to share it with me,
And the love which my spirit hath painted
    It never hath found but in *thee*.

Then when nature around me is smiling,
    The last smile which answers to mine,
I do not believe it beguiling,
    Because it reminds me of thine ;
And when winds are at war with the ocean,
    As the breasts I believed in with me,
If their billows excite an emotion,
    It is that they bear me from *thee*.

Though the rock of my last hope is shivered,
    And its fragments are sunk in the wave,
Though I feel that my soul is delivered
    To pain — it shall not be its slave.
There is many a pang to pursue me :
    They may crush, but they shall not contemn —
They may torture, but shall not subdue me —
    'T is of *thee* that I think — not of them.

Though human, thou didst not deceive me,
    Though woman, thou didst not forsake,
Though loved, thou forborest to grieve me,
    Though slandered, thou never couldst shake, —
Though trusted, thou didst not disclaim me,
    Though parted, it was not to fly,
Though watchful, 't was not to defame me,
    Nor mute, that the world might belie.

Yet I blame not the world, nor despise it,
  Nor the war of the many with one —
If my soul was not fitted to prize it,
  'T was folly not sooner to shun :
And if dearly that error hath cost me,
  And more than I once could foresee,
I have found that whatever it lost me,
  It could not deprive me of *thee*.

From the wreck of the past, which hath perished,
  Thus much I at least may recall,
It hath taught me that what I most cherished
  Deserved to be dearest of all :
In the desert a fountain is springing,
  In the wide waste there still is a tree,
And a bird in the solitude singing,
  Which speaks to my spirit of *thee*.

Although the rhythm here is one of the most difficult, the versification could scarcely be improved. No nobler *theme* ever engaged the pen of poet. It is the soul-elevating idea, that no man can consider himself entitled to complain of Fate while, in his adversity, he still retains the unwavering love of woman.

From Alfred Tennyson — although in perfect sincerity I regard him as the noblest poet that ever lived — I have left myself time to cite only a very brief specimen. I call him, and *think* him the noblest of poets — *not* because the impressions he produces are, at *all* times, the most profound — *not* because the poetical excitement which he induces is, at *all* times, the most intense — but because it *is*, at all times, the most ethereal — in other words, the most elevating and the most pure. No poet is so little of the earth, earthy. What I am about to read is from his last long poem, " The Princess " :

  Tears, idle tears, I know not what they mean,
  Tears from the depth of some divine despair
  Rise in the heart, and gather to the eyes,
  In looking on the happy Autumn-fields,
  And thinking of the days that are no more.

Fresh as the first beam glittering on a sail,
That brings our friends up from the underworld,
Sad as the last which reddens over one
That sinks with all we love below the verge;
So sad, so fresh, the days that are no more.

Ah, sad and strange as in dark summer dawns
The earliest pipe of half-awaken'd birds
To dying ears, when unto dying eyes
The casement slowly grows a glimmering square;
So sad, so strange, the days that are no more.

Dear as remember'd kisses after death,
And sweet as those by hopeless fancy feign'd
On lips that are for others; deep as love,
Deep as first love, and wild with all regret;
O Death in Life, the days that are no more.

Thus, although in a very cursory and imperfect manner,
I have endeavoured to convey to you my conception of the
Poetic Principle. It has been my purpose to suggest that,
while this Principle itself is, strictly and simply, the Human
Aspiration for Supernal Beauty, the manifestation of the
Principle is always found in an *elevating excitement of the
Soul* — quite independent of that passion which is the in-
toxication of the Heart — or of that Truth which is the
satisfaction of the Reason. For, in regard to Passion, alas!
its tendency is to degrade, rather than to elevate the Soul.
Love, on the contrary — Love — the true, the divine Eros
— the Uranian, as distinguished from the Dionæan Venus
— is unquestionably the purest and truest of all poetical
themes. And in regard to Truth — if, to be sure, through
the attainment of a truth, we are led to perceive a harmony
where none was apparent before, we experience, at once,
the true poetical effect — but this effect is referable to the
harmony alone, and not in the least degree to the truth
which merely served to render the harmony manifest.

We shall reach, however, more immediately a distinct
conception of what the true Poetry is, by mere reference to
a few of the simple elements which induce in the Poet himself the true poetical effect. He recognises the ambrosia

which nourishes his soul, in the bright orbs that shine in Heaven — in the volutes of the flower — in the clustering of low shrubberies — in the waving of the grain-fields — in the slanting of tall, Eastern trees — in the blue distance of mountains — in the grouping of clouds — in the twinkling of half-hidden brooks — in the gleaming of silver rivers — in the repose of sequestered lakes — in the star-mirroring depths of lonely wells. He perceives it in the songs of birds — in the harp of Æolus — in the sighing of the night-wind — in the repining voice of the forest — in the surf that complains to the shore — in the fresh breath of the woods — in the scent of the violet — in the voluptuous perfume of the hyacinth — in the suggestive odour that comes to him, at eventide, from far-distant, undiscovered islands, over dim oceans, illimitable and unexplored. He owns it in all noble thoughts — in all unworldly motives — in all holy impulses — in all chivalrous, generous, and self-sacrificing deeds. He feels it in the beauty of woman — in the grace of her step — in the lustre of her eye — in the melody of her voice — in her soft laughter — in her sigh — in the harmony of the rustling of her robes. He deeply feels it in her winning endearments — in her burning enthusiasms — in her gentle charities — in her meek and devotional endurances — but above all — ah, far above all — he kneels to it — he worships it in the faith, in the purity, in the strength, in the altogether divine majesty — of her *love*.

Let me conclude — by the recitation of yet another brief poem — one very different in character from any that I have before quoted. It is by Motherwell, and is called "The Song of the Cavalier." With our modern and altogether rational ideas of the absurdity and impiety of warfare, we are not precisely in that frame of mind best adapted to sympathise with the sentiments, and thus to appreciate the real excellence of the poem. To do this fully, we must identify ourselves, in fancy, with the soul of the old cavalier.

Then mounte ! then mounte, brave gallants, all,
   And don your helmes amaine :
Deathe's couriers, Fame and Honour, call
   Us to the field againe.
No shrewish teares shall fill our eye
   When the sword-hilt 's in our hand, —
Heart-whole we 'll part, and no whit sighe
   For the fayrest of the land ;
Let piping swaine, and craven wight,
   Thus weepe and puling crye,
Our business is like men to fight,
   And hero-like to die !

MARGARET FULLER OSSOLI

1810 – 1850

A SHORT ESSAY ON CRITICS

[From " The Dial," 1840. Reprinted in " Art, Literature, and the Drama," 1859]

A N essay on Criticism were a serious matter; for, though this age be emphatically critical, the writer would still find it necessary to investigate the laws of criticism as a science, to settle its conditions as an art. Essays, entitled critical, are epistles addressed to the public, through which the mind of the recluse relieves itself of its impressions. Of these the only law is, " Speak the best word that is in thee." Or they are regular articles got up to order by the literary hack writer, for the literary mart, and the only law is to make them plausible. There is not yet deliberate recognition of a standard of criticism, though we hope the always strengthening league of the republic of letters must ere long settle laws on which its Amphictyonic council may act. Meanwhile let us not venture to write on criticism, but, by classifying the critics, imply our hopes and thereby our thoughts.

First, there are the subjective class, (to make use of a convenient term, introduced by our German benefactors). These are persons to whom writing is no sacred, no reverend employment. They are not driven to consider, not forced upon investigation by the fact, that they are deliberately giving their thoughts an independent existence, and that it may live to others when dead to them. They know no agonies of conscientious research, no timidities of self-respect. They see no ideal beyond the present hour, which makes its mood an uncertain tenure. How things affect them now they know; let the future, let the whole take care

of itself.   They state their impressions as they rise, of other
men's spoken, written, or acted thoughts.   They never
dream of going out of themselves to seek the motive, to
trace the law of another nature.   They never dream that
there are statures which cannot be measured from their
point of view.   They love, they like, or they hate ; the
book is detestable, immoral, absurd, or admirable, noble, of
a most approved scope ; — these statements they make
with authority, as those who bear the evangel of pure
taste and accurate judgment, and need be tried before no
human synod.   To them it seems that their present position
commands the universe.

Thus the essays on the works of others, which are called
criticisms, are often, in fact, mere records of impressions.
To judge of their value you must know where the man was
brought up, under what influences, — his nation, his church,
his family even.   He himself has never attempted to estimate the value of these circumstances, and find a law or
raise a standard above all circumstances, permanent against
all influence.   He is content to be the creature of his place,
and to represent it by his spoken and written word.   He
takes the same ground with a savage, who does not hesi-
tate to say of the product of a civilization on which he could
not stand, " It is bad," or " It is good."

The value of such comments is merely reflex.   They
characterize the critic.   They give an idea of certain influences on a certain act of men in a certain time or place.
Their absolute, essential value is nothing.   The long review,
the eloquent article by the man of the nineteenth century,
are of no value by themselves considered, but only as
samples of their kind.   The writers were content to tell
what they felt, to praise or to denounce without needing to
convince us or themselves.   They sought not the divine
truths of philosophy, and she proffers them not if unsought.

Then there are the apprehensive.   These can go out of
themselves and enter fully into a foreign existence.   They
breathe its life ; they live in its law ; they tell what it meant,

and why it so expressed its meaning.   They reproduce the
work of which they speak, and make it better known to us
in so far as two statements are better than one.   There are
beautiful specimens in this kind.   They are pleasing to us
as bearing witness of the genial sympathies of nature.
They have the ready grace of love with somewhat of the
dignity of disinterested friendship.   They sometimes give
more pleasure than the original production of which they
treat, as melodies will sometimes ring sweetlier in the echo.
Besides there is a peculiar pleasure in a true response ; it
is the assurance of equipoise in the universe.   These, if not
true critics, come nearer the standard than the subjective
class, and the value of their work is ideal as well as historical.

Then there are the comprehensive, who must also be apprehensive.   They enter into the nature of another being
and judge his work by its own law.   But having done so,
having ascertained his design and the degree of his success
in fulfilling it, thus measuring his judgment, his energy, and
skill, they do also know how to put that aim in its place, and
how to estimate its relations.   And this the critic can only do
who perceives the analogies of the universe, and how they
are regulated by an absolute, invariable principle.   He can
see how far that work expresses this principle, as well as
how far it is excellent in its details.   Sustained by a principle, such as can be girt within no rule, no formula, he can
walk around the work, he can stand above it, he can uplift
it, and try its weight.   Finally, he is worthy to judge it.

Critics are poets cut down, says some one by way of
jeer ; but, in truth, they are men with the poetical temperament to apprehend, with the philosophical tendency to investigate.   The maker is divine ; the critic sees this divine,
but brings it down to humanity by the analytic process.
The critic is the historian who records the order of creation.
In vain for the maker, who knows without learning it, but
not in vain for the mind of his race.

The critic is beneath the maker, but is his needed friend.
What tongue could speak but to an intelligent ear, and every

noble work demands its critic. The richer the work, the more severe should be its critic; the larger its scope, the more comprehensive must be his power of scrutiny. The critic is not a base caviller, but the younger brother of genius. Next to invention is the power of interpreting invention; next to beauty the power of appreciating beauty.

And of making others appreciate it; for the universe is a scale of infinite gradation, and, below the very highest, every step is explanation down to the lowest. Religion, in the two modulations of poetry and music, descends through an infinity of waves to the lowest abysses of human nature. Nature is the literature and art of the divine mind; human literature and art the criticism on that; and they, too, find their criticism within their own sphere.

The critic, then, should be not merely a poet, not merely a philosopher, not merely an observer, but tempered of all three. If he criticise the poem, he must want nothing of what constitutes the poet, except the power of creating forms and speaking in music. He must have as good an eye and as fine a sense; but if he had as fine an organ for expression also, he would make the poem instead of judging it. He must be inspired by the philosopher's spirit of inquiry and need of generalization, but he must not be constrained by the hard cemented masonry of method to which philosophers are prone. And he must have the organic acuteness of the observer, with a love of ideal perfection, which forbids him to be content with mere beauty of details in the work or the comment upon the work.

There are persons who maintain, that there is no legitimate criticism, except the reproductive; that we have only to say what the work is or is to us, never what it is not. But the moment we look for a principle, we feel the need of a criterion, of a standard; and then we say what the work is *not*, as well as what it *is;* and this is as healthy though not as grateful and gracious an operation of the mind as the other. We do not seek to degrade but to classify an object by stating what it is not. We detach the part from the whole, lest it stand between us and the whole. When we have ascertained in what degree it manifests the whole, we may safely restore it to its place, and love or admire it there ever after.

The use of criticism, in periodical writing is to sift, not to stamp a work. Yet should they not be "sieves and drainers for the use of luxurious readers," but for the use of earnest inquirers, giving voice and being to their objections, as well as stimulus to their sympathies. But the critic must not be an infallible adviser to his reader. He must not tell him what books are not worth reading, or what must be thought of them when read, but what he read in them. Wo to that coterie where some critic sits despotic, intrenched behind the infallible "We." Wo to that oracle who has infused such soft sleepiness, such a gentle dulness into his atmosphere, that when he opes his lips no dog will bark. It is this attempt at dictatorship in the reviewers, and the indolent acquiescence of their readers, that has brought them into disrepute. With such fairness did they make out their statements, with such dignity did they utter their verdicts, that the poor reader grew all too submissive. He learned his lesson with such docility, that the greater part of what will be said at any public or private meeting can be foretold by any one who has read the leading periodical works for twenty years back. Scholars sneer at and would fain dispense with them altogether; and the public, grown lazy and helpless by this constant use of props and stays, can now scarce brace itself even to get through a magazine article, but reads in the daily paper laid beside the breakfast plate a short notice of the last number of the long established and popular review, and thereupon passes its judgment and is content.

Then the partisan spirit of many of these journals has made it unsafe to rely upon them as guide-books and expurgatory indexes. They could not be content merely to stimulate and suggest thought, they have at last become powerless to supersede it.

From these causes and causes like these, the journals have lost much of their influence. There is a languid feeling about them, an inclination to suspect the justice of their verdicts, the value of their criticisms. But their golden age cannot be quite past. They afford too convenient a vehicle for the transmission of knowledge ; they are too natural a feature of our time to have done all their work yet. Surely they may be redeemed from their abuses, they may be turned to their true uses. But how?

It were easy to say what they should *not* do. They should not have an object to carry or a cause to advocate, which obliges them either to reject all writings which wear the distinctive traits of individual life, or to file away what does not suit them, till the essay, made true to their design, is made false to the mind of the writer. An external consistency is thus produced, at the expense of all salient thought, all genuine emotion of life, in short, and all living influence. Their purpose may be of value, but by such means was no valuable purpose ever furthered long. There are those, who have with the best intention pursued this system of trimming and adaptation, and thought it well and best to

"Deceive their country for their country's good."

But their country cannot long be so governed. It misses the pure, the full tone of truth ; it perceives that the voice is modulated to coax, to persuade, and it turns from the judicious man of the world, calculating the effect to be produced by each of his smooth sentences, to some earnest voice which is uttering thoughts, crude, rash, ill-arranged it may be, but true to one human breast, and uttered in full faith, that the God of Truth will guide them aright.

And here, it seems to me, has been the greatest mistake in the conduct of these journals. A smooth monotony has been attained, an uniformity of tone, so that from the title of a journal you can infer the tenor of all its chapters. But nature is ever various, ever new, and so should be her daughters, art and literature. We do not want merely a polite response to what we thought before, but by the freshness of thought in other minds to have new thought awakened in our own.   We do not want stores of information only, but to be roused to digest these into knowledge.   Able and experienced men write for us, and we would know what they think, as they think it not for us but for themselves. We would live with them, rather than be taught by them how to live ; we would catch the contagion of their mental activity, rather than have them direct us how to regulate our own.   In books, in reviews, in the senate, in the pulpit, we wish to meet thinking men, not schoolmasters or pleaders. We wish that they should do full justice to their own view, but also that they should be frank with us, and, if now our superiors, treat us as if we might some time rise to be their equals.   It is this true manliness, this firmness in his own position, and this power of appreciating the position of others, that alone can make the critic our companion and friend.   We would converse with him, secure that he will tell us all his thought, and speak as man to man.   But if he adapts his work to us, if he stifles what is distinctively his, if he shows himself either arrogant or mean, or, above all, if he wants faith in the healthy action of free thought, and the safety of pure motive, we will not talk with him, for we cannot confide in him.   We will go to the critic who trusts Genius and trusts us, who knows that all good writing must be spontaneous, and who will write out the bill of fare for the public as he read it for himself, —

> " Forgetting vulgar rules, with spirit free
> To judge each author by his own intent,
> Nor think one standard for all minds is meant."

Such an one will not disturb us with personalities, with sectarian prejudices, or an undue vehemence in favour of petty plans or temporary objects.   Neither will he disgust us by smooth obsequious flatteries and an inexpressive, lifeless gentleness.   He will be free and make free from the mechanical and distorting influences we hear complained of on every side. He will teach us to love wisely what we before loved well, for he knows the difference between censoriousness and discernment, infatuation and reverence ; and while delighting in the genial melodies of Pan, can perceive, should Apollo bring his lyre into audience, that there may be strains more divine than those of his native groves.

AMERICAN LITERATURE;

ITS POSITION IN THE PRESENT TIME, AND PROSPECTS FOR THE FUTURE

[From " Papers on Literature and Art," 1846. Reprinted in "Art, Literature and the Drama," 1859]

SOME thinkers may object to this essay, that we are about to write of that which has, as yet, no existence.

For it does not follow because many books are written by persons born in America that there exists an American literature. Books which imitate or represent the thoughts and life of Europe do not constitute an American literature. Before such can exist, an original idea must animate this nation and fresh currents of life must call into life fresh thoughts along its shores.

We have no sympathy with national vanity. We are not anxious to prove that there is as yet much American literature. Of those who think and write among us in the methods and of the thoughts of Europe, we are not impatient; if their minds are still best adapted to such food and such action. If their books express life of mind and character in graceful forms, they are good and we like them. We consider them as colonists and useful schoolmasters to our people in a transition state; which lasts rather longer than is occupied in passing, bodily, the ocean which separates the new from the old world.

We have been accused of an undue attachment to foreign continental literature, and, it is true, that in childhood, we had well nigh "forgotten our English," while constantly reading in other languages. Still, what we loved in the literature of continental Europe was the range and force of ideal manifestation in forms of national and individual greatness. A model was before us in the great Latins of simple masculine minds seizing upon life with unbroken power. The stamp both of nationality and individuality was very strong upon them; their lives and thoughts stood out in clear and bold relief. The English character has the iron force of the Latins, but not the frankness and expansion. Like their fruits, they need a summer sky to give them more sweetness and a richer flavour. This does not apply to Shakspeare, who has all the fine side of English genius, with the rich colouring, and more fluent life, of the Catholic countries. Other poets, of England also, are expansive more or less, and soar freely to seek the blue sky, but take it as a whole, there is in English literature, as in English character, a reminiscence of walls and ceilings, a tendency to the arbitrary and conventional that repels a mind trained in admiration of the antique spirit. It is only in later days that we are learning to prize the peculiar greatness which a thousand times outweighs this fault, and which has enabled English genius to go forth from its insular position and conquer such vast dominion in the realms both of matter and of mind.

Yet there is, often, between child and parent, a reaction from excessive influence having been exerted, and such an one we have experienced, in behalf of our country, against England. We use her language, and receive, in torrents, the influence of her thought, yet it is, in many respects, uncongenial and injurious to our constitution. What suits Great Britain, with her insular position and consequent need to concentrate and intensify her life, her limited monarchy, and spirit of trade, does not suit a mixed race, continually enriched with new blood from other stocks the most unlike that of our first descent, with ample field and verge enough to range in and leave every impulse free, and abundant opportunity to develope a genius, wide and full as

our rivers, flowery, luxuriant and impassioned as our vast
prairies, rooted in strength as the rocks on which the Puritan
fathers landed.

That such a genius is to rise and work in this hemisphere
we are confident; equally so that scarce the first faint
streaks of that day's dawn are yet visible. It is sad for
those that foresee, to know they may not live to share its
glories, yet it is sweet, too, to know that every act and
word, uttered in the light of that foresight, may tend to
hasten or ennoble its fulfilment.

That day will not rise till the fusion of races among us is
more complete. It will not rise till this nation shall attain
sufficient moral and intellectual dignity to prize moral and
intellectual, no less highly than political, freedom, not till,
the physical resources of the country being explored, all its
regions studded with towns, broken by the plow, netted
together by railways and telegraph lines, talent shall be
left at leisure to turn its energies upon the higher department of man's existence. Nor then shall it be seen till
from the leisurely and yearning soul of that riper time
national ideas shall take birth, ideas craving to be clothed
in a thousand fresh and original forms.

Without such ideas all attempts to construct a national
literature must end in abortions like the monster of Frank-
enstein, things with forms, and the instincts of forms, but
soulless, and therefore revolting. We cannot have expression till there is something to be expressed.

The symptoms of such a birth may be seen in a longing
felt here and there for the sustenance of such ideas. At
present, it shows itself, where felt, in sympathy with the
prevalent tone of society, by attempts at external action,
such as are classed under the head of social reform. But
it needs to go deeper, before we can have poets, needs to
penetrate beneath the springs of action, to stir and remake
the soil as by the action of fire.

Another symptom is the need felt by individuals of being
even sternly sincere. This is the one great means by which

alone progress can be essentially furthered. Truth is the nursing mother of genius. No man can be absolutely true to himself, eschewing cant, compromise, servile imitation, and complaisance, without becoming original, for there is in every creature a fountain of life which, if not choked back by stones and other dead rubbish, will create a fresh atmosphere, and bring to life fresh beauty. And it is the same with the nation as with the individual man.

The best work we do for the future is by such truth. By use of that, in whatever way, we harrow the soil and lay it open to the sun and air. The winds from all quarters of the globe bring seed enough, and there is nothing wanting but preparation of the soil, and freedom in the atmosphere, for ripening of a new and golden harvest.

We are sad that we cannot be present at the gathering in of this harvest. And yet we are joyous, too, when we think that though our name may not be writ on the pillar of our country's fame, we can really do far more towards rearing it, than those who come at a later period and to a seemingly fairer task. *Now*, the humblest effort, made in a noble spirit, and with religious hope, cannot fail to be even infinitely useful. Whether we introduce some noble model from another time and clime, to encourage aspiration in our own, or cheer into blossom the simplest wood-flower that ever rose from the earth, moved by the genuine impulse to grow, independent of the lures of money or celebrity; whether we speak boldly when fear or doubt keep others silent, or refuse to swell the popular cry upon an unworthy occasion, the spirit of truth, purely worshipped, shall turn our acts and forbearances alike to profit, informing them with oracles which the latest time shall bless.

Upon present circumstances the amount of talent and labour given to writing ought to surprise us. Literature is in this dim and struggling state, and its pecuniary results exceedingly pitiful. From many well known causes it is impossible for ninety-nine out of the hundred, who wish to use the pen, to ransom, by its use, the time they need.

This state of things will have to be changed in some way. No man of genius writes for money; but it is essential to the free use of his powers, that he should be able to disembarrass his life from care and perplexity. This is very difficult here; and the state of things gets worse and worse, as less and less is offered in pecuniary meed for works demanding great devotion of time and labour (to say nothing of the ether engaged) and the publisher, obliged to regard the transaction as a matter of business, demands of the author to give him only what will find an immediate market, for he cannot afford to take anything else. This will not do! When an immortal poet was secure only of a few copyists to circulate his works, there were princes and nobles to patronize literature and the arts. Here is only the public, and the public must learn how to cherish the nobler and rarer plants, and to plant the aloe, able to wait a hundred years for its bloom, or its garden will contain, presently, nothing but potatoes and pot-herbs. We shall have, in the course of the next two or three years, a convention of authors to inquire into the causes of this state of things and propose measures for its remedy. Some have already been thought of that look promising, but we shall not announce them till the time be ripe; that date is not distant, for the difficulties increase from day to day, in consequence of the system of cheap publication, on a great scale.

The ranks that led the way in the first half century of this republic were far better situated than we, in this respect. The country was not so deluged with the dingy page, reprinted from Europe, and patriotic vanity was on the alert to answer the question, "Who reads an American book?" And many were the books written, worthy to be read, as any out of the first class in England. They were, most of them, except in their subject matter, English books.

The list is large, and, in making some cursory comments, we do not wish to be understood as designating *all* who are worthy of notice, but only those who present themselves to our minds with some special claims. In history there has been nothing done to which the world at large has not been eager to award the full meed of its deserts. Mr. Prescott, for instance, has been greeted with as much warmth abroad as here. We are not disposed to undervalue his industry and power of clear and elegant arrangement. The richness and freshness of his materials is such that a sense of enchantment must be felt in their contemplation. We must regret, however, that they should have been first presented to the public by one who possesses nothing of the higher powers of the historian, great leading views, or discernment as to the motives of action and the spirit of an era. Considering the splendour of the materials the books are wonderfully tame, and every one must feel that having once passed through them and got the sketch in the mind, there is nothing else to which it will recur. The absence of thought, as to that great picture of Mexican life, with its heroisms, its terrible but deeply significant superstitions, its admirable civic refinement, seems to be quite unbroken.

Mr. Bancroft is a far more vivid writer; he has great resources and great command of them, and leading thoughts by whose aid he groups his facts. But we cannot speak fully of his historical works, which we have only read and referred to here and there.

In the department of ethics and philosophy, we may inscribe two names as likely to live and be blessed and honoured in the later time. These are the names of Channing and of Emerson.

Dr. Channing had several leading thoughts which corresponded with the wants of his time, and have made him in it a father of thought. His leading idea of "the dignity of human nature" is one of vast results, and the peculiar form in which he advocated it had a great work to do in this new world. The spiritual beauty of his writings is very great; they are all distinguished for sweetness, elevation, candour, and a severe devotion to truth. On great questions, he took middle ground, and sought a panoramic view; he wished also to stand high, yet never forgot what was above more than what was around and beneath him. He was not well acquainted with man on the impulsive and passionate side of his nature, so that his view of character was sometimes narrow, but it was always noble. He exercised an expansive and purifying power on the atmosphere, and stands a godfather at the baptism of this country.

The Sage of Concord has a very different mind, in every thing except that he has the same disinterestedness and dignity of purpose, the same purity of spirit. He is a profound thinker. He is a man of ideas, and deals with causes rather than effects. His ideas are illustrated from a wide range of literary culture and refined observation, and embodied in a style whose melody and subtle fragrance enchant those who stand stupified before the thoughts themselves, because their utmost depths do not enable them to sound his shallows. His influence does not yet extend over a wide space; he is too far beyond his place and his time, to be felt at once or in full, but it searches deep, and yearly widens its circles. He is a harbinger of the better day. His beautiful elocution has been a great aid to him in opening the way for the reception of his written word.

In that large department of literature which includes descriptive sketches, whether of character or scenery, we are already rich. Irving, a genial and fair nature, just what he ought to be, and would have been, at any time of the world, has drawn the scenes amid which his youth was spent in their primitive lineaments, with all the charms of his graceful jocund humour. He has his niche and need never be deposed; it is not one that another could occupy.

The first enthusiasm about Cooper having subsided, we remember more his faults than his merits. His ready resentment and way of showing it in cases which it is the wont of gentlemen to pass by in silence, or meet with a good humoured smile, have caused unpleasant associations with his name, and his fellow citizens, in danger of being tormented by suits for libel, if they spoke freely of him, have ceased to speak of him at all. But neither these causes, nor the baldness of his plots, shallowness of thought, and poverty in the presentation of character, should make us forget the grandeur and originality of his sea-sketches, nor the redemption from oblivion of our forest-scenery, and the noble romance of the hunter-pioneer's life. Already, but for him, this fine page of life's romance would be almost forgotten. He has done much to redeem these irrevocable beauties from the corrosive acid of a semi-civilized invasion.[1]

[1] Since writing the above we have read some excellent remarks by Mr. W. G. Simms on the writings of Cooper. We think the reasons are given for the powerful interest excited by Hawk Eye and the Pilot, with great discrimination and force.

"They both think and feel, with a highly individual nature, that has been taught, by constant contemplation, in scenes of solitude. The vast unbroken ranges of forest to its one lonely occupant press upon the mind with the same sort of solemnity which one feels condemned to a life of partial isolation upon the ocean. Both are permitted that degree of commerce with their fellow beings, which suffices to maintain in strength the sweet and sacred sources of their humanity. . . . The very isolation to which, in the most successful of his stories, Mr. Cooper subjects his favourite personages, is, alone, a proof of his strength and genius. While the ordinary writer, the man of mere talent, is compelled to look around him among masses for his material, he contents himself with one man, and flings him upon the wilderness. The picture, then, which follows, must be one of intense individuality. Out of this one man's nature, his moods and fortunes, he spins his story. The agencies and dependencies are few. With the self-reliance which is only found in true genius, he goes forward into the wilderness, whether of land or ocean ; and the vicissitudes of either region, acting upon the natural resources of one man's mind, furnish the whole material of his work-shop. This mode of performance is highly dramatic, and thus it is that his scout, his trapper, his hunter, his pilot, all live to our eyes and thoughts, the perfect ideals of moral individuality."

Miss Sedgwick and others have portrayed, with skill and feeling, scenes and personages from the revolutionary time. Such have a permanent value in proportion as their subject is fleeting. The same charm attends the spirited delineations of Mrs. Kirkland, and that amusing book, " A New Purchase." The features of Hoosier, Sucker, and Wolverine life are worth fixing ; they are peculiar to the soil, and indicate its hidden treasures ; they have, also, that charm which simple life, lived for its own sake, always has, even in rude and all but brutal forms.

What shall we say of the poets? The list is scanty ; amazingly so, for there is nothing in the causes that paralyze other kinds of literature that could affect lyrical and narrative poetry. Men's hearts beat, hope, and suffer always, and they must crave such means to vent them ; yet of the myriad leaves garnished with smooth stereotyped rhymes that issue yearly from our press, you will not find, one time in a million, a little piece written from any such impulse, or with the least sincerity or sweetness of tone. They are written for the press, in the spirit of imitation or vanity, the paltriest offspring of the human brain, for the heart disclaims, as the ear is shut against them. This is the kind of verse which is cherished by the magazines as a correspondent to the tawdry pictures of smiling milliners' dolls in the frontispiece. Like these they are only a fashion, a fashion based on no reality of love or beauty. The inducement to write them consists in a little money, or more frequently the charm of seeing an anonymous name printed at the top in capitals.

We must here, in passing, advert also to the style of story current in the magazines, flimsy beyond any texture that was ever spun or even dreamed of by the mind of man, in any other age and country. They are said to be " written for the seamstresses," but we believe that every way injured class could relish and digest better fare even at the end of long days of exhausting labour. There are exceptions to this censure ; stories by Mrs. Child have been published in the magazines, and now and then good ones by Mrs. Stephens and others; but, take them generally, they are calculated to do a positive injury to the public mind, acting as an opiate, and of an adulterated kind, too.

But to return to the poets. At their head Mr. Bryant stands alone. His range is not great, nor his genius fertile. But his poetry is purely the language of his inmost nature, and the simple lovely garb in which his thoughts are arranged, a direct gift from the Muse. He has written nothing that is not excellent, and the atmosphere of his verse refreshes and composes the mind, like leaving the highway to enter some green, lovely, fragrant wood.

Halleck and Willis are poets of society. Though the former has written so little, yet that little is full of fire, — elegant, witty, delicate in sentiment. It is an honour to the country that these occasional sparks, struck off from the flint of commercial life, should have kindled so much flame as they have. It is always a consolation to see one of them sparkle amid the rubbish of daily life. One of his poems has been published within the last year, written, in fact, long ago, but new to most of us, and it enlivened the literary thoroughfare, as a green wreath might some dusty, musty hall of legislation.

Willis has not the same terseness or condensed electricity. But he has grace, spirit, at times a winning pensiveness, and a lively, though almost wholly sensuous, delight in the beautiful.

Dana has written so little that he would hardly be seen in a more thickly garnished galaxy. But the masculine strength of feeling, the solemn tenderness and refined thought displayed in such pieces as the " Dying Raven," and the " Husband and Wife's Grave," have left a deep impression on the popular mind.

Longfellow is artificial and imitative. He borrows incessantly, and mixes what he borrows, so that it does not appear to the best advantage. He is very faulty in using broken or mixed metaphors. The ethical part of his writing has a hollow, second-hand sound. He has, however, elegance, a love of the beautiful, and a fancy for what is large and manly, if not a full sympathy with it. His verse breathes at times much sweetness ; and, if not allowed to supersede what is better may promote a taste for good poetry. Though imitative, he is not mechanical.

We cannot say as much for Lowell, who, we must declare it, though to the grief of some friends, and the disgust of more, is absolutely wanting in the true spirit and tone of poesy. His interest in the moral questions of the day has supplied the want of vitality in himself ; his great facility at versification has enabled him to fill the ear with a copious stream of pleasant sound. But his verse is stereotyped ; his thought sounds no depth, and posterity will not remember him.

R. W. Emerson, in melody, in subtle beauty of thought and expression, takes the highest rank upon this list. But his poems are mostly philosophical, which is not the truest kind of poetry. They want the simple force of nature and passion, and, while they charm the ear and interest the mind, fail to wake far-off echoes in the heart. The imagery wears a symbolical air, and serves rather as illustration, than to delight us by fresh and glowing forms of life.

We must here mention one whom the country has not yet learned to honour, perhaps never may, for he wants artistic skill to give complete form to his inspiration. This is William Ellery Channing, nephew and namesake of Dr. C., a volume of whose poems, published three or four years ago in Boston, remains unknown, except to a few friends, nor, if known, would they probably, excite sympathy, as those which have been published in the periodicals have failed to do so. Yet some of the purest tones of the lyre are his, the finest inspirations as to the feelings and passions of men, deep spiritual insight, and an entire originality in the use of his means. The frequently unfinished and obscure state of his poems, a passion for forcing words out of their usual meaning into one which they may appropriately bear, but which comes upon the reader with an unpleasing and puzzling surprise, may repel, at first glance, from many of these poems, but do not mar the following sublime description of the beings we want, to rule, to redeem, to re-create this nation, and under whose reign alone can there be an American literature, for then only could we have life worth recording. The simple grandeur of this poem as a whole, must be felt by every one, while each line and thought will be found worthy of earnest contemplation and satisfaction after the most earnest life and thought.

> Hearts of Eternity! hearts of the deep!
> Proclaim from land to sea your mighty fate;
> How that for you no living comes too late;
> How ye cannot in Theban labyrinth creep;
> How ye great harvests from small surface reap;
> Shout, excellent band, in grand primeval strain,
> Like midnight winds that foam along the main,
> And do all things rather than pause to weep.
> A human heart knows naught of littleness,
> Suspects no man, compares with no man's ways,
> Hath in one hour most glorious length of days,
> A recompense, a joy, a loveliness;
> Like eaglet keen, shoots into azure far,
> And always dwelling nigh is the remotest star.

A series of poems, called "Man in the Republic," by Cornelius Mathews, deserves a higher meed of sympathy than it has received. The thoughts and views are strong and noble, the exhibition of them imposing. In plastic power this writer is deficient. His prose works sin in exuberance, and need consolidating and chastening. We find fine things, but not so arranged as to be seen in the right places and by the best light. In his poems Mr. Mathews is unpardonably rough and rugged; the poetic substance finds no musical medium in which to flow. Yet there *is* poetic substance which makes full chords, if not a harmony. He holds a worthy sense of the vocation of the poet, and worthily expresses it thus: —

To strike or bear, to conquer or to yield
Teach thou ! O topmost crown of duty, teach,
What fancy whispers to the listening ear,
At hours when tongue nor taint of care impeach
The fruitful calm of greatly silent hearts ;
When all the stars for happy thought are set,
And, in the secret chambers of the soul,
All blessed powers of joyful truth are met ;
Though calm and garlandless thou mayst appear,
The world shall know thee for its crowned seer.

A considerable portion of the hope and energy of this country still turns towards the drama, that greatest achievement when wrought to perfection of human power. For ourselves, we believe the day of the regular drama to be past ; and, though we recognize the need of some kind of spectacle and dramatic representation to be absolutely coincident with an animated state of the public mind, we have thought that the opera, ballet, pantomime and briefer, more elastic forms, like the *vaudeville* of the French theatre, or the *proverb* of the social party, would take the place of elaborate tragedy and comedy.

But those who find the theatres of this city well filled all the year round by an audience willing to sit out the heroisms of Rolla, and the sentimentalism and stale morality of such a piece as we were doomed to listen to while the Keans were here, ("Town and Country" was its name,) still think there is room for the regular drama, if genius should engage in its creation. Accordingly there have been in this country, as well as in England, many attempts to produce dramas suitable for action no less than for the closet. The actor, Murdoch, about to devote himself with enthusiasm and hope to prop up a falling profession, is to bring out a series of plays written, not merely *for* him, but because his devotion is likely to furnish fit occasion for their appearance. The first of these, "Witchcraft, a tragedy," brought out successfully upon the boards at Philadelphia, we have read, and it is a work of strong and majestic lineaments ; a fine originality is shown in the conception, by which the love of a son for a mother is made a sufficient *motiv* (as the Germans call the ruling impulse of a work) in the production of tragic interest; no less original is the attempt, and delightful the success, in making an aged woman a satisfactory heroine to the piece through the greatness of her soul, and the magnetic influence it exerts on all around her, till the ignorant and superstitious fancy that the sky darkens and the winds wait upon her as she walks on the lonely hill-side near her hut to commune with the Past, and seek instruction from Heaven.   The working of her character on the other agents of the piece is depicted with force and nobleness.   The deep love of her son for her, the little tender, simple ways in which he shows it, having preserved the purity and poetic spirit of childhood by never having been weaned from his first love, a mother's love, the anguish of his soul when he too becomes infected with distrust, and cannot discriminate the natural magnetism of a strong nature from the spells and lures of sorcery, the final triumph of his faith, all offered the highest scope to genius and the power of moral perception in the actor.   There are highly poetic intimations of those lowering days with their veiled skies, brassy light, and sadly whispering winds, very common in Massachusetts, so ominous and brooding seen from any point, but from the idea of witchcraft, invested with an awful significance.   We do not know, however, that this could bring it beyond what it has appeared to our own sane mind, as if the air was thick with spirits, in an equivocal and surely sad condition, whether of purgatory or downfall; and the air was vocal with all manner of dark intimations. We are glad to see this mood of nature so fitly characterized.

The sweetness and *naiveté* with which the young girl is made to describe the effects of love upon her, as supposing them to proceed from a spell, are also original, and there is no other way in which this revelation could have been induced that would not have injured the beauty of the character and position.   Her visionary sense of her lover, as an ideal figure, is of a high order of poetry, and these facts have very seldom been brought out from the cloisters of the mind into the light of open day.

The play is very deficient as regards rhythm; indeed, we might say there is no apparent reason why the lines should begin with capital letters. The minor personages are mere caricatures, very coarsely drawn; all the power is concentrated on the main characters and their emotions. So did not Shakspeare, does not ever the genuine dramatist, whose mind teems with " the fulness of forms." As Raphael in his most crowded groups can put in no misplaced or imperfect foot or hand, neither neglect to invest the least important figure of his backgrounds with every characteristic trait, nor could spare the invention of the most beautiful *coiffure* and accessories for the humblest handmaid of his Madonnas, so doth the great artist always clothe the whole picture with full and breathing life, for it appears so before his mental eye. But minds not perfectly artistical, yet of strong conceptions, subordinate the rest to one or two leading figures, and the imperfectly represented life of the others incloses them, as in a frame.

In originality of conception and resting the main interest upon force of character in a woman, this drama naturally leads us to revert to a work in the department of narrative fiction, which, on similar grounds, comes to us as a harbinger of the new era. This book is " Margaret, or the Real and Ideal," a work which has appeared within the past year; and, considering its originality and genuineness, has excited admiration and sympathy amazingly soon. Even some leading reviews, of what Byron used to speak of as the " garrison " class, (a class the most opposite imaginable to that of Garrison abolitionists,) have discussed its pretensions and done homage to its merits. It is a work of great power and richness, a genuine disclosure of the life of mind and the history of character. Its descriptions of scenery and the common people, in the place and time it takes up, impart to it the highest value as a representative of transient existence, which had a great deal of meaning.

The beautiful simplicity of action upon and within the mind of Margaret, Heaven lying so clearly about her in the infancy of the hut of drunkards, the woods, the village, and their ignorant, simply human denizens, her unconscious growth to the stature of womanhood, the flow of life impelled by her, the spiritual intimations of her dreams, the prophecies of music in the character of Chilion, the *naive* discussion of the leading reform movements of the day in their rudimental forms, the archness, the humour, the profound religious faith, make of this book an aviary from which doves shall go forth to discover and report of all the green spots of promise in the land. Of books like this, as good, and still better, our new literature shall be full ; and, though one swallow does not make a summer, yet we greet, in this one " Yankee novel," the sufficient earnest of riches that only need the skill of competent miners to be made current for the benefit of man.

Meanwhile, the most important part of our literature, while the work of diffusion is still going on, lies in the journals, which monthly, weekly, daily, send their messages to every corner of this great land, and form, at present, the only efficient instrument for the general education of the people.

Among these, the Magazines take the lowest rank. Their object is principally to cater for the amusement of vacant hours, and, as there is not a great deal of wit and light talent in this country, they do not even this to much advantage. More wit, grace, and elegant trifling, embellish the annals of literature in one day of France than in a year of America.

The Reviews are more able. If they cannot compare, on equal terms, with those of France, England, and Germany, where, if genius be rare, at least a vast amount of talent and culture are brought to bear upon all the departments of knowledge, they are yet very creditable to a new country, where so large a portion of manly ability must be bent on making laws, making speeches, making

rail-roads and canals. They are, however, much injured
by a partisan spirit, and the fear of censure from their own
public. This last is always slow death to a journal; its
natural and only safe position is *to lead;* if, instead, it bows
to the will of the multitude, it will find the ostracism of
democracy far more dangerous than the worst censure of a
tyranny could be. It is not half so dangerous to a man to
be immured in a dungeon alone with God and his own clear
conscience, as to walk the streets fearing the scrutiny of a
thousand eyes, ready to veil, with anxious care, whatever
may not suit the many-headed monster in its momentary
mood. Gentleness is dignified, but caution is debasing;
only a noble fearlessness can give wings to the mind, with
which to soar beyond the common ken, and learn what may
be of use to the crowd below. Writers have nothing to do
but to love truth fervently, seek justice according to their
ability, and then express what is in the mind; they have
nothing to do with consequences, God will take care of
those. The want of such noble courage, such faith in the
power of truth and good desire, paralyze mind greatly in
this country. Publishers are afraid; authors are afraid;
and if a worthy resistance is not made by religious souls,
there is danger that all the light will soon be put under
bushels, lest some wind should waft from it a spark that
may kindle dangerous fire.

For want of such faith, and the catholic spirit that flows
from it, we have no great leading Review. The North
American was once the best. While under the care of
Edward Everett, himself a host in extensive knowledge,
grace and adroitness in applying it, and the power of enforcing grave meanings by a light and flexible satire that
tickled while it wounded, it boasted more force, more life,
a finer scope of power. But now, though still exhibiting
ability and information upon special points, it is entirely
deficient in great leadings, and the *vivida vis*, but ambles
and jogs at an old gentlemanly pace along a beaten path
that leads to no important goal.

Several other journals have more life, energy and directness than this, but there is none which occupies a truly
great and commanding position, a beacon light to all who
sail that way.   In order to this, a journal must know how
to cast aside all local and temporary considerations when
new convictions command, and allow free range in its columns, to all kinds of ability, and all ways of viewing subjects.
That would give it a life, rich, bold various.

The life of intellect is becoming more and more determined to the weekly and daily papers, whose light leaves
fly so rapidly and profusely over the land.   Speculations
are afloat, as to the influence of the electric telegraph upon
their destiny, and it seems obvious that it should raise their
character by taking from them in some measure, the office
of gathering and dispersing the news, and requiring of them
rather to arrange and interpret it.

This mode of communication is susceptible of great excellence in the way of condensed essay, narrative, criticism, and is the natural receptacle for the lyrics of the day.
That so few good ones deck the poet's corner, is because
the indifference or unfitness of editors, as to choosing and
refusing, makes this place, at present, undesirable to the
poet.   It might be otherwise.

The means which this organ affords of diffusing knowledge
and sowing the seeds of thought where they may hardly fail
of an infinite harvest, cannot be too highly prized by the discerning and benevolent.   Minds of the first class are generally indisposed to this kind of writing ; what must be done
on the spur of the occasion and cast into the world so incomplete, as the hurried off-spring of a day or hour's labour
must generally be, cannot satisfy their judgment, or do justice to their powers.   But he who looks to the benefit of
others, and sees with what rapidity and ease instruction and
thought are assimilated by men, when they come thus, as it
were, on the wings of the wind, may be content, as an un-
honoured servant to the grand purposes of Destiny, to work
in such a way at the Pantheon which the Ages shall com-

plete, on which his name may not be inscribed, but which will breathe the life of his soul.

The confidence in uprightness of intent, and the safety of truth, is still more needed here than in the more elaborate kinds of writing, as meanings cannot be fully explained nor expressions revised. Newspaper writing is next door to conversation, and should be conducted on the same principles. It has this advantage : we address, not our neighbour, who forces us to remember his limitations and prejudices, but the ideal presence of human nature as we feel it ought to be and trust it will be. We address America rather than Americans.

A worthy account of the vocation and duties of the journalist, is given by Cornelius Mathews. Editors, generally, could not do better than every New Year's day to read and insert the following verses.

As shakes the canvass of a thousand ships,
   Struck by a heavy land-breeze, far at sea,
Ruffle the thousand broad sheets of the land,
   Filled with the people's breath of potency.

A thousand images the hour will take,
   From him who strikes, who rules, who speaks, who sings,
Many within the hour their grave to make,
   Many to live, far in the heart of things.

A dark-dyed spirit he, who coins the time,
   To virtue's wrong, in base disloyal lies,
Who makes the morning's breath, the evening's tide,
   The utterer of his blighting forgeries.

How beautiful who scatters, wide and free,
   The gold-bright seeds of loved and loving truth !
By whose perpetual hand, each day supplied,
   Leaps to new life the empire's heart of youth.

To know the instant and to speak it true,
   Its passing lights of joy, its dark, sad cloud,
To fix upon the unnumbered gazers' view,
   Is to thy ready hand's broad strength allowed.

There is an inwrought life in every hour,
　Fit to be chronicled at large and told.
'T is thine to pluck to light its secret power,
　And on the air its many-colored heart unfold.

The angel that in sand-dropped minutes lives,
　Demands a message cautious as the ages,
Who stuns, with dusk-red words of hate his ear,
　That mighty power to boundless wrath enrages.

This feeling of the dignity of his office, honour and power in fulfilling it, are not common in the journalist, but, where they exist, a mark has been left fully correspondent to the weight of the instrument. The few editors of this country who, with mental ability and resource, have combined strength of purpose and fairness of conduct, who have never merged the man and the gentleman in the partisan, who have been willing to have all sides fully heard, while their convictions were clear on one, who have disdained groundless assaults or angry replies, and have valued what was sincere, characteristic and free, too much to bend to popular errors they felt able to correct, have been so highly prized that it is wonderful that more do not learn the use of this great opportunity. It will be learned yet; the resources of this organ of thought and instruction begin to be understood, and shall yet be brought out and used worthily.

We see we have omitted honoured names in this essay. We have not spoken of Brown, as a novelist by far our first in point of genius and instruction as to the soul of things. Yet his works have fallen almost out of print. It is their dark, deep gloom that prevents their being popular, for their very beauties are grave and sad. But we see that Ormond is being republished at this moment. The picture of Roman character, of the life and resources of a single noble creature, of Constantia alone, should make that book an object of reverence. All these novels should be republished; if not favorites, they should at least not be lost sight of, for there will always be some who find in such powers of mental analysis the only response to their desires.

We have not spoken of Hawthorne, the best writer of the day, in a similar range with Irving, only touching many more points and discerning far more deeply. But we have omitted many things in this slight sketch, for the subject, even in this stage, lies as a volume in our mind, and cannot be unrolled in completeness unless time and space were more abundant. Our object was to show that although by a thousand signs, the existence is foreshown of those forces which are to animate an American literature, that faith, those hopes are not yet alive which shall usher it into a homogeneous or fully organized state of being. The future is glorious with certainties for those who do their duty in the present, and, lark-like, seeking the sun, challenge its eagles to an earthward flight, where their nests may be built in our mountains, and their young raise their cry of triumph, unchecked by dullness in the echoes.

JAMES RUSSELL LOWELL

1819 – 1891

EMERSON

[*From "A Fable for Critics," 1848*]

" THERE comes Emerson first, whose rich words,
      every one,
Are like gold nails in temples to hang trophies on,
Whose prose is grand verse, while his verse, the Lord
      knows,
Is some of it pr—   No, 't is not even prose;
I 'm speaking of metres; some poems have welled
From those rare depths of soul that have ne'er been
      excelled;
They 're not epics, but that doesn't matter a pin,
In creating, the only hard thing 's to begin;
A grass-blade 's no easier to make than an oak;
If you 've once found the way, you 've achieved the grand
      stroke;
In the worst of his poems are mines of rich matter.
But thrown in a heap with a crash and a clatter;
Now it is not one thing nor another alone
Makes a poem, but rather the general tone,
The something pervading, uniting the whole,
The before unconceived, unconceivable soul,
So that just in removing this trifle or that, you
Take away, as it were, a chief limb of the statue;
Roots, wood, bark, and leaves singly perfect may be,
But, clapt hodge-podge together, they don't make a tree.

" But, to come back to Emerson (whom, by the way,
I believe we left waiting), — his is, we may say,
A Greek head on right Yankee shoulders, whose range

Has Olympus for one pole, for t' other the Exchange ;
He seems, to my thinking (although I 'm afraid
The comparison must, long ere this, have been made),
A Plotinus-Montaigne, where the Egyptian's gold mist
And the Gascon's shrewd wit cheek-by-jowl coexist ;
All admire, and yet scarcely six converts he 's got
To I don't (nor they either) exactly know what ;
For though he builds glorious temples, 't is odd
He leaves never a doorway to get in a god.
'T is refreshing to old-fashioned people like me
To meet such a primitive Pagan as he,
In whose mind all creation is duly respected
As parts of himself — just a little projected ;
And who 's willing to worship the stars and the sun,
A convert to — nothing but Emerson.
So perfect a balance there is in his head,
That he talks of things sometimes as if they were dead ;
Life, nature, love, God, and affairs of that sort,
He looks at as merely ideas ; in short,
As if they were fossils stuck round in a cabinet,
Of such vast extent that our earth 's a mere dab in it ;
Composed just as he is inclined to conjecture her,
Namely, one part pure earth, ninety-nine parts pure lecturer ;
You are filled with delight at his clear demonstration,
Each figure, word, gesture, just fits the occasion,
With the quiet precision of science he 'll sort 'em,
But you can't help suspecting the whole a *post mortem.*

    " There are persons, mole-blind to the soul's make and
        style,
Who insist on a likeness 'twixt him and Carlyle ;
To compare him with Plato would be vastly fairer,
Carlyle 's the more burly, but E. is the rarer ;
He sees fewer objects, but clearlier, truelier,
If C. 's as original, E. 's more peculiar ;
That he 's more of a man you might say of the one,
Of the other he 's more of an Emerson ;

C. 's the Titan, as shaggy of mind as of limb, —
E. the clear-eyed Olympian, rapid and slim ;
The one 's two thirds Norseman, the other half Greek,
Where the one 's most abounding, the other 's to seek ;
C.'s generals require to be seen in the mass, —
E.'s specialties gain if enlarged by the glass ;
C. gives nature and God his own fits of the blues,
And rims common-sense things with mystical hues, —
E. sits in a mystery calm and intense,
 And looks coolly around him with sharp common-sense ;
C. shows you how every-day matters unite
With the dim transdiurnal recesses of night, —
While E., in a plain, preternatural way,
Makes mysteries matters of mere every day ;
C. draws all his characters quite *à la* Fuseli, —
Not sketching their bundles of muscles and thews illy,
He paints with a brush so untamed and profuse,
They seem nothing but bundles of muscles and thews ;
E. is rather like Flaxman, lines strait and severe,
And a colorless outline, but full, round, and clear ; —
To the men he thinks worthy he frankly accords
The design of a white marble statue in words.
C. labors to get at the centre, and then
Take a reckoning from there of his actions and men ;
E. calmly assumes the said centre as granted,
And, given himself, has whatever is wanted.

   " He has imitators in scores, who omit
No part of the man but his wisdom and wit, —
Who go carefully o'er the sky-blue of his brain,
And when he has skimmed it once, skim it again ;
If at all they resemble him, you may be sure it is
Because their shoals mirror his mists and obscurities,
As a mud-puddle seems deep as heaven for a minute,
While a cloud that floats o'er is reflected within it.

WHITTIER

[*From " A Fable for Critics," 1848*]

" THERE is Whittier, whose swelling and vehement
        heart
Strains the strait-breasted drab of the Quaker apart,
And reveals the live Man, still supreme and erect,
Underneath the bemummying wrappers of sect;
There was ne'er a man born who had more of the swing
Of the true lyric bard and all that kind of thing;
And his failures arise (though he seem not to know it)
From the very same cause that has made him a poet, —
A fervor of mind which knows no separation
'Twixt simple excitement and pure inspiration,
As my Pythoness erst sometimes erred from not knowing
If 't were I or mere wind through her tripod was blowing;
Let his mind once get head in its favorite direction
And the torrent of verse bursts the dams of reflection,
While, borne with the rush of the metre along,
The poet may chance to go right or go wrong,
Content with the whirl and delirium of song;
Then his grammar 's not always correct, nor his rhymes,
And he 's prone to repeat his own lyrics sometimes,
Not his best, though, for those are struck off at white-heats
When the heart in his breast like a trip-hammer beats,
And can ne'er be repeated again any more
Than they could have been carefully plotted before:
Like old what 's-his-name there at the battle of Hastings
(Who, however, gave more than mere rhythmical bastings),
Our Quaker leads off metaphorical fights
For reform and whatever they call human rights,

Both singing and striking in front of the war,
And hitting his foes with the mallet of Thor;
Anne haec, one exclaims, on beholding his knocks,
Vestis filii tui, O leather-clad Fox?
Can that be thy son, in the battle's mid din,
Preaching brotherly love and then driving it in
To the brain of the tough old Goliath of sin,
With the smoothest of pebbles from Castaly's spring
Impressed on his hard moral sense with a sling?

" All honor and praise to the right-hearted bard
Who was true to The Voice when such service was hard,
Who himself was so free he dared sing for the slave
When to look but a protest in silence was brave;
All honor and praise to the women and men
Who spoke out for the dumb and the down-trodden then!
It needs not to name them, already for each
I see History preparing the statue and niche;
They were harsh, but shall *you* be so shocked at hard words
Who have beaten your pruning-hooks up into swords,
Whose rewards and hurrahs men are surer to gain
By the reaping of men and of women than grain?
Why should *you* stand aghast at their fierce wordy war, if
You scalp one another for Bank or for Tariff?
Your calling them cut-throats and knaves all day long
Doesn't prove that the use of hard language is wrong;
While the World's heart beats quicker to think of such men
As signed Tyranny's doom with a bloody steel-pen,
While on Fourth-of-Julys beardless orators fright one
With hints at Harmodius and Aristogeiton,
You need not look shy at your sisters and brothers
Who stab with sharp words for the freedom of others; —
No, a wreath, twine a wreath for the loyal and true
Who, for sake of the many, dared stand with the few,
Not of blood-spattered laurel for enemies braved,
But of broad, peaceful oak-leaves for citizens saved!

THOREAU

[*Published in " The North American Review," 1865. Reprinted in " My Study Windows," 1871. Copyright, 1871, by James Russell Lowell.*]

WHAT contemporary, if he was in the fighting period of his life, (since Nature set limits about her conscription for spiritual fields, as the state does in physical warfare,) will ever forget what was somewhat vaguely called the "Transcendental Movement" of thirty years ago? Apparently set astir by Carlyle's essays on the "Signs of the Times," and on "History," the final and more immediate impulse seemed to be given by "Sartor Resartus." At least the republication in Boston of that wonderful Abraham à Sancta Clara sermon on Falstaff's text of the miserable forked radish gave the signal for a sudden mental and moral mutiny. *Ecce nunc tempus acceptabile!* was shouted on all hands with every variety of emphasis, and by voices of every conceivable pitch, representing the three sexes of men, women, and Lady Mary Wortley Montagues. The nameless eagle of the tree Ygdrasil was about to sit at last, and wild-eyed enthusiasts rushed from all sides, each eager to thrust under the mystic bird that chalk egg from which the new and fairer Creation was to be hatched in due time. *Redeunt Saturnia regna,* — so far was certain, though in what shape, or by what methods, was still a matter of debate. Every possible form of intellectual and physical dyspepsia brought forth its gospel. Bran had its prophets, and the presartorial simplicity of Adam its martyrs, tailored impromptu from the tar-pot by incensed neighbors, and sent forth to illustrate the " feathered Mercury," as defined by Webster and Worcester. Plainness of speech was carried to a pitch that would have taken away the breath of George Fox ; and even swearing had its evangelists, who answered a simple inquiry after their health with an elaborate ingenuity of imprecation that might have been honorably mentioned by Marlborough in general orders. Everybody had a mission (with a capital M) to attend to everybody-else's business. No brain but had its private maggot, which must have found pitiably short commons sometimes. Not a few impecunious zealots abjured the use of money (unless earned by other people), professing to live on the internal revenues of the spirit. Some had an assurance of instant millennium so soon as hooks and eyes should be substituted for buttons. Communities were established where everything was to be common but common-sense. Men renounced their old gods, and hesitated only whether to bestow their furloughed allegiance on Thor or Budh. Conventions were held for every hitherto inconceivable purpose. The belated gift of tongues, as among the Fifth Monarchy men, spread like a contagion, rendering its victims incomprehensible to all Christian men ; whether equally so to the most distant possible heathen or not was unexperimented, though many would have subscribed liberally that a fair trial might be made. It was the pentecost of Shinar. The day of utterances reproduced the day of rebuses and anagrams, and there was nothing so simple that uncial letters and the style of Diphilus the Labyrinth could not turn it into a riddle. Many foreign revolutionists out of work added to the general misunderstanding their contribution of broken English in every most ingenious form of fracture. All stood ready at a moment's notice to reform everything but themselves. The general motto was : —

> " And we 'll *talk* with them, too,
> And take upon 's the mystery of things
> As if we were God's spies."

Nature is always kind enough to give even her clouds a humorous lining. I have barely hinted at the comic side of the affair, for the material was endless. This was the whistle and trailing fuse of the shell, but there was a very solid and serious kernel, full of the most deadly explosiveness. Thoughtful men divined it, but the generality suspected nothing. The word "transcendental" then was the maid of all work for those who could not think, as "Pre-Raphaelite" has been more recently for people of the same limited housekeeping. The truth is, that there was a much nearer metaphysical relation and a much more distant æsthetic and literary relation between Carlyle and the Apostles of the Newness, as they were called in New England, than has commonly been supposed. Both represented the reaction and revolt against *Philisterei*, a renewal of the old battle begun in modern times by Erasmus and Reuchlin, and continued by Lessing, Goethe, and, in a far narrower sense, by Heine in Germany, and of which Fielding, Sterne, and Wordsworth in different ways have been the leaders in England. It was simply a struggle for fresh air, in which, if the windows could not be opened, there was danger that panes would be broken, though painted with images of saints and martyrs. Light, colored by these reverend effigies, was none the more respirable for being picturesque. There is only one thing better than tradition, and that is the original and eternal life out of which all tradition takes its rise. It was this life which the reformers demanded, with more or less clearness of consciousness and expression, life in politics, life in literature, life in religion. Of what use to import a gospel from Judæa, if we leave behind the soul that made it possible, the God who keeps it forever real and present? Surely Abana and Pharpar *are* better than Jordan, if a living faith be mixed with those waters and none with these.

Scotch Presbyterianism as a motive of spiritual progress was dead; New England Puritanism was in like manner

dead ; in other words, Protestantism had made its fortune
and no longer protested ; but till Carlyle spoke out in the
Old World and Emerson in the New, no one had dared
to proclaim, *Le roi est mort: vive le roi!* The meaning
of which proclamation was essentially this : the vital spirit
has long since departed out of this form once so kingly,
and the great seal has been in commission long enough ;
but meanwhile the soul of man, from which all power
emanates and to which it reverts, still survives in undimin-
ished royalty ; God still survives, little as you gentlemen
of the Commission seem to be aware of it, — nay, will
possibly outlive the whole of you, incredible as it may
appear.   The truth is, that both Scotch Presbyterianism
and New England Puritanism made their new avatar in
Carlyle and Emerson, the heralds of their formal decease,
and the tendency of the one toward Authority and of the
other toward Independency might have been prophesied
by whoever had studied history.   The necessity was not
so much in the men as in the principles they represented
and the traditions which overruled them.   The Puritanism
of the past found its unwilling poet in Hawthorne, the
rarest creative imagination of the century, the rarest in
some ideal respects since Shakespeare ; but the Puritanism
that cannot die, the Puritanism that made New England
what it is, and is destined to make America what it should
be, found its voice in Emerson.   Though holding himself
aloof from all active partnership in movements of reform,
he has been the sleeping partner who has supplied a great
part of their capital.

The artistic range of Emerson is narrow, as every well-read
critic must feel at once ; and so is that of Æschylus, so is that
of Dante, so is that of Montaigne, so is that of Schiller, so is
that of nearly every one except Shakespeare ; but there is a
gauge of height no less than of breadth, of individuality as
well as of comprehensiveness, and, above all, there is the
standard of genetic power, the test of the masculine as
distinguished from the receptive minds.   There are stamin-

ate plants in literature, that make no fine show of fruit, but without whose pollen, quintessence of fructifying gold, the garden had been barren. Emerson's mind is emphatically one of these, and there is no man to whom our æsthetic culture owes so much. The Puritan revolt had made us ecclesiastically and the Revolution politically independent, but we were still socially and intellectually moored to English thought, till Emerson cut the cable and gave us a chance at the dangers and the glories of blue water. No man young enough to have felt it can forget or cease to be grateful for the mental and moral *nudge* which he received from the writings of his high-minded and brave-spirited countryman. That we agree with him, or that he always agrees with himself, is aside from the question; but that he arouses in us something that we are the better for having awakened, whether that something be of opposition or assent, that he speaks always to what is highest and least selfish in us, few Americans of the generation younger than his own would be disposed to deny. His oration before the Phi Beta Kappa Society at Cambridge, some thirty years ago, was an event without any former parallel in our literary annals, a scene to be always treasured in the memory for its picturesqueness and its inspiration. What crowded and breathless aisles, what windows clustering with eager heads, what enthusiasm of approval, what grim silence of foregone dissent! It was our Yankee version of a lecture by Abelard, our Harvard parallel to the last public appearances of Schelling.

I said that the Transcendental Movement was the protestant spirit of Puritanism seeking a new outlet and an escape from forms and creeds which compressed rather than expressed it. In its motives, its preaching, and its results, it differed radically from the doctrine of Carlyle. The Scotchman, with all his genius, and his humor gigantesque as that of Rabelais, has grown shriller and shriller with years, degenerating sometimes into a common scold, and emptying very unsavory vials of wrath on the head of the sturdy British Socrates of worldly common-sense. The teaching of Emerson tended much more exclusively to self-culture and the independent development of the individual man. It seemed to many almost Pythagorean in its voluntary seclusion from commonwealth affairs. Both Carlyle and Emerson were disciples of Goethe, but Emerson in a far truer sense; and while the one, from his bias toward the eccentric, has degenerated more and more into mannerism, the other has clarified steadily toward perfection of style, — exquisite fineness of material, unobtrusive lowness of tone and simplicity of fashion, the most high-bred garb of expression. Whatever may be said of his thought, nothing can be finer than the delicious limpidness of his phrase. If it was ever questionable whether democracy could develop a gentleman, the problem has been affirmatively solved at last. Carlyle, in his cynicism and his admiration of force in and for itself, has become at last positively inhuman; Emerson, reverencing strength, seeking the highest outcome of the individual, has found that society and politics are also main elements in the attainment of the desired end, and has drawn steadily manward and worldward. The two men represent respectively those grand personifications in the drama of Æschylus, Βία and Κράτος.

Among the pistillate plants kindled to fruitage by the Emersonian pollen, Thoreau is thus far the most remarkable; and it is something eminently fitting that his posthumous works should be offered us by Emerson, for they are strawberries from his own garden. A singular mixture of varieties, indeed, there is; — alpine, some of them, with the flavor of rare mountain air; others wood, tasting of sunny roadside banks or shy openings in the forest; and not a few seedlings swollen hugely by culture, but lacking the fine natural aroma of the more modest kinds. Strange books these are of his, and interesting in many ways, — instructive chiefly as showing how considerable a crop may be raised on a comparatively narrow close of mind, and

how much a man may make of his life if he will assiduously
follow it, though perhaps never truly finding it at last.

I have just been renewing my recollection of Mr.
Thoreau's writings, and have read through his six volumes
in the order of their production. I shall try to give an
adequate report of their impression upon me both as critic
and as mere reader. He seems to me to have been a man
with so high a conceit of himself that he accepted without
questioning, and insisted on our accepting, his defects and
weaknesses of character as virtues and powers peculiar to
himself. Was he indolent, he finds none of the activities
which attract or employ the rest of mankind worthy of
him. Was he wanting in the qualities that make success,
it is success that is contemptible, and not himself that
lacks persistency and purpose. Was he poor, money was
an unmixed evil. Did his life seem a selfish one, he condemns doing good as one of the weakest of superstitions.
To be of use was with him the most killing bait of the
wily tempter Uselessness. He had no faculty of generalization from outside of himself, or at least no experience
which would supply the material of such, and he makes
his own whim the law, his own range the horizon of the
universe. He condemns a world, the hollowness of whose
satisfactions he had never had the means of testing, and
we recognize Apemantus behind the mask of Timon. He
had little active imagination; of the receptive he had
much. His appreciation is of the highest quality; his critical power, from want of continuity of mind, very limited
and inadequate. He somewhere cites a simile from Ossian,
as an example of the superiority of the old poetry to the
new, though, even were the historic evidence less convinc-
ing, the sentimental melancholy of those poems should be
conclusive of their modernness. He had none of the
artistic mastery which controls a great work to the serene
balance of completeness, but exquisite mechanical skill in
the shaping of sentences and paragraphs, or (more rarely)
short bits of verse for the expression of a detached thought,

sentiment, or image. His works give one the feeling of a
sky full of stars, — something impressive and exhilarating
certainly, something high overhead and freckled thickly
with spots of isolated brightness ; but whether these have
any mutual relation with each other, or have any concern
with our mundane matters, is for the most part matter of
conjecture, — astrology as yet, and not astronomy.

It is curious, considering what Thoreau afterwards became, that he was not by nature an observer. He only
saw the things he looked for, and was less poet than
naturalist. Till he built his Walden shanty, he did not
know that the hickory grew in Concord. Till he went to
Maine, he had never seen phosphorescent wood, a phenomenon early familiar to most country boys. At forty he
speaks of the seeding of the pine as a new discovery,
though one should have thought that its gold-dust of blowing
pollen might have earlier drawn his eye. Neither his
attention nor his genius was of the spontaneous kind. He
discovered nothing. He thought everything a discovery
of his own, from moonlight to the planting of acorns and
nuts by squirrels. This is a defect in his character, but
one of his chief charms as a writer. Everything grows
fresh under his hand. He delved in his mind and nature ;
he planted them with all manner of native and foreign
seeds, and reaped assiduously. He was not merely solitary,
he would be isolated, and succeeded at last in almost per-
suading himself that he was autochthonous. He valued
everything in proportion as he fancied it to be exclusively
his own. He complains in " Walden " that there is no one
in Concord with whom he could talk of Oriental literature,
though the man was living within two miles of his hut who
had introduced him to it. This intellectual selfishness becomes sometimes almost painful in reading him. He
lacked that generosity of " communication " which Johnson
admired in Burke. De Quincey tells us that Wordsworth
was impatient when any one else spoke of mountains, as if
he had a peculiar property in them. And we can readily

understand why it should be so: no one is satisfied with another's appreciation of his mistress. But Thoreau seems to have prized a lofty way of thinking (often we should be inclined to call it a remote one) not so much because it was good in itself as because he wished few to share it with him. It seems now and then as if he did not seek to lure others up "above our lower region of turmoil," but to leave his own name cut on the mountain peak as the first climber. This itch of originality infects his thought and style. To be misty is not to be mystic. He turns commonplaces end for end, and fancies it makes something new of them. As we walk down Park Street, our eye is caught by Dr. Winship's dumb-bells, one of which bears an inscription testifying that it is the heaviest ever put up at arm's length by any athlete; and in reading Mr. Thoreau's books we cannot help feeling as if he sometimes invited our attention to a particular sophism or parodox as the biggest yet maintained by any single writer. He seeks, at all risks, for perversity of thought, and revives the age of *concetti* while he fancies himself going back to a pre-classical nature. "A day," he says, "passed in the society of those Greek sages, such as described in the Banquet of Xenophon, would not be comparable with the dry wit of decayed cranberry-vines and the fresh Attic salt of the moss-beds." It is not so much the True that he loves as the Out-of-the-Way. As the Brazen Age shows itself in other men by exaggeration of phrase, so in him by extravagance of statement. He wishes always to trump your suit and to *ruff* when you least expect it. Do you love Nature because she is beautiful? He will find a better argument in her ugliness. Are you tired of the artificial man? He instantly dresses you up an ideal in a Penobscot Indian, and attributes to this creature of his otherwise-mindedness as peculiarities things that are common to all woodsmen, white or red, and this simply because he has not studied the pale-faced variety.

This notion of an absolute originality, as if one could have a patent-right in it, is an absurdity. A man cannot escape in thought, any more than he can in language, from the past and the present. As no one ever invents a word, and yet language somehow grows by general contribution and necessity, so it is with thought. Mr. Thoreau seems to me to insist in public on going back to flint and steel, when there is a match-box in his pocket which he knows very well how to use at a pinch. Originality consists in power of digesting and assimilating thoughts, so that they become part of our life and substance. Montaigne, for example, is one of the most original of authors, though he helped himself to ideas in every direction. But they turn to blood and coloring in his style, and give a freshness of complexion that is forever charming. In Thoreau much seems yet to be foreign and unassimilated, showing itself in symptoms of indigestion. A preacher-up of Nature, we now and then detect under the surly and stoic garb something of the sophist and the sentimentalizer. I am far from implying that this was conscious on his part. But it is much easier for a man to impose on himself when he measures only with himself. A greater familiarity with ordinary men would have done Thoreau good, by showing him how many fine qualities are common to the race. The radical vice of his theory of life was that he confounded physical with spiritual remoteness from men. A man is far enough withdrawn from his fellows if he keep himself clear of their weaknesses. He is not so truly withdrawn as exiled, if he refuse to share in their strength. "Solitude," says Cowley, "can be well fitted and set right but upon a very few persons. They must have enough knowledge of the world to see the vanity of it, and enough virtue to despise all vanity." It is a morbid self-consciousness that pronounces the world of men empty and worthless, before trying it, the instinctive evasion of one who is sensible of some innate weakness, and retorts the accusation of it before any has made it but himself. To a healthy mind, the world is a constant challenge of opportunity. Mr. Thoreau had not a healthy mind, or he would not have been so fond of prescribing. His whole life was a search for the doctor. The old mystics had a wiser sense of what the world was worth. They ordained a severe apprenticeship to law, and even ceremonial, in order to the gaining of freedom and mastery over these. Seven years of service for Rachel were to be rewarded at last with Leah. Seven other years of faithfulness with her were to win them at last the true bride of their souls. Active Life was with them the only path to the Contemplative.

Thoreau had no humor, and this implies that he was a sorry logician. Himself an artist in rhetoric, he confounds thought with style when he undertakes to speak of the latter. He was forever talking of getting away from the world, but he must be always near enough to it, nay, to the Concord corner of it, to feel the impression he makes there. He verifies the shrewd remark of Sainte-Beuve, " On touche encore à son temps et très-fort, même quand on le repousse." This egotism of his is a Stylites pillar after all, a seclusion which keeps him in the public eye. The dignity of man is an excellent thing, but therefore to hold one's self too sacred and precious is the reverse of excellent. There is something delightfully absurd in six volumes addressed to a world of such " vulgar fellows " as Thoreau affirmed his fellowmen to be. I once had a glimpse of a genuine solitary who spent his winters one hundred and fifty miles beyond all human communication, and there dwelt with his rifle as his only confidant. Compared with this, the shanty on Walden Pond has something the air, it must be confessed, of the Hermitage of La Chevrette. I do not believe that the way to a true cosmopolitanism carries one into the woods or the society of musquashes. Perhaps the narrowest provincialism is that of Self; that of Kleinwinkel is nothing to it. The natural man, like the singing birds, comes out of the forest as inevitably as the natural bear and the wildcat stick there. To seek to be natural implies a consciousness that forbids all naturalness forever. It is as easy — and no easier — to be natural in a *salon* as in a swamp, if one do not aim at it, for what we call unnaturalness always has its spring in a man's thinking too much about himself. " It is impossible," said Turgot, " for a vulgar man to be simple."

I look upon a great deal of the modern sentimentalism about Nature as a mark of disease. It is one more symptom of the general liver-complaint. To a man of wholesome constitution the wilderness is well enough for a mood or a vacation, but not for a habit of life. Those who have most loudly advertised their passion for seclusion and their intimacy with nature, from Petrarch down, have been mostly sentimentalists, unreal men, misanthropes on the spindle side, solacing an uneasy suspicion of themselves by professing contempt for their kind. They make demands on the world in advance proportioned to their inward measure of their own merit, and are angry that the world pays only by the visible measure of performance. It is true of Rousseau, the modern founder of the sect, true of Saint Pierre, his intellectual child, and of Châteaubriand, his grandchild, the inventor, we might almost say, of the primitive forest, and who first was touched by the solemn falling of a tree from natural decay in the windless silence of the woods. It is a very shallow view that affirms trees and rocks to be healthy, and cannot see that men in communities are just as true to the laws of their organization and destiny ; that can tolerate the puffin and the fox, but not the fool and the knave ; that would shun politics because of its demagogues, and snuff up the stench of the obscene fungus. The divine life of Nature is more wonderful, more various, more sublime in man than in any other of her works, and the wisdom that is gained by commerce with men, as Montaigne and Shakespeare gained it, or with one's own soul among men, as Dante, is the most delightful, as it is the most precious, of all. In outward nature it is still man that interests us, and we care far less for the things seen than the way in which they are seen by poetic eyes like Wordsworth's or Thoreau's, and the reflections they cast there. To hear the to-do that is often made over the simple fact that a man sees the image of himself in the outward world, one is reminded of a savage when he for the first time catches a glimpse of himself in a looking-glass. "Venerable child of Nature," we are tempted to say, "to whose science in the invention of the tobacco-pipe, to whose art in the tattooing of thine undegenerate hide not yet enslaved by tailors, we are slowly striving to climb back, the miracle thou beholdest is sold in my unhappy country for a shilling!" If matters go on as they have done, and everybody must needs blab of all the favors that have been done him by roadside and riverbrink and woodland walk, as if to kiss and tell were no longer treachery, it will be a positive refreshment to meet a man who is as superbly indifferent to Nature as she is to him. By and by we shall have John Smith, of No. - 12 - 12th Street, advertising that he is not the J. S. who saw a cow-lily on Thursday last, as he never saw one in his life, would not see one if he could, and is prepared to prove an alibi on the day in question.

Solitary communion with Nature does not seem to have been sanitary or sweetening in its influence on Thoreau's character. On the contrary, his letters show him more cynical as he grew older. While he studied with respectful attention the minks and woodchucks, his neighbors, he looked with utter contempt on the august drama of destiny of which his country was the scene, and on which the curtain had already risen. He was converting us back to a state of nature "so eloquently," as Voltaire said of Rousseau, "that he almost persuaded us to go on all fours," while the wiser fates were making it possible for us to walk erect for the first time. Had he conversed more with his fellows, his sympathies would have widened with the assurance that his peculiar genius had more appreciation, and his writings a larger circle of readers, or at least a warmer one, than he dreamed of. We have the highest testimony [1] to the natural

---

[1] Mr. Emerson, in the Biographical Sketch prefixed to the *Excursions.*

sweetness, sincerity, and nobleness of his temper, and in his
books an equally irrefragable one to the rare quality of his
mind.   He was not a strong thinker, but a sensitive feeler.
Yet his mind strikes us as cold and wintry in its purity.   A
light snow has fallen everywhere in which he seems to
come on the track of the shier sensations that would elsewhere leave no trace.   We think greater compression would
have done more for his fame.   A feeling of sameness comes
over us as we read so much.   Trifles are recorded with an
over-minute punctuality and conscientiousness of detail.
He registers the state of his personal thermometer thirteen
times a day.   We cannot help thinking sometimes of the
man who

> " Watches, starves, freezes, and sweats
> To learn but catechisms and alphabets
> Of unconcerning things, matters of fact,"

and sometimes of the saying of the Persian poet, that
" when the owl would boast, he boasts of catching mice at
the edge of a hole."   We could readily part with some of
his affectations.   It was well enough for Pythagoras to say,
once for all, " When I was Euphorbus at the siege of
Troy " ; not so well for Thoreau to travesty it into
" When I was a shepherd on the plains of Assyria."   A
naïve thing said over again is anything but naïve.   But with
every exception, there is no writing comparable with
Thoreau's in kind, that is comparable with it in degree
where it is best ; where it disengages itself, that is, from the
tangled roots and dead leaves of a second-hand Orientalism,
and runs limpid and smooth and broadening as it runs, a
mirror for whatever is grand and lovely in both worlds.

George Sand says neatly, that " Art is not a study of
positive reality," (*actuality* were the fitter word,) "but a
seeking after ideal truth."   It would be doing very inadequate justice to Thoreau if we left it to be inferred that
this ideal element did not exist in him, and that too in larger
proportion, if less obtrusive, than his nature-worship.   He

took nature as the mountain-path to an ideal world. If
the path wind a good deal, if he record too faithfully every
trip over a root, if he botanize somewhat wearisomely, he
gives us now and then superb outlooks from some jutting
crag, and brings us out at last into an illimitable ether,
where the breathing is not difficult for those who have any
true touch of the climbing spirit. His shanty-life was a
mere impossibility, so far as his own conception of it goes,
as an entire independency of mankind. The tub of
Diogenes had a sounder bottom. Thoreau's experiment
actually presupposed all that complicated civilization which
it theoretically abjured. He squatted on another man's
land; he borrows an axe; his boards, his nails, his bricks,
his mortar, his books, his lamp, his fish-hooks, his plough,
his hoe, all turn state's evidence against him as an accom-
plice in the sin of that artificial civilization which rendered
it possible that such a person as Henry D. Thoreau should
exist at all. *Magnis tamen excidit ausis.* His aim was a
noble and a useful one, in the direction of " plain living and
high thinking." It was a practical sermon on Emerson's
text that " things are in the saddle and ride mankind," an
attempt to solve Carlyle's problem (condensed from Johnson) of " lessening your denominator." His whole life was
a rebuke of the waste and aimlessness of our American
luxury, which is an abject enslavement to tawdry uphol-
stery. He had " fine translunary things " in him. His
better style as a writer is in keeping with the simplicity and
purity of his life. We have said that his range was narrow,
but to be a master is to be a master. He had caught his
English at its living source, among the poets and prose-
writers of its best days; his literature was extensive and
recondite; his quotations are always nuggets of the purest
ore : there are sentences of his as perfect as anything in the
language, and thoughts as clearly crystallized; his metaphors
and images are always fresh from the soil; he had watched
Nature like a detective who is to go upon the stand; as
we read him, it seems as if all-out-of-doors had kept a

diary and become its own Montaigne ; we look at the land-scape as in a Claude Lorraine glass ; compared with his, all other books of similar aim, even White's " Selborne," seem dry as a country clergyman's meteorological journal in an old almanac. He belongs with Donne and Browne and Novalis ; if not with the originally creative men, with the scarcely smaller class who are peculiar, and whose leaves shed their invisible thought-seed like ferns.

WALT WHITMAN
1819–1892

FIRST PREFACE TO "LEAVES
OF GRASS"

[*From " Leaves of Grass," 1855*]

A MERICA does not repel the past, or what the past
has produced under its forms, or amid other politics,
or the idea of castes, or the old religions — accepts the
lesson with calmness — is not impatient because the slough
still sticks to opinions and manners in literature, while the
life which served its requirements has passed into the new
life of the new forms — perceives that the corpse is slowly
borne from the eating and sleeping rooms of the house —
perceives that it waits a little while in the door — that it
was fittest for its days — that its action has descended to the
stalwart and well-shaped heir who approaches — and that
he shall be fittest for his days.

The Americans of all nations at any time upon the earth,
have probably the fullest poetical nature. The United
States themselves are essentially the greatest poem. In the
history of the earth hitherto, the largest and most stirring
appear tame and orderly to their ampler largeness and stir.
Here at last is something in the doings of man that corre-
sponds with the broadcast doings of the day and night.
Here is action untied from strings, necessarily blind to particulars and details, magnificently moving in masses. Here
is the hospitality which for ever indicates heroes. Here
the performance, disdaining the trivial, unapproach'd in the
tremendous audacity of its crowds and groupings, and the
push of its perspective, spreads with crampless and flowing
breadth, and showers its prolific and splendid extravagance.
One sees it must indeed own the riches of the summer and

winter, and need never be bankrupt while corn grows from the ground, or the orchards drop apples, or the bays contain fish, or men beget children upon women.

Other states indicate themselves in their deputies — but the genius of the United States is not best or most in its executives or legislatures, nor in its ambassadors or authors, or colleges or churches or parlors, nor even in its newspapers or inventors — but always most in the common people, south, north, west, east, in all its States, through all its mighty amplitude. The largeness of the nation, however, were monstrous without a corresponding largeness and generosity of the spirit of the citizen. Not swarming states, nor streets and steamships, nor prosperous business, nor farms, nor capital, nor learning, may suffice for the ideal of man — nor suffice the poet. No reminiscences may suffice either. A live nation can always cut a deep mark, and can have the best authority the cheapest — namely, from its own soul. This is the sum of the profitable uses of individuals or states, and of present action and grandeur, and of the subjects of poets. (As if it were necessary to trot back generation after generation to the eastern records! As if the beauty and sacredness of the demonstrable must fall behind that of the mythical! As if men do not make their mark out of any times! As if the opening of the western continent by discovery, and what has transpired in North and South America, were less than the small theatre of the antique, or the aimless sleep-walking of the middle ages!) The pride of the United States leaves the wealth and finesse of the cities, and all returns of commerce and agriculture, and all the magnitude of geography or shows of exterior victory, to enjoy the sight and realization of full-sized men, or one full-sized man unconquerable and simple.

The American poets are to enclose old and new, for America is the race of races. The expression of the American poet is to be transcendent and new. It is to be indirect, and not direct or descriptive or epic. Its quality goes through these to much more. Let the age and wars of other nations be chanted, and their eras and characters be illustrated, and that finish the verse. Not so the great psalm of the republic. Here the theme is creative, and has vista. Whatever stagnates in the flat of custom or obedience or legislation, the great poet never stagnates. Obedience does not master him, he masters it. High up out of reach he stands, turning a concentrated light — he turns the pivot with his finger — he baffles the swiftest run- ners as he stands, and easily overtakes and envelopes them. The time straying toward infidelity and confections and per- siflage he withholds by steady faith. Faith is the antiseptic of the soul — it pervades the common people and preserves them — they never give up believing and expecting and trusting. There is that indescribable freshness and uncon- sciousness about an illiterate person, that humbles and mocks the power of the noblest expressive genius. The poet sees for a certainty how one not a great artist may be just as sacred and perfect as the greatest artist.

The power to destroy or remould is freely used by the greatest poet, but seldom the power of attack. What is past is past. If he does not expose superior models, and prove himself by every step he takes, he is not what is wanted. The presence of the great poet conquers — not parleying, or struggling, or any prepared attempts. Now he has passed that way, see after him ! There is not left any vestige of despair, or misanthropy, or cunning, or exclusive- ness, or the ignominy of a nativity or color, or delusion of hell or the necessity of hell — and no man thenceforward shall be degraded for ignorance or weakness or sin. The greatest poet hardly knows pettiness or triviality. If he breathes into anything that was before thought small, it dilates with the grandeur and life of the universe. He is a seer — he is individual — he is complete in himself — the others are as good as he, only he sees it, and they do not. He is not one of the chorus — he does not stop for any regulation — he is the president of regulation. What the eyesight does to the rest, he does to the rest. Who knows the curious mystery of the eyesight? The other senses corroborate themselves, but this is removed from any proof but its own, and foreruns the identities of the spiritual world. A single glance of it mocks all the investigations of man, and all the instruments and books of the earth, and all reasoning. What is marvellous? what is unlikely? what is impossible or baseless or vague — after you have once just open'd the space of a peach-pit, and given audience to far and near, and to the sunset, and had all things enter with electric swiftness, softly and duly, without confusion or jostling or jam?

The land and sea, the animals, fishes and birds, the sky of heaven and the orbs, the forests, mountains and rivers, are not small themes — but folks expect of the poet to indicate more than the beauty and dignity which always attach to dumb real objects — they expect him to indicate the path between reality and their souls. Men and women perceive the beauty well enough — probably as well as he. The passionate tenacity of hunters, woodmen, early risers, cultivators of gardens and orchards and fields, the love of healthy women for the manly form, seafaring persons, drivers of horses, the passion for light and the open air, all is an old varied sign of the unfailing perception of beauty, and of a residence of the poetic in out-door people. They can never be assisted by poets to perceive — some may, but they never can. The poetic quality is not marshal'd in rhyme or uniformity, or abstract addresses to things, nor in melancholy complaints or good precepts, but is the life of these and much else, and is in the soul. The profit of rhyme is that it drops seeds of a sweeter and more luxuriant rhyme, and of uniformity that it conveys itself into its own roots in the ground out of sight. The rhyme and uniformity of perfect poems show the free growth of metrical laws, and bud from them as unerringly and loosely as lilacs and roses on a bush, and take shapes as compact as the shapes of chestnuts and oranges, and melons and pears, and shed the perfume impalpable to form. The fluency and ornaments of the finest poems or music or orations or recitations, are not independent but dependent. All beauty comes from beautiful blood and a beautiful brain. If the greatnesses are in conjunction in a man or woman, it is enough — the fact will prevail through the universe ; but the gaggery and gilt of a million years will not prevail. Who troubles himself about his ornaments or fluency if lost. This is what you shall do : Love the earth and sun and the animals, despise riches, give alms to every one that asks, stand up for the stupid and crazy, devote your income and labor to others, hate tyrants, argue not concerning God, have patience and indulgence toward the people, take off your hat to nothing known or unknown, or to any man or number of men — go freely with powerful uneducated persons, and with the young, and with the mothers of families — re-examine all you have been told in school or church or in any book, and dismiss whatever insults your own soul ; and your very flesh shall be a great poem, and have the richest fluency, not only in its words, but in the silent lines of its lips and face, and between the lashes of your eyes, and in every motion and joint of your body. The poet shall not spend his time in unneeded work. He shall know that the ground is already plough'd and manured ; others may not know it, but he shall. He shall go directly to the creation. His trust shall master the trust of everything he touches — and shall master all attachment.

The known universe has one complete lover, and that is the greatest poet. He consumes an eternal passion, and is indifferent which chance happens, and which possible contingency of fortune or misfortune, and persuades daily and hourly his delicious pay. What balks or breaks others is fuel for his burning progress to contact and amorous joy. Other proportions of the reception of pleasure dwindle to nothing to his proportions. All expected from heaven or from the highest, he is rapport with in the sight of the daybreak, or the scenes of the winter woods, or the presence of children playing, or with his arm round the neck of a man or woman. His love above all love has leisure and expanse — he leaves room ahead of himself. He is no irresolute or suspicious lover — he is sure — he scorns intervals. His experience and the showers and thrills are not for nothing. Nothing can jar him — suffering and darkness cannot — death and fear cannot. To him complaint and jealousy and envy are corpses buried and rotten in the earth — he saw them buried. The sea is not surer of the shore, or the shore of the sea, than he is the fruition of his love, and of all perfection and beauty.

The fruition of beauty is no chance of miss or hit — it is as inevitable as life — it is exact and plumb as gravitation. From the eyesight proceeds another eyesight, and from the hearing proceeds another hearing, and from the voice proceeds another voice, eternally curious of the harmony of things with man. These understand the law of perfection in masses and floods — that it is profuse and impartial — that there is not a minute of the light or dark, nor an acre of the earth and sea, without it — nor any direction of the sky, nor any trade or employment, nor any turn of events. This is the reason that about the proper expression of beauty there is precision and balance. One part does not need to be thrust above another. The best singer is not the one who has the most lithe and powerful organ. The pleasure of poems is not in them that take the handsomest measure and sound.

Without effort, and without exposing in the least how it is done, the greatest poet brings the spirit of any or all events and passions and scenes and persons, some more and some less, to bear on your individual character as you hear or read. To do this well is to compete with the laws that pursue and follow Time. What is the purpose must surely be there, and the clue of it must be there — and the faintest indication is the indication of the best, and then becomes the clearest indication. Past and present and future are not disjoin'd but join'd. The greatest poet forms the consistence of what is to be, from what has been and is. He drags the dead out of their coffins and stands them again on their feet. He says to the past, Rise and walk before me that I may realize you. He learns the lesson — he places himself where the future becomes present. The greatest poet does not only dazzle his rays over character and scenes and passions — he finally ascends, and finishes all — he exhibits the pinnacles that no man can tell what they are for, or what is beyond — he glows a moment on the extremest verge. He is most wonderful in his last half-hidden smile or frown; by that flash of the moment of parting the one that sees it shall be encouraged or terrified afterward for many years. The greatest poet does not moralize or make applications of morals — he knows the soul. The soul has that measureless pride which consists in never acknowledging any lessons or deductions but its own. But it has sympathy as measureless as its pride, and the one balances the other, and neither can stretch too far while it stretches in company with the other. The inmost secrets of art sleep with the twain. The greatest poet has lain close betwixt both, and they are vital in his style and thoughts.

The art of art, the glory of expression and the sunshine of the light of letters, is simplicity. Nothing is better than simplicity — nothing can make up for excess, or for the lack of definiteness. To carry on the heave of impulse and pierce intellectual depths and give all subjects their articulations, are powers neither common nor very uncommon. But to speak in literature with the perfect rectitude and insouciance of the movements of animals, and the unimpeachableness of the sentiment of trees in the woods and grass by the roadside, is the flawless triumph of art. If you have look'd on him who has achiev'd it you have look'd on one of the masters of the artists of all nations and times. You shall not contemplate the flight of the gray gull over the bay, or the mettlesome action of the blood horse, or the tall leaning of sunflowers on their stalk, or the appear-

ance of the sun journeying through heaven, or the appearance of the moon afterward, with any more satisfaction
than you shall contemplate him. The great poet has less
a mark'd style, and is more the channel of thoughts and
things without increase or diminution, and is the free
channel of himself. He swears to his art, I will not be
meddlesome, I will not have in my writing any elegance,
or effect, or originality, to hang in the way between me
and the rest like curtains. I will have nothing hang in the
way, not the richest curtains. What I tell I tell for precisely what it is. Let who may exalt or startle or fascinate
or soothe, I will have purposes as health or heat or snow
has, and be as regardless of observation. What I experience
or portray shall go from my composition without a shred of
my composition. You shall stand by my side and look in
the mirror with me.

The old red blood and stainless gentility of great poets
will be proved by their unconstraint. A heroic person
walks at his ease through and out of that custom or prece-
dent or authority that suits him not. Of the traits of the
brotherhood of first-class writers, savans, musicians, inventors and artists, nothing is finer than silent defiance
advancing from new free forms. In the need of poems,
philosophy, politics, mechanism, science, behavior, the craft
of art, an appropriate native grand opera, shipcraft, or any
craft, he is greatest for ever and ever who contributes the
greatest original practical example. The cleanest expression is that which finds no sphere worthy of itself, and
makes one.

The messages of great poems to each man and woman
are, Come to us on equal terms, only then can you understand us. We are no better than you, what we inclose
you inclose, what we enjoy you may enjoy. Did you suppose there could be only one Supreme? We affirm there
can be unnumber'd Supremes, and that one does not
countervail another any more than one eyesight counter-
vails another — and that men can be good or grand only

of the consciousness of their supremacy within them. What do you think is the grandeur of storms and dismemberments, and the deadliest battles and wrecks, and the wildest fury of the elements, and the power of the sea, and the motion of Nature, and the throes of human desires, and dignity and hate and love? It is that something in the soul which says, Rage on, whirl on, I tread master here and everywhere — Master of the spasms of the sky and of the shatter of the sea, Master of nature and passion and death, and of all terror and all pain.

The American bards shall be mark'd for generosity and affection, and for encouraging competitors. They shall be Kosmos, without monopoly or secrecy, glad to pass anything to any one — hungry for equals night and day. They shall not be careful of riches and privilege — they shall be riches and privilege — they shall perceive who the most affluent man is. The most affluent man is he that confronts all the shows he sees by equivalents out of the stronger wealth of himself. The American bard shall delineate no class of persons, nor one or two out of the strata of interests, nor love most nor truth most, nor the soul most, nor the body most — and not be for the Eastern States more than the Western, or the Northern States more than the Southern.

Exact science and its practical movements are no checks on the greatest poet, but always his encouragement and support. The outset and remembrance are there — there the arms that lifted him first, and braced him best — there he returns after all his goings and comings. The sailor and traveler — the anatomist, chemist, astronomer, geologist, phrenologist, spiritualist, mathematician, historian, and lexicographer, are not poets, but they are the lawgivers of poets, and their construction underlies the structure of every perfect poem. No matter what rises or is utter'd, they sent the seed of the conception of it — of them and by them stand the visible proofs of souls. If there shall be love and content between the father and the son, and if the greatness of the son is the exuding of the greatness of the father, there shall be love between the poet and the man of demonstrable science. In the beauty of poems are henceforth the tuft and final applause of science.

Great is the faith of the flush of knowledge, and of the investigation of the depths of qualities and things. Cleaving and circling here swells the soul of the poet, yet is president of itself always. The depths are fathomless, and therefore calm. The innocence and nakedness are resumed — they are neither modest nor immodest. The whole theory of the supernatural, and all that was twined with it or educed out of it, departs as a dream. What has ever happen'd — what happens, and whatever may or shall happen, the vital laws inclose all. They are sufficient for any case and for all cases — none to be hurried or retarded — any special miracle of affairs or persons inadmissible in the vast clear scheme where every motion and every spear of grass, and the frames and spirits of men and women and all that concerns them, are unspeakably perfect miracles, all referring to all, and each distinct and in its place. It is also not consistent with the reality of the soul to admit that there is anything in the known universe more divine than men and women.

Men and women, and the earth and all upon it, are to be taken as they are, and the investigation of their past and present and future shall be unintermitted, and shall be done with perfect candor. Upon this basis philosophy speculates, ever looking towards the poet, ever regarding the eternal tendencies of all toward happiness, never inconsistent with what is clear to the senses and to the soul. For the eternal tendencies of all toward happiness make the only point of sane philosophy. Whatever comprehends less than that — whatever is less than the laws of light and of astronomical motion — or less than the laws that follow the thief, the liar, the glutton and the drunkard, through this life and doubtless afterward — or less than vast stretches of time, or the slow formation of density, or the patient upheaving of strata — is of no account. Whatever would put God in a poem or system of philosophy as contending against some being or influence, is also of no account. Sanity and ensemble characterize the great master — spoilt in one principle, all is spoilt. The great master has nothing to do with miracles. He sees health for himself in being one of the mass — he sees the hiatus in singular eminence. To the perfect shape comes common ground. To be under the general law is great, for that is to correspond with it. The master knows that he is unspeakably great, and that all are unspeakably great — that nothing, for instance, is greater than to conceive children, and bring them up well — that to *be* is just as great as to perceive or tell.

In the make of the great masters the idea of political liberty is indispensable. Liberty takes the adherence of heroes wherever man and woman exist — but never takes any adherence or welcome from the rest more than from poets. They are the voice and exposition of liberty. They out of ages are worthy the grand idea — to them it is confided, and they must sustain it. Nothing has precedence of it, and nothing can warp or degrade it.

As the attributes of the poets of the kosmos concentre in the real body, and in the pleasure of things, they possess the superiority of genuineness over all fiction and romance. As they emit themselves, facts are shower'd over with light — the daylight is lit with more volatile light — the deep between the setting and rising sun goes deeper many fold. Each precise object or condition or combination or process exhibits a beauty — the multiplication table its — old age its — the carpenter's trade its — the grand opera its — the huge-hull'd clean-shap'd New York clipper at sea under steam or full sail gleams with unmatch'd beauty — the American circles and large harmonies of government gleam with theirs — and the commonest definite intentions and actions with theirs. The poets of the kosmos advance through all interpositions and coverings and turmoils and stratagems to first principles. They are of use — they dissolve poverty from its need, and riches from its conceit. You large proprietor, they say, shall not realize or perceive more than any one else. The owner of the library is not he who holds a legal title to it, having bought and paid for it. Any one and every one is owner of the library, (indeed he or she alone is owner,) who can read the same through all the varieties of tongues and subjects and styles, and in whom they enter with ease, and make supple and powerful and rich and large.

These American States, strong and healthy and accomplish'd, shall receive no pleasure from violations of natural models, and must not permit them. In paintings or mouldings or carvings in mineral or wood, or in the illustrations of books or newspapers, or in the patterns of woven stuffs, or anything to beautify rooms or furniture or costumes, or to put upon cornices or monuments, or on the prows or sterns of ships, or to put anywhere before the human eye indoors or out, that which distorts honest shapes, or which creates unearthly beings or places or contingencies, is a nuisance and revolt. Of the human form especially, it is so great it must never be made ridiculous. Of ornaments to a work nothing outre can be allow'd — but those ornaments can be allow'd that conform to the perfect facts of the open air, and that flow out of the nature of the work, and come irrepressibly from it, and are necessary to the completion of the work. Most works are most beautiful without ornament. Exaggerations will be revenged in human physiology. Clean and vigorous children are jetted and conceiv'd only in those communities where the models of natural forms are public every day. Great genius and the people of these States must never be demean'd to romances. As soon as histories are properly told, no more need of romances.

The great poets are to be known by the absence in them of tricks, and by the justification of perfect personal candor. All faults may be forgiven of him who has perfect candor. Henceforth let no man of us lie, for we have seen that openness wins the inner and outer world, and that there is no single exception, and that never since our earth gather'd itself in a mass have deceit or subterfuge or prevarication attracted its smallest particle or the faintest tinge of a shade — and that through the enveloping wealth and rank of a state, or the whole republic of states, a sneak or sly person shall be discover'd and despised — and that the soul has never once been fool'd and never can be fool'd — and thrift without the loving nod of the soul is only a fœtid puff — and there never grew up in any of the continents of the globe, nor upon any planet or satellite, nor in that condition which precedes the birth of babes, nor at any time during the changes of life, nor in any stretch of abeyance or action of vitality, nor in any process of formation or reformation anywhere, a being whose instinct hated the truth.

Extreme caution or prudence, the soundest organic health, large hope and comparison and fondness for women and children, large alimentiveness and destructiveness and causality, with a perfect sense of the oneness of nature, and the propriety of the same spirit applied to human affairs, are called up of the float of the brain of the world to be parts of the greatest poet from his birth out of his mother's womb, and from her birth out of her mother's. Caution seldom goes far enough. It has been thought that the prudent citizen was the citizen who applied himself to solid gains, and did well for himself and for his family, and completed a lawful life without debt or crime. The greatest poet sees and admits these economies as he sees the economies of food and sleep, but has higher notions of prudence than to think he gives much when he gives a few slight attentions at the latch of the gate. The premises of the prudence of life are not the hospitality of it, or the ripeness and harvest of it. Beyond the independence of a little sum laid aside for burial-money, and of a few clap-boards around and shingles overhead on a lot of American soil own'd, and the easy dollars that supply the

year's plain clothing and meals, the melancholy prudence
of the abandonment of such a great being as a man is, to
the toss and pallor of years of money-making, with all their
scorching days and icy nights, and all their stifling deceits
and underhand dodgings, or infinitesimals of parlors, or
shameless stuffing while others starve, and all the loss of the
bloom and odor of the earth, and of the flowers and atmosphere, and of the sea, and of the true taste of the women
and men you pass or have to do with in youth or middle
age, and the issuing sickness and desperate revolt at the
close of a life without elevation or naiveté, (even if you
have achiev'd a secure 10,000 a year, or election to Congress or the Governorship,) and the ghastly chatter of a
death without serenity or majesty, is the great fraud upon
modern civilization and forethought, blotching the surface
and system which civilization undeniably drafts, and moisten-
ing with tears the immense features it spreads and spreads
with such velocity before the reach'd kisses of the soul.

Ever the right explanation remains to be made about
prudence. The prudence of the mere wealth and respecta-
bility of the most esteem'd life appears too faint for the eye
to observe at all, when little and large alike drop quietly
aside at the thought of the prudence suitable for immortality. What is the wisdom that fills the thinness of a
year, or seventy or eighty years — to the wisdom spaced
out by ages, and coming back at a certain time with strong
reinforcements and rich presents, and the clear faces of
wedding-guests as far as you can look, in every direction,
running gaily toward you? Only the soul is of itself — all
else has reference to what ensues. All that a person does
or thinks is of consequence. Nor can the push of charity
or personal force ever be anything else than the profoundest
reason, whether it brings argument to hand or no. No
specification is necessary — to add or subtract or divide
is in vain. Little or big, learn'd or unlearn'd, white or
black, legal or illegal, sick or well, from the first inspiration
down the windpipe to the last expiration out of it, all that

a male or female does that is vigorous and benevolent and clean is so much sure profit to him or her in the unshakable order of the universe, and through the whole scope of it forever. The prudence of the greatest poet answers at last the craving and glut of the soul, puts off nothing, permits no let-up for its own case or any case, has no particular sabbath or judgment day, divides not the living from the dead, or the righteous from the unrighteous, is satisfied with the present, matches every thought or act by its correlative, and knows no possible forgiveness or deputed atonement.

The direct trial of him who would be the greatest poet is to-day. If he does not flood himself with the immediate age as with vast oceanic tides — if he be not himself the age transfigur'd, and if to him is not open'd the eternity which gives similitude to all periods and locations and processes, and animate and inanimate forms, and which is the bond of time, and rises up from its inconceivable vagueness and infiniteness in the swimming shapes of to-day, and is held by the ductile anchors of life, and makes the present spot the passage from what was to what shall be, and commits itself to the representation of this wave of an hour, and this one of the sixty beautiful children of the wave — let him merge in the general run, and wait his development.

Still the final test of poems, or any character or work, remains. The prescient poet projects himself centuries ahead, and judges performer or performance after the changes of time. Does it live through them? Does it still hold on untired? Will the same style, and the direction of genius to similar points, be satisfactory now? Have the marches of tens and hundreds and thousands of years made willing detours to the right hand and the left hand for his sake? Is he beloved long and long after he is buried? Does the young man think often of him? and the young woman think often of him? and do the middle-aged and the old think of him?

A great poem is for ages and ages in common, and for all degrees and complexions, and all departments and sects, and for a woman as much as a man, and a man as much as a woman. A great poem is no finish to a man or woman, but rather a beginning. Has any one fancied he could sit at last under some due authority, and rest satisfied with explanations, and realize, and be content and full? To no such terminus does the greatest poet bring — he brings neither cessation nor shelter'd fatness and ease. The touch of him, like Nature, tells in action. Whom he takes he takes with firm sure grasp into live regions previously unattain'd — thenceforward is no rest — they see the space and ineffable sheen that turn the old spots and lights into dead vacuums. Now there shall be a man cohered out of tumult and chaos — the elder encourages the younger and shows him how — they two shall launch off fearlessly together till the new world fits an orbit for itself, and looks unabash'd on the lesser orbits of the stars, and sweeps through the ceaseless rings, and shall never be quiet again.

There will soon be no more priests. Their work is done. A new order shall arise, and they shall be the priests of man, and every man shall be his own priest. They shall find their inspiration in real objects to-day, symptoms of the past and future. They shall not deign to defend immortality or God, or the perfection of things, or liberty, or the exquisite beauty and reality of the soul. They shall arise in America, and be responded to from the remainder of the earth.

The English language befriends the grand American expression — it is brawny enough, and limber and full enough. On the tough stock of a race who through all change of circumstance was never without the idea of political liberty, which is the animus of all liberty, it has attracted the terms of daintier and gayer and subtler and more elegant tongues. It is the powerful language of resistance — it is the dialect of common sense. It is the speech of the proud and melancholy races, and of all who aspire. It is the chosen tongue to express growth, faith, self-esteem, freedom, justice, equality, friendliness, amplitude, prudence, decision, and courage. It is the medium that shall wellnigh express the inexpressible.

No great literature, nor any like style of behavior or oratory, or social intercourse or household arrangements, or public institutions, or the treatment by bosses of employ'd people, nor executive detail, or detail of the army and navy, nor spirit of legislation or courts, or police or tuition or architecture, or songs or amusements, can long elude the jealous and passionate instinct of American standards. Whether or no the sign appears from the mouths of the people, it throbs a live interrogation in every freeman's and freewoman's heart, after that which passes by, or this built to remain. Is it uniform with my country? Are its disposals without ignominious distinctions? Is it for the ever-growing communes of brothers and lovers, large, well united, proud, beyond the old models, generous beyond all models? Is it something grown fresh out of the fields, or drawn from the sea for use to me to-day here? I know that what answers for me, an American, in Texas, Ohio, Canada, must answer for any individual or nation that serves for a part of my materials. Does this answer? Is it for the nursing of the young of the republic? Does it solve readily with the sweet milk of the nipples of the breasts of the Mother of Many Children.

America prepares with composure and good-will for the visitors that have sent word. It is not intellect that is to be their warrant and welcome. The talented, the artist, the ingenious, the editor, the statesman, the erudite, are not unappreciated — they fall in their place and do their work. The soul of the nation also does its work. It rejects none, it permits all. Only toward the like of itself will it advance half-way. An individual is as superb as a nation when he has the qualities which make a superb nation. The soul of the largest and wealthiest and proudest nation may well go half-way to meet that of its poets.

EDWIN PERCY WHIPPLE

1819 – 1886

THACKERAY

[*Published in " The Christian Examiner," 1864. Reprinted in
" Character and Characteristic Men," 1866. Copyright, 1894, by
Charlotte B. Whipple.*]

THE death of Thackeray has elicited from the press
both of England and the United States a series of
warm testimonials to the genius of the writer and the character of the man. The majority of them bear the marks of
proceeding from personal friends or acquaintances, and the
majority of them resent with special heat the imputation
that the object of their eulogy was, in any respect, a cynic.
A shrewd suspicion arises that such agreement in selecting
the topic of defence indicates an uneasy consciousness of a
similar agreement, in the reading public, as to the justice
of the charge. If this were so, we should think the question was settled against the eulogists. As the inmost individuality of a man of genius inevitably escapes in his writings,
and as the multitude of readers judge of him by the general
impression his works have left on their minds, their intelligent verdict in regard to his real disposition and nature
carries with it more authority than the testimony of his
chance companions. Acres of evidence concerning the
correct life and benevolent feelings of Smollett and Wieland
can blind no discerning eye to the palpable fact that sensu-
ality and misanthropy entered largely into the composition
of the author of " Roderick Random," and that a profound
disbelief in what commonly goes under the name of virtue,
and a delight in toying with voluptuous images, characterized the historian of " Agathon." The world has little to
do with the outward life a man of genius privately leads, in

comparison with the inward life he universally diffuses ; and an author who contrives to impress fair-minded readers that his mind is tainted with cynical views of man and society, can hardly pass as a genial lover of his race on the strength of certificates that he has performed individual acts of kindness and good-will. The question relates to the kind of influence he exercises on those he has never seen or known. What this influence is, in the case of Thackeray, we by no means think is expressed in so blunt and rough a term as " cynical," and those who use it must be aware that it but coarsely conveys the notion they have of the individuality of the writer they seek to characterize. But clear perceptions often exist in persons who lack the power, or shirk the labor, of giving exact definitions ; and among the readers of Thackeray who quietly take in the subtile essence of his personality, there is less disagreement in their impressions than in their statements. To give what seems to us a fair transcript of the general feeling respecting the writer and the man will be the object of the present paper.

And, first, to exclude him at once from the class and company of the great masters of characterization, we must speak of his obvious limitations. He is reported to have said of himself, that he " had no head above his eyes " ; and a man who has no head above his eyes is not an observer after the fashion of Shakespeare, or Cervantes, or Goethe, or Scott, or even of Fielding. The eye observes only what the mind, the heart, and the imagination are gifted to see ; and sight must be reinforced by insight before souls can be discerned as well as manners, ideas as well as objects, realities and relations as well as appearances and accidental connections.

But, without taking an epigram of humorous self-depreciation as the statement of a fact, it is still plain that Thackeray was not a philosopher or a poet, in the sense in which a great novelist or dramatist possesses the qualities of either. He had no conception of causes and principles, no grasp of human nature, as distinguished from the pe-

culiarities of individuals, no perception of the invisible
foundations of visible things, no strictly creative power.
The world drifted before his eyes as his stories drift to
their conclusion; and as to the meaning or purpose or law
of the phenomenon, he neither knew nor sought to know.
This peculiar scepticism, the result not of the exercise,
but the absence, of philosophical thought, is characteristic
of the " Bohemian " view of life; and, among a certain
class, whose ideal of wisdom is not so much to know as to
be "knowing," this ignorant indifference to principles is
one of Thackeray's chief claims to distinction.   His philosophy is the vanity of all things, and the enjoyment of
as many as you can.   His superficiality in this respect is
evident the moment we pass to some dramatist or novelist
who seizes the substance of human nature and human life,
and represents things in their vital relations, instead of in
the mechanical juxtaposition in which they " happen " to
be observed.   Shakespeare's plot, for example, is a combination of events; Thackeray's story, a mere procession of
incidents.   Shakespeare knew woman as well as women,
and created Cleopatra and Cordelia; Thackeray sharply
scrutinized a certain number of women, and fashioned Becky
Sharp and Amelia.   The gulf between the two writers, in
respect to naturalness, to a knowledge of human nature,
and to individual characterizations, is as wide as that which
yawned between Lazarus and Dives.   They never can be
brought into the same class, without a flippant and heed-
less oversight of the distinction between kinds of genius,
and of their different positions in the sliding-scale of minds.
   Connected with this lack of high thought and imagination, is a lack of great passions, and an absence of sympathy
with them in life.   They are outside of Thackeray's world.
When he touches on them, it is with a fleer of incredulity:
he has a suspicion of private theatricals; he is curious to
see the dressing for the part; he keeps a bright lookout to
detect the stage-strut in the hero's stride, and ironically
encores the impassioned declamation.   In nothing does he

better succeed in taking the romance from life, than in this oversight of the reality of great passions in his quick pene- tration through all the masks of their imitators. He is so bent on stripping the king's robes from the limbs of the thief, that he has lost the sense of kingly natures. His world is, to a great extent, a world in which the grand and the noble are "left out in the cold," and the prominence given to the mean and the common. He takes the real heart and vitality out of mankind, calls what remains by the name of human nature, and adopts a theory of life which makes all history impossible, — except the "History of Pendennis." An amusing illustration of this defect is ob- servable in one of his "Roundabout Papers," written during the Confederate Rebellion. He had travelled all over the United States with the sharpest eye that any tourist ever brought with him across the Atlantic ; but he saw nothing of the essential character of the people, and he could not for the life of him imagine, after his return, why we went to war. While North and South were engaged in their fierce death-grapple, he had no perception of the ideas at stake, or the passions in operation. He took a kindly view of both parties in the contest. "How hospitable they were, those Southern men ! " They gave him excellent claret in New Orleans. "Find me," he says, "speaking ill of such a country ! " A Southern acquaintance sent him a case of Medoc, just as he was starting for a voyage up the Missis- sippi. "Where are you," he exclaims, "honest friends, who gave me of your kindness and your cheer? May I be considerably boiled, blown up, and snagged, if I speak hard words of you. May claret turn sour ere I do ! " This may be geniality, but it is the geniality of indifference to great things. A nation in its death-throes, — one side passion- ately battling for the most gigantic of shams as well as iniquities, — the land flooded with blood, — and still the good-natured "delineator of human nature" utterly unable to account for the strange phenomena, is only sure that the Southerners cannot be so bad and wrong as they are represented, for did they not give him "that excellent light claret"?

Another defect of Thackeray, and the consequence of those we have mentioned, is the limitation of the range of his observation and the comparative poverty of his materials. Because he confines himself to the delineation of actual life, he is sometimes absurdly considered to include it, when, in fact, he only includes a portion, and that a relatively small portion. A man may have a wide experience of the world without knowing experimentally much of Thackeray's world; and those whose knowledge of the world is chiefly confined to what they obtain from the novelists of manners and society, soon learn that Thackeray's predecessors and Thackeray's contemporaries contain much which Thackeray overlooks. He is only one of a large number of observers, each with a special aptitude for some particular province of actual life, each repairing certain deficiencies of the others, and all combined falling short of the immense variety of the facts. In his own domain he is a master, but his mastery comes from his keen and original perception of what has been frequently observed before, rather than from his discovery of a new field of observation. After generalizing the knowledge of life and the types of character we have obtained through his writings, we find they are not so much additions to our knowledge as verifications and revivals of it. The form rather than the substance is what is new, and the superficiality of thought underlying the whole representation is often painfully evident. The maxims which may be deduced from the incidents and characters would make but an imperfect manual of practical wisdom.

We now come, by the method of exclusion, to the positive qualities of Thackeray, and to the direction and scope of his powers. Gifted originally with a joyous temperament, a vigorous understanding, a keen sensibility, and a decided, though somewhat indolent self-reliance, he appears, before he came before the world as a writer, to have seen through most of the ordinary forms of human pretension, and to have had a considerable experience of human rascality. He lost a fortune in the process of learning the various vanities, follies, and artifices he afterwards exposed, and thus may be considered to have fairly earned the right to be their satirist. A man who has been deceived by a hypocrite or cheated by a rogue describes hypocrites and rogues from a sharper insight, and with a keener scorn, than a man who knows them only from the observation of their victims. Truisms brighten into truths, and hearsays into certainties, under the touch of such an artist. As a man's powers are determined in their direction by his materials, — as what he has seen, known, and assimilated becomes a part of his intellect and individuality, — Thackeray obeyed the mere instinct of his genius in becoming the delineator of manners and the satirist of shams. The artificial — sometimes as complicated with the natural, sometimes as entirely overlaying it, sometimes as almost extinguishing it — was the field where his powers could obtain their appropriate exercise. They had indeed grown into powers by the nutriment derived from it, and took to their game as the duck takes to the water. From the worst consequences of this perilous mental direction he was saved by his tenderness of heart, and his love and appreciation of simple, unpretending moral excellence. He never hardened into misanthropy or soured into cynicism. Much of his representation of life is necessarily ungenial, for it is the representation of the selfish, the dissolute, the hard-hearted, and the worthless. Those who accuse him of cynicism for the manner in which he depicted these must expect a toleration after the fashion of the Regent Duke of Orleans, "who thought," says Macaulay, "that he and his fellow-creatures were Yahoos," but then he thought "the Yahoo was a very agreeable sort of animal." Thackeray's standard of human nature was not high, and his peculiar talent lay in delineating specimens of it lower than his own standard, but the wholesome impulses of his heart taught him when to use the lash and the scourge. The general impression his individuality leaves on the mind is not that of a cynic, but of a sceptic. He takes the world as he finds it; usually treats of it in a tone of good-natured banter; is pleased when he can praise, and often grieved when he is compelled to censure; touches lightly, but surely, on follies, and only kindles into wrath at obdurate selfishness or malignity; hardly thinks the world can be bettered; and dismisses it as something whose ultimate purpose it is impossible to explain. He records that portion which passes under his own microscopic vision, and leaves to others the task of reconciling the facts with accredited theories.

In his earliest works the satirist is predominant over the humorist. He adopted the almost universal policy of Englishmen who wish to attract public attention, — the policy of assault. Mr. Bull can only be roused into the admission of a writer's ability by feeling the smart of his whip on his hide. Sydney Smith, Macaulay, Carlyle, Kingsley, Ruskin, Thackeray, having something to say to him, began with shrieking out that he was a fool and a rogue; and, thus gaining his ear, proceeded to state their reasons for so injurious an opinion, with a plentiful mixture all the time of opprobrious epithets to prevent a relapse into insensibility. This system naturally tends to make authors exaggerate things out of their relations in order to give immediate effect to their special view, and the habit of indiscriminate assault frequently survives the necessity for its exercise. Thackeray appears at first to have considered that his business was to find fault; to carry into literature the functions of the detective police; to pry into the haunts, and arrest the persons, of scoundrels who evaded the ordinary operations of the law. The most fashionable clubs and drawing-rooms were invaded, to catch scamps whom a common policeman would have sought in low alleys and hells. The successful exposer found a saturnine enjoyment in the confusion and scandal which his ingenuity and pertinacity wrought among "respectable" people, and his taste for the sport was naturally increased by its indulgence, and his success in its prosecution. He contracted a morbid liking for tainted character, and his sharp glance and fine scent were exercised to discover the taint in characters generally sound and healthy. The latent weaknesses, foibles, follies, vices, of the intelligent and good became the objects of his search, somewhat to the exclusion of their nobler and predominant qualities, and the result was, in many instances, wofully partial estimates and exhibitions of men and women. The truth was truth only from the satirist's point of view.

But all these earlier works — " The Yellowplush Correspondence," " The Confessions of Fitz-Boodle," " The Luck of Barry Lyndon," " Men's Wives," " The Book of Snobs," not to mention others — have the one merit of being readable, — a merit which Thackeray never lost. The fascination they exert is in spite of the commonness of their materials. The charm comes from the writer, and his mode of treatment. The wit and the humor, so " bittersweet "; the fine fancy and delicate observation; the eye for ludicrous situations; the richness, raciness, and occasional wildness of the comic vein; the subtilty of the unexpected strokes of pathos; the perfect obedience of the style to the mind it expresses; and the continual presence of the writer himself, making himself the companion of the reader, — gossiping, hinting, sneering, laughing, crying, as the narrative proceeds, — combine to produce an effect which nobody, to say the least, ever found dull. The grace, flexibility, and easy elegance of the style are especially notable. It is utterly without pretension, and partakes of the absolute sincerity of the writer; it is talk in print, seemingly as simple as the most familiar private chat, yet as delicate in its felicities as the most elaborate composition.

In " Vanity Fair," the first novel which gave the author wide celebrity, we have all the qualities we have noticed cast into the frame of a story, — a story which has a more connected interest and a more elastic movement than its successors, though we cannot think that it equals some of them in general power of thought, observation, and characterization. The moral, if moral it have, is that the Amelias of the world, with all their simplicity and ignorance, will, in the long run, succeed better than the Becky Sharps, with all their evil knowledge and selfish acuteness. Amelia is evidently as much the favorite of the author's heart as Becky is of his brain, and he has expended nearly as much skill in the delineation of the one as of the other. The public, however, was prepared for the first, but the second took it by surprise. It was the most original female character of its kind that had appeared in contemporary fiction, and the raciness and never-faltering courage with which the character was developed, through all the phases of her career, seemed an insult to the sex. "Cynic!" cried the ladies. The truth, in this case, was the cause of offence. The Sharps wisely held their tongues, and left the denial of the possibility of such a woman to those who had happily never made her acquaintance. Thackeray had evidently seen her, and seen also the Marquis of Steyne. The latter represents a class of titled reprobates in England and on the Continent, whom other novelists have repeatedly attempted to domesticate in the domain of romance, but have failed from ignorance or exaggeration. The peculiarity of the Marquis is that a long life of habitual and various vice has spread a thick scurf over his soul, so that he has lost by degrees all consciousness of the existence of such an organ. Few felons have gone to the gallows or the gibbet with such an oblivion of the immortal part of them as this noble Marquis exhibits in going to his daily dissoluteness and depravity. The character is in some respects a horrible one, but it is probably true. Shakespeare makes Emilia wish that the "pernicious soul" of Iago "may rot half a grain a day"; and it would certainly seem that the soul may, by a course of systematic and cynical depravity, be completely covered up, if it may not be gradually consumed.

"The History of Pendennis" has more variety of character, and more minute analysis of feeling, than "Vanity Fair," but the story drifts and drags. Though Mrs. Pendennis and Laura rank high among Thackeray's good women, his genius is specially seen in Blanche Amory, a most perfect and masterly exhibition of the union of selfishness and malice with sentimentality, resulting, as it seems to us, in a character more wicked and heartless than that of Becky Sharp. Major Pendennis and she carry off the honors of the book, — a book which, with all its wealth of wit, humor, and worldly knowledge, still leaves the saddest impression on the mind of all of Thackeray's works. It is enjoyed while we are engaged in reading its many-peopled pages; the separate scenes and incidents are full of matter; but it wants unity and purpose, and the wide information of the superficies of life it conveys is of the kind which depresses rather than exhilarates. The gloss is altogether taken both from literature and society, and the subtle scepticism of the author's view of life is destructive of those illusions which are beneficent, as well as of those delusions which are mischievous. There are certain habits, prejudices, opinions, and preconceptions, which, though they cannot stand the test of relentless criticism, are still bound up with virtues, and are at some periods of life the conditions both of action and good action. They should be unlearned by experience, if unlearned at all. To begin life with a theoretical disbelief in them, is to anticipate experience at the cost often of destroying ambition and weakening will. Thackeray in this novel gives a great deal of that sort of information which is not practically so good as the ignorance of enthusiasm and the error of faith. We assent as we read, and congratulate ourselves on being so much more knowing than our neighbors; but at the end we find that, while our eyes have been opened, the very sources of volition have been touched with paralysis.

"The History of Henry Esmond" is an attempt to look at the age of Queen Anne through the eyes of a contemporary, and to record the result of the inspection in the style of the period. It is, on the whole, successful. The diction of the book is exquisite; pleasant glimpses are given of the memorable men of the era, — literary, political, and military, and the languid pace with which the story rambles to its conclusion provokes just that tranquil interest with which Esmond himself recalls in memory the incidents of his career. Both persons and scenes have the visionary grace and remoteness which objects take when seen through the thin and shining mist of imaginative recollection. Beatrix Esmond, the heroine, is another of Thackeray's studies in perverted feminine character, and is worthy of the delineator of Becky and Blanche. The picture of the old age of this pernicious beauty, given in " The Virginians," is equally skilful and true. The defect in the plot of " Henry Esmond " is obvious to every reader. Lady Castlewood, whom the author intends to represent as the ideal of a noble woman, loves the lover of her daughter, and is swayed by passions and placed in situations degrading to womanhood; while Esmond himself, put forward as a high-toned gentleman and chivalrous man of honor, is so demoralized by his passion for a jilt, that he enters into a conspiracy to overturn the government, and involve England in civil war, simply to please her, and with a profound disbelief in the cause for which he is to draw his sword. The atrocious villany of such conduct, from which a Marquis of Steyne would have recoiled, appears to Thackeray simply the weakness of a noble nature.

"The Newcomes " is perhaps the most genial of the author's works, and the one which best exhibits the maturity and the range of his powers. It seems written with a pen diamond-pointed, so glittering and incisive is its slightest touch. The leading idea is the necessary unhappiness of marriage without mutual love, no matter what other motive, selfish or generous, may prompt it; and the worldly view of the matter, as contrasted with the romantic, has never been combated with more unanswerable force than by this realist and man of the world. The practical argument loses none of its power by being given in instances, instead of declamations or syllogisms. The sincerity and conscientiousness of Thackeray's mind, and the absence in him of any pretension to emotions he does not feel and ideas he does not believe, are very marked in this book. He has the honesty of a clear-sighted and clear-headed witness on the stand, stating facts as they appear to him, and on the watch to escape being perjured by yielding to the impulses either of amiability or malice. In the versatile characterization of the work, two inimitable personages stand out as the best expression of Thackeray's heart, — Colonel Newcome and Madame de Florac. Ethel Newcome seems to us, on the whole, an ambitious failure, lacking the usual vitality of the author's feminine characters, and wrought out with set purpose against his grain to show that he could conceive and delineate "a young lady." It is hard for the reader to share Clive's passion for her, for she never arrives in the book to substantial personality. She brings to mind Adam, in the German play, who is represented as passing across the stage, "going to be created." Rosey Mackenzie has infinitely more life. Lady Kew is a good female counterpart of the Marquis of Steyne ; Madame d'Ivry is Blanche Amory grown up ; Mrs. Mackenzie is petty malice and selfishness personified ; and all three are masterpieces in their several kinds. Indeed, the ingenious contrivances of human beings to torment each other were never better set forth than in these "Memoirs of a Respectable Family."

We have no space to do even partial justice to "The Virginians," "Lovel the Widower," and "The Adventures of Philip." Attractive as these are, they furnish no specially novel illustrations of Thackeray's powers, and exhibit no change in the point of view from which he surveyed life. Perhaps as he grew older there was a more obvious desire on his part to appear amiable. He celebrates the kindly virtues. He protests against being called a cynic ; condescends to interrupt the course of his story to answer petulant criticism petulantly ; and relaxes somewhat from his manly and resolute tone. The struggle between his feelings and his obstinate intellectual habit of minutely inspecting defects is obvious on his page. He likes good people, yet cannot help indulging in a sly, mischievous cut at their faults, and then seems vexed that he yields to the temptation. His humility is often that of a person who tells his neighbor that he is a fool and then adds, " but so are we all, more or less "; the particular fool pointed out having a dim intuition that the rapid generalization at the end is intended rather to indicate the wisdom of the generalizer than his participation in the universal folly. A covert insult thus lurks under his ostentatious display of charity. And then in his jets of geniality there is something suspicious. He condescends; he slaps on the back; he patronizes in praising; he is benevolent from pity; and, with a light fleer or vanishing touch of sarcasm, he hints that it is a superior intelligence that is thus disporting in the levities of good-fellowship.

One thing remains to be said regarding the collective impression left on the mind by Thackeray's works. That impression, sharply scrutinized, we will venture to say is this, that life as he represents it is life not worth the living. It is doubtless very entertaining to read about, and it is not without instruction; but who would wish to go through the labor and vexation of leading it? Who would desire to be any one of the characters, good or bad, depicted in it? Who would consider its pleasures and rewards as any compensation for its struggles, disappointments, and disillusions? Who, if called upon to accept existence under its conditions, would not, on the whole, consider existence a bore or a burden, rather than a blessing? This can, we think, be said of no other delineator of human life and human character of equal eminence; and it points to that pervading scepticism, in Thackeray's mind, which is felt to be infused into the inmost substance of his works. Deficient in those qualities and beliefs which convey inspiration as well as information, which impart heat to the will as well as light to the intellect, — lacking the insight of principles and the experience of great passions and uplifting sentiments, — his representation even of the actual world excludes the grand forces which really animate and move it, and thus ignores those deeper elements which give to life earnestness, purpose, and glow.

EDMUND CLARENCE STEDMAN

1833 –

THE FACULTY DIVINE

[*From " The Nature and Elements of Poetry," 1892.   Copyright,
1892, by Edmund Clarence Stedman.*]

POETIC expression is that of light from a star, our
straightest message from the inaccessible human soul.
Critics may apply their spectral analysis to   Unde aether
the beam, but without such a process our sym-   sidera pascit ?
pathetic instinct tells us how fine, how rude,   *— Lucr.*
how rare or common, are the primal constituents from
which its vibrations are derived.   The heat-rays, the light,
the actinic, — these may be combined in ever various proportions, but to make a vivid expression they must in some
proportion come together.   Behind the action at their
starting-place glows and pulsates a spirit of mysterious and
immortal force, the " vital spark," to comprehend which
were to lay hold upon divinity itself.   As to the poet's
share of this, Wordsworth, that inspired schoolmaster with
the gift to create a soul under the ribs of pedantry, con-
ceived his impressive title, — " the faculty divine."   Before
approaching more closely to this radiant source, we have to
touch upon one remaining element which seems most of all
to excite its activity, and to which, in truth, a whole discourse might be devoted as equitably as to truth, or beauty,
or imagination.

I have laid stress, heretofore, upon the passion which so
vivifies all true poetry that certain thinkers believe the art
has no other office than to give emotion vent.
And I have just said that, while poetry which is   **Passion.**
not imaginative cannot be great, the utterance which lacks
passion is seldom imaginative.   It may tranquillize, but it

seldom exalts and thrills. Therefore, what is this quality which we recognize as passion in imaginative literature? What does Milton signify, in his masterly tractate on education, by the element of poetry which, as we have seen, he mentions last, as if to emphasize it? Poetry, he says, is simple, — and so is all art at its best; it is sensuous, — and thus related to our mortal perceptions; lastly, it is passionate, — and this, I think, it must be to be genuine.

In popular usage the word "passion" is almost a synonym for love, and we hear of "poets of passion," votaries **Not an** of Eros or Anteros, as the case may be. Love **epithet of** has a fair claim to its title of the master pas- **love alone.** sion, despite the arguments made in behalf of friendship and ambition respectively, and whether supremacy over human conduct, or its service to the artistic imagination, be the less. Almost every narrative-poem, novel, or drama, whatsoever other threads its coil may carry, seems to have love for a central strand. Love has the heart of youth in it,

> " — and the heart
> Giveth grace unto every art."

Love, we know, has brought about historic wars and treaties, has founded dynasties, made and unmade chiefs and cabinets, inspired men to great deeds or lured them to evil: in our own day has led more than one of its subjects to imperil the liberty of a nation, if not to deem, with Dryden's royal pair, "the world well lost." A strenuous passion indeed, and one the force of which pervades imaginative literature.

But if Milton had used the word "impassioned," his meaning would be plainer to the vulgar apprehension. **Passion and** Poetic passion is intensity of emotion. Abso- **Imagination.** lute sincerity banishes artifice, ensures earnest and natural expression; then beauty comes without effort, and the imaginative note is heard. We have the increased

stress of breath, the tone, and volume, that sway the listener.   You cannot fire his imagination, you cannot rouse
your own, in quite cold blood.   Profound emotion seems,
also, to find the aptest word, the strongest utterance, — not
the most voluble or spasmodic, — and to be content with
it.   Wordsworth speaks of "thoughts that do often lie too
deep for tears," while Mill says that "the poetry of a poet
is Feeling itself, using thought only as a means of expression."   The truth is that passion uses the imagination to
supply conceptions for its language.   On the other hand,
the poet, imagining situations and experiences, becomes
excited through dwelling on them.   But whether passion or
imagination be first aroused, they speed together like the
wind-sired horses of Achilles.

The mere artisan in verse, however adroit, will do well
to keep within his liberties.   Sometimes you find one affec-
ing the impassioned tone.   It is a dangerous
test.   His wings usually melt in the heat of the
flame he would approach.   Passion has a finer
art than that of the æsthete with whom beauty
is the sole end.   Sappho illustrated this, even among the
Greeks, with whom art and passion were one.   Keats felt
that "the excellence of every art is its intensity, capable
of making all disagreeables evaporate, from their being in
close relations with beauty and truth."   Passion rises above
the sensuous, certainly above the merely sensual, or it has
no staying power.   I heard a wit say of a certain painting
that it was "repulsive equally to the artist, the moralist,
and the voluptuary."   Even in love there must be something ideal, or it is soon outlawed of art.   A few of Swinburne's early lyrics, usually classed as erotic, with all their
rhythmic beauty, are not impassioned.   His true genius,
his sacred rage, break forth in measures burning with devotion to art, to knowledge, or to liberty.   There is more
real passion in one of the resonant "Songs before Sunrise"
than in all the studiously erotic verse of the period, his own
included.

Emotion must be unaffected and ideal.

The idea that poetry is uttered emotion, though now somewhat in abeyance, is on the whole modern. It was **Recognition of this force in art.** distinctive with the romantic school, until the successors of Scott and Byron allied a new and refined tenderness to beauty. The first rush had been that of splendid barbarians. It is so true that strong natures recognize the force of passion, that even Wordsworth, conscious of great moods, was led to confess that "poetry is the spontaneous outflow of powerful feelings," and saved himself by adding that it takes "its origin from emotion recollected in tranquillity." Poets do retain the impressions of rare moments, and express them at their own time. But "the passion of Wordsworth," **Wordsworth's emotional limits.** under which title I have read an ingenious plea for it by Dr. Coan, was at its best very serene, and not of a kind to hasten dangerously his heart-beats. Like Goethe, he regarded human nature from without; furthermore, he studied by choice a single class of people, whose sensibilities were not so acute, say what you will, as those of persons wonted to varied and dramatic experiences. The highest passion of his song was inspired by inanimate nature; it was a tide of exaltation and worship, the yearning of a strong spirit to be at one with the elements. Add to this his occasional notes of feeling: the pathos of love in his thought of Lucy: —

> "But she is in her grave, and, oh,
> The difference to me!"

the pathos of broken comradeship in the quatrain: —

> "Like clouds that rake the mountain-summits,
> Or waves that own no curbing hand,
> How fast has brother followed brother
> From sunshine to the sunless land!"

include also his elevated religious and patriotic moods, and we have Wordsworth's none too frequent episodes of intense expression.

All passion obtains relief by rhythmic utterance in music or speech; it is soothed like Saul in his frenzy by the minstrel harp of David. But the emotion which The quality of Feeling. most usually gives life to poetry is not that of fits of passion, but, as in the verses just quoted, of the universal moods embraced in the word "feeling." Out of natural feeling, one touch of which "makes the whole world kin," come the lyrics and popular verse of all nations; it is the fountain of spontaneous song. Take the poetry of this class from Southern literatures, such as the Italian and Spanish, and you leave only their masterpieces. At first thought, it seems more passionate than our own, and certainly it is more sonorous. But Anglo-Saxon words are deep and strong, although there is a good deal of insularity in the song from "The Princess" : —

> "O tell her, Swallow, thou that knowest each,
> That bright and fierce and fickle is the South,
> And dark and true and tender is the North."

If this be so, they should wed indissolubly, for each must be the other's complement. Scottish verse is full of sentiment, often with the added force of pathos. Voices of the heart. For pure feeling we all carry in our hearts "Auld Lang Syne," "The Land o' the Leal," Motherwell's "Jeanie Morrison," and "My heid is like to rend, Willie." Robert Burns is first and always the poet of natural emotion, and his fame is a steadfast lesson to minstrels that if they wish their fellow-men to feel for and with them, they must themselves have feeling. Only from the depths of a great soul could come the stanzas of "Highland Mary" and "To Mary in Heaven." He touches chords for high and low alike in the unsurpassable "Farewell" : —

> "Had we never loved sae kindly,
> Had we never loved sae blindly,
> Never met or never parted,
> We had ne'er been broken-hearted!"

His lyrics of joy, ambition, patriotism, are all virile with the feeling of a brave and strong nature.

English emotional verse is more self-conscious, and often flooded with sentimentalism. Yet Byron's fame rests upon his intensity, whether that of magnificent apostrophes, or of his personal poems, among which none is more genuine than his last lyric, written upon completing his thirty-sixth year. In the Victorian period the regard for art has covered sentiment with an aristocratic reserve, but Hood was a poet of emotion in his beautiful songs and ballads no less than in " The Bridge of Sighs."

English sentiment.

From the middle register of emotion, poetry rises to the supreme, such as that of Shelley's " Lines to an Indian Air," or the more spiritual ecstasy of his invocation to the West Wind :

The ecstasy of song.

> " Make me thy lyre, even as the forest is :
> What if my leaves are falling like its own !
> The tumult of its mighty harmonies
> Will take from both a deep autumnal tone,
> Sweet though in sadness. Be thou, spirit fierce,
> My spirit ! Be thou me, impetuous one ! "

Of recent English lyrical poets Mrs. Browning is one of the most impassioned. Her lips were touched with fire ; her songs were magnetic with sympathy, ardor, consecration. But our women poets of the century usually have written from the heart ; none more so than Emma Lazarus, whose early verse had been that of an art-pupil, and who died young, — but not before she seized the harp of Judah and made it give out strains that all too briefly renewed the ancient fervor and inspiration.

" Das Ewig-weibliche."

Every note of emotion has its varying organ-stops : religious feeling, for instance, whether perfectly allied with music in cloistral hymns, or expressed objectively in studies like Tennyson's "St. Agnes" and "Sir Galahad," and Elizabeth Lloyd's "Milton in his Blindness," or rising to the eloquent height of Coleridge's Chamouni Hymn. So it is with martial songs and national hymns, from Motherwell's "Cavalier's Song," and Campbell's " Ye Mariners of Eng-

" Fill all the stops of Life with tuneful breath."

land," to the Marseillaise hymn, to " My Maryland " and the " Battle Hymn of the Republic." It is the passion of Lowell's " Memorial Odes " that so lifts their rhythm and argument. With Poe, beauty was a passion, but always hovering with strange light above some haunted tomb. Emerson exhibits the intensity of joy as he listens to nature's "perfect rune." On the one side we have Poe avowing that the " tone " of the highest manifestations of beauty is one of sadness. "Beauty of whatever kind," he said, "in its supreme development, invariably excites the sensitive soul to tears." This is the key-note of our romanticism, of which there has been no more sensitive exemplar than Poe, — Grecian as he was at times in his sense of form. But far more Grecian, in temper and philosophy, was Emerson, who found the poet's royal trait to be his cheerfulness, without which "no man can be a poet, for beauty is his aim. . . . Beauty, the spirit of joy and hilarity, he sheds upon the universe." What diverse interpretations, each a lesson to those who would limit the uncharted range of feeling and art! Yet it is easy to comprehend what Poe meant, and to confess that mortal joy is less intense of expression than mortal grief. And it was Emerson himself who, in his one outburst of sorrow, gave us the most impassioned of American lyrics, the "Threnody" for his lost child, — his "hyacinthine boy." " Threnody." This free and noble poem — even for its structural beauty, so uncommon in Emerson's work — must rank with memorable odes. But the poet's faith, thought, imagination, are all quickened by his sorrow, so that the "Threnody" is one of the most consolatory as well as melodiously ideal elegies in the language.

Taken for all in all, Whittier, "our bard and prophet best-beloved," that purely American minstrel, so virginal and so impassioned, at once the man of peace and the poet militant, is the Sir Galahad of American song. He has read the hearts of

Exquisite sadness and enraptured joy.

Emerson's " Threnody."

Whittier's impulsive glow.

his own people, and chanted their emotions, and powerfully affected their convictions. His lyrics of freedom and
reform, in his own justified language, were " words wrung
from the nation's heart, forged at white heat." Longfellow's national poems, with all their finish, cannot rival
the natural art of Whittier's; they lack the glow, the
earnestness, the intense characterization, of such pieces
as " Randolph of Roanoke," " Ichabod," and " The Lost
Occasion." The Quaker bard, besides, no less than Longfellow, is a poet of sympathy. Human feeling, derived
from real life and environment, is the charm of " Snow-
Bound," even more than its absolute transcript of nature.
Years enough have passed since it was written for us to
see that, within its range, it is not inferior to " The
Deserted Village," " The Cotter's Saturday Night," and
" Tam O'Shanter."

Mark Pattison justly declared that " poets of the first
order " always have felt that " human action or passion " is
Art's highest the highest theme. These are the topics of
theme. Homer, Dante, Milton, Goethe, Hugo. Dante,
while perceiving by the smiling of the stars, and by the increasing beauty and divineness of Beatrice, that she is
translating him to the highest spheres, still clings to his
love for the woman. Its blood-red strand connects his
Paradise with earth. The Faust-Margaret legend is human
The human to the radiant end. Rossetti's " The Blessed
element. Damozel " idealizes the naïve materialism of
the cathedral ages. The motive of that prismatic ballad is
the deathless human passion of the sainted maiden. Her
arms make warm the bar of Heaven on which she leans,
still mortal in her immortality, waiting for the soul of her
lover. Such is the poetic instinct that no creature can be
finer in quality, however advanced in power, than man
himself; that the emotions of his soul are of the uttermost
account. Rossetti was ever an impassioned poet, in whom
were blended Northern and Italian types. His series of
sonnets, " The House of Life," quivers with feeling. Chris-

tina Rossetti, his sister, holds her eminence not by the variety and extent of her verse, but for its emotion deed inwrought.   Tennyson's career indicates that From youth the line of advance for a poet is that of greater to age. intensity ; nevertheless, he has furnished a typical example of the national repugnance to throwing wide the gates of that deep-set but rugged castle, an English heart. His sense of beauty and art at first was all in all, although such poems as " Locksley Hall " and " The Sisters " — such a line as that from the former, —

"And our spirits rushed together at the touching of the lips," —

showed him capable of taking up the " Harp of Life." Throughout his long idyllic reign, he grew upon the whole more impassioned in thought and dramatic conception, — yet the proof of this is not found in his dramas, but in portions of " In Memoriam," in powerful studies like " Lucretius " and " Rizpah," and in the second part of " Locksley Hall."   Great poets confront essentials as they approach their earthly resolution.

Thus far I have referred only to the emotion of the poet's own soul, often the more intense and specific from its limits of range.   The creative masters give us all the hues of life's " dome of many-colored The objective creation of glass," as caught from their interior points of impassioned view.   What is life but the speech and action types. of us all, under stress of countless motives and always of that blind emotion which Schopenhauer termed the World-Will?   It is at the beck of the strong invoker that these modes of feeling come arrayed for action, and not in single spies, but far more various than the passions which Collins's Muse drew around her cell.   Such are the throes of Homer's personages within and without the walls of Troy. The intense and natural emotion of Priam and Achilles, of Hector and Andromache and Helen, has made them imperishable.   The heroic epics have gone with their ages, and for every romantic and narrative poem we have a hundred novels; but the drama remains, with its range for the display of passion's extreme types. The keen satisfaction we take in an exhibition, not of the joy and triumph alone, but of the tragedy, the crime, the failure of lives that ape our own, is not morbid, but elevating. We know by instinct that they are right who declare all passion good *per se;* we feel that it is a good servant if a bad master, and bad only when it goes awry, and that the exhibition of its force both enhances and instructs the force

Exaltation. within each soul of us. Again, the poet who broods on human passion and its consequent action attains his highest creative power: he rises, as we say, at each outbreak and crisis, and the actor impersonating his conception must rise accordingly, or disappoint the audience which knows that such culminations are his opportunities, above the realistic level of a well-conceived play. More than all, and as I have suggested in a former lecture, the

Intense sensations enhance the worth of life. soul looks tranquilly on, knowing that it, no more than its prototypes, can be harmed by any mischance. "Agonies" are merely "its changes of garments." They are forms of *experience*. The soul desires *all* experiences; to touch this planetary life at all points, to drink not of triumph and delight alone; it needs must drain its portion of anguish, failure, wrong. It would set, like the nightingale, its breast against the thorn. Its greatest victory is when it is most agonized. When all is lost, when the dark tower is reached, then Childe Roland dauntless winds his blast upon the slug-horn. Its arms scattered, its armor torn away, the soul, "the victor-victim," slips from mortal encumbrance and soars freer than ever. *Victor atque victima, atque ideo victor quia victima.* This is the constant lesson of the lyrics and plays and studies of Browning, the most red-blooded and impassioned of modern dramatic poets; a wise and great master, whose imagination, if it be less strenuous than his insight and feeling, was yet sufficient to derive from history and experience more types of human passion than have been marshalled by any compeer. I have been struck by a critic's quotation of a passage from Beyle (written in 1817) which says that, after centuries of artificiality, it must be the office of the coming artist to express "states of soul," — that that is what a Michelangelo would do with modern sculpture. In truth the potent artist, the great poet, is he who makes us realize the emotions of those who experience august extremes of fortune. For what can be of more value than intense and memorable sensations? What else make up that history which alone is worth the name of life?

The most dramatic effects are often those which indicate suppressed passion — that the hounds are ready to slip the leash. These are constantly utilized _{Reserved power.} by Browning; they characterize the Puritan repression in Hawthorne's romances and Mrs. Stoddard's novels, and the weird power of Emily Brontë's "Wuthering Heights." In the drama, above all, none but a robustious periwig-pated fellow is expected to "tear a passion to tatters." Nor can dramatic heights be of frequent occurrence: they must rise like mountains from a plain to produce their effect, and even then be capped with clouds — must have something left untold. A poem at concert-pitch from first to last is ineffective. See with what relief of commonplace or humor Shakespeare sets off his supreme crises: the banter with Osric before the death of Hamlet; the potter and babble of the peasant who brings the aspic to Cleopatra. In the silent arts, as in nature, the prevailing mood is equable, and must be caught. The picture on your walls that displays nature in her ordinary mien, and not in a vehement and exceptional phase, is the one which does not weary you. But poetry, with its time-extension, has the freedom of dramatic contrasts — of _{True naturalism.} tranquillity and passion according to nature's own allotment. With this brave advantage, naturalism is ignoble which restricts itself to the ordinary, and is indeed

grossly untrue to our life, at times so concentrated and
electric.

The ideal of dramatic intensity — that is, of *imagined*
feeling — is reached when the expression is as inevitable as
that of a poet's outburst under stress of per-
Absolute
dramatic sonal emotion. You are conscious, for exam-
passion. ple, that one must endure a loss as irreparable
as that which Cowper bemoaned, before he can realize the
pathos and beauty of the monody " On the Receipt of my
Mother's Picture " : —

> " O that those lips had language ! Life has passed
> With me but roughly since I heard thee last."

But you also feel, and as strongly, that only one who has
been agonized by the final surrender, whether to violence
or death, of an adored child, can fully comprehend that
passionate wail of Constance bereft of Arthur : —

> " Grief fills the room up of my absent child,
> Lies in his bed, walks up and down with me,
> Puts on his pretty looks, repeats his words,
> Remembers me of all his gracious parts,
> Stuffs out his vacant garments with his form ;
> Then have I reason to be fond of grief."

Shakespeare's dramas hold the stage, and if his stronger
characters are not impersonated so frequently as of old,
they are still the chief rôles of great actors, and are supported with a fitness of detail unattained before. The
grand drama, then, is the most efficient form of poetry in
an unideal period to conserve a taste for something imagi-
Modern native and impassioned. But, with a public
equanimity. bred to reserve, our new plays and poems on
the whole avoid extremes of feeling, which, alike in life and
literature, are not " good form." What we do accept is
society drama, chiefly that which turns upon the Parisian
notion of life as it is. But whether the current drama,
poetic or otherwise, reflects life as it is, is a question upon
which I do not enter. I have referred to the lack of pas-

sion in modern poetry. The minor emotions are charmingly, if lightly, expressed. Humor, for instance, is given a play almost Catullian; and that Mirth is a feeling, if not a passion, is the lyrical justification of some of our felicitous modern song. Many of our poets realize that we have rounded a beautiful but too prolonged idyllic period; they amuse themselves with idly touching the strings, while awaiting some new dispensation — the stimulus of a motive, the example of a leader. Emotion cannot be always sustained; there must be intervals of rest. But each generation desires to be moved, to be thrilled; and they are mistaken who conceive the poetic imagination to be out of date and minstrelsy a foible of the past.

As it is, we hear much talk, on the part of those observers whose business it is to record the movement of a single day, about the decline of ideality. Whenever one of the elder luminaries goes out, the cry is *An idle outcry.* raised, Who will there be to take his place? What lights will be left when the constellation of which he was a star shall have vanished? The same cry has gone up from every generation in all eras. Those who utter it are like water-beetles perceiving only the ripples, comprehending little of the great waves of thought and expression, upon which we are borne along. The truth is that, alike in savagery and civilization, there never is a change from stagnation to life, from bondage to freedom, from apathy to feeling and passion, that does not beget its poets. At such a period we have the making of new names in song, as surely as deeds and fame in great wars come to men unknown before. It is true that the greatest compositions, in all the arts, are usually produced at culminating epochs of national development. But the period of that eminent group, the "elder American poets," surely has not been that of our full development. Theirs has been the first inspiring rise of the foot-hills, above which — after a stretch of mesa, or even a slight descent — range upon range are still to rise before we reach that culminating sierra-top whose height none yet can measure. Throughout this mountain-climbing, every time that a glowing and original poet appears, his art will be in vogue again.

Now, is such a poet the child of his period, or does he come as if by warrant and create an environment for himself? From the first it seemed to me a flaw in the armor of Taine, otherwise our most catholic exponent of the principles of art, that he did not allow for the irrepressibleness of genius, for the historic evidence that now and then "God lets loose a man in the world." Such a man, it is true, must be of ingrained power to overcome an adverse situation; his very originality will for a long time, as in the recent cases of Wordsworth and Browning, stand in his way, even if in the end it secures for him a far more exceeding crown of glory. If the situation is ripe for him, then his course is smooth, his work is instantly recognizable. First, then, the poet is needed. He must possess, besides imaginative and emotional endowments, the special gifts which, however cultivable, come only at birth — "the vision and the faculty divine," and a certain strong compulsion to their exercise. But these gifts, under such compulsion, constitute what we mean by the poet's genius.

In our age of distributed culture, it has become a matter of doubt — even among men reared upon the Shorter Catechism — whether there is any predestination and foreordination of the elect in art, literature, or action. Many deem this a superstition which has too long prevailed. That it has impressed mankind everywhere and always is a matter of record. I have much faith in a universal instinct; and I believe that I still have with me the majority even of modern realists, and that the majority is right, in refusing to discredit the gift of high and exceptional qualities to individuals predestined by heredity or otherwise, and I believe that without this gift — traditionally called genius — no poet

When comes the poet.

The Faculty Divine.

Genius: whether it is "the inspired gift of God."

has afforded notable delight and service. I know that men
of genius often waive their claim ; that Buffon said genius
was " but long-continued patience " ; that Carlyle wrote, it
" means transcendent capacity for taking trouble, first of
all " ; that one eminent modern writer, though in a passing
mood, announced : " There is no ' genius ' ; there is only
the mastery which comes to natural aptitude from the hard-
est study of any art or science." But these are the sur-
mises of men whose most original work comes from them
so easily that they do not recognize the value of the gift
that makes it natural. They honestly lay more stress upon
the merit of the hard labor which genius unconsciously
drives them to undertake. I say " drives them," and call
to mind Lowell's acute distinction : " Talent is that which
is in a man's power ; genius is that in whose power a man
is." Carlyle's whole career proves that he simply wished
to recognize the office laid upon genius of taking " infinite
trouble." His prevailing tone is unmistakable : " Genius,"
he says, " is the inspired gift of God."   " It is the clearer
presence of God Most High in a man ; " and again,
" Genius, Poet, do we know what those words mean?   An
inspired Soul once more vouchsafed to us, direct from
Nature's own fire-heat, to see the Truth, and speak it, or
do it." His whole philosophy of sway by divine right is a
genius-worship.   Even Mr. Howells's phrase, " natural aptitude," if raised to the highest power, is a recognition of
something behind mere industry. It is what forces the
hero, the artist, the poet, to be absorbed in a special office,
and decides his choice of it.[1]

---

[1] Nothing of late has seemed apter than a criticism of the
Saturday Review upon certain outgivings of the academicians,
Sir Frederick Leighton and Sir John Millais, quite in the line
of the industrial theory from which the present writer is dissent-
ing. The reviewer, commenting upon these didactic paradoxes,
asserts that all the truth which is in them amounts to just this :
" That the intuitive perceptions and rapidity of combination
which constitute genius, whether in action or speculation, in

The world is equipped with steadfast workers whose natural taste and courageous, strenuous labor do not lift them quite above the mediocre. The difference between these, the serviceable rank and file, and the originative leaders, is one of kind, not of degree. However admirable their skill and service in time become, they do not get far apart from impressions common to us all. We cannot dispense with their army in executive and mechanical fields of action. It is a question whether they are so essential to arts of taste and investigation; to philosophy, painting, music; to the creative arts of the novelist and poet. But with respect to these, it would be most unjust to confound them with the upstarts whose condign suppression is a desirable thing for both the public and themselves, — claimants really possessed of less than ordinary sense. Such is the fool of the family who sets up for a " genius " ; the weakling of the borough, incapable of practical work, or too lazy to follow it, but with a fondness for fine things and a knack of imitating them. Such are the gadflies of every art, pertinaciously forcing themselves upon attention, and lowering their assumed crafts in the esteem of a community.

Talent and executive service.

Pretension.

It is wise to discriminate, also, between genius and natural fineness of taste. The latter, joined with equally natural ambition, has made many a life unhappy that had peculiar opportunities for delight. For surely it is a precious thing to discern and enjoy the beautiful. Taste in art, in selection, in conduct, is the charm that makes for true aristocracy, a

Taste, as distinguished from artistic genius.

scientific discovery or inventive art or imaginative creation, open out so many new problems and ideas as to involve in their adjustment and development the most arduous labor and the most unwearied patience. But without the primal perception the labor will be vanity and the patience akin to despair. Perhaps it is important to keep in mind that labor without the appropriate capacity is even more fruitless than aptitude without industry."

gift unspoiled but rather advanced by gentle breeding, a grace in man, and adorable in woman; it is something to rest content with, the happier inasmuch as you add to the happiness of others. It is the nimbus of many a household, beautifying the speech and bearing of the members, who, if they are wise, realize that their chief compensation is a more tranquil study and possession of the beautiful than the fates allot to those who create it. Hephaistos, the grim, sooty, halt artificer of all things fair, found small comfort even in the possession of Aphrodite, the goddess who inspired him. The secret of happiness, for a refined nature, is a just measure of limitations. Taste is not always original, creative. There are no more pathetic lives than the lives of those who know and love the beautiful, and who surrender its enjoyment in a vain struggle to produce it. Their failures react upon finely sensitive natures, and often end in sadness, even misanthrophy, and disillusionment when the best of life is over.

Men of talent and experience do learn to concentrate their powers on certain occasions, and surprise us with strokes like those of genius. That is where they write "better than they can," as our Autocrat so cleverly has put it. But such efforts are exhausting and briefly sustained. I know it is said that genius also expires when its work is done; but who is to measure its reservoir of force, or to gauge the unseen current which replenishes it?

Fortunate moments.

That there is something which comes without effort, yet impels its possessor to heroic labor, is immemorially verified. It whispered melodies to Mozart almost in his boyhood, made him a composer at five, —at seven the author of an opus, four sonatas for piano and violin; and it so drew him on to victorious industry, that he asserted in after life: "No one has taken such pains with the study of composition as I!" It made the child Clairon, as she refused to learn to sew, cry out under brutal punishment: "Kill me! You had better do so, for

Congenital gift.

if you don't I shall be an actress ! " Dickens declared
that he did not invent his work : " I see it," he said, "and
write it down." [1] Sidney Lanier, in nervous crises, would
seem to hear rich music. It was an inherited gift. Thus
equipped with a rhythmical sense beyond that of other poets,
he turned to poetry as to the supreme art. Now, the finer
and more complex the gift, the longer exercise is needful
for its full mastery. He strove to make poetry do what
painting has done better, and to make it do what only music
hitherto has done. If he could have lived three lives, he
would have adjusted the relations of these arts as far as possible to his own satisfaction. I regard his work, striking
as it is, as merely tentative from his own point of view. It
was as if a discoverer should sail far enough to meet the
floating rock-weed, the strayed birds, the changed skies,
that betoken land ahead ; should even catch a breath of
fragrance wafted from outlying isles, and then find his
bark sinking in the waves before he could have sight of the
promised continent.

In our day, when talent is so highly skilled and industry
so habitual, people detect the genius of a poet or tale-writer
through its originality, perhaps first of all. It
Originality. has a different note, even in the formative and
imitative period, and it soon has a different message, —
perhaps one from a new field. The note is its style ; the
message involves an exhibition of creative power. Genius
does not borrow its main conceptions. As I have said, it

---

[1] Hartmann's scientific definition, which I cited in a former
lecture, — " Genius is the activity and efflux of the intellect
freed from the domination of the conscious Will," — finds its
counterpart in the statement by F. W. H. Myers, concerning the action of the " Subliminal Consciousness." This, Mr.
Myers says, has to do with " the initiation and control of organic processes, which the conscious will cannot reach. . . .
Perhaps we seldom give the name of genius to any piece of
work into which some uprush of subliminal faculty has not
entered." (See the *Journal of the Society for Psychical Research*, February, 1892.)

reveals a more or less populous world of which it is the maker and showman. Here it rises above taste, furnishing new conditions, to the study of which taste may profitably apply itself. It is neither passion nor imagination, but it takes on the one and makes a language of the other. Genius of the universal kind is never greater **Transfiguration.** than in imparting the highest interest to good and ordinary and admirable characters; while a limited faculty can design only vicious or eccentric personages effectively, depending on their dramatic villainy or their grotesqueness for a hold upon our interest. Véron has pointed out this inferiority of Balzac and Dickens to Shakespeare and Molière — and he might have added, to Thackeray also. In another way the genius of many poets is limited,— that of Rossetti, of Poe, for example, — poets of few, though striking, tones and of isolated temperaments. Genius of the more universal type is marked by a sound and healthy judgment. You may dismiss with small **Sanity.** respect the notion of Fairfield, Lombroso, and their like, that genius is the symptom of neurotic disorder — that all who exhibit it are more or less mad. This generalization involves a misconception of the term; they apply it to the abnormal excess, the morbid action, of a special faculty, while true genius consists in the creative gift of one or more faculties at the highest, sustained by the sane coöperation of the possessor's other physical and mental endowments. Again, what we term common sense is the genius of man as a race, the best of sense because the least ratiocinative. Nearly every man has thus a spark of **Wisdom.** genius in the conduct of life. A just balance between instinct, or understanding, and reason, or intellectual method, is true wisdom. It requires years for a man of constructive talent — a writer who forms his plans in advance — for such a man to learn to be flexible, to be obedient **Obedience to** to his sudden intuitions and to modify his de- **the vision.** sign accordingly. You will usually do well to follow a clew that comes to you in the heat of work — in fact, to lay aside for the moment the part which you had designed to complete at once, and to lay hold of the new matter before that escapes you. The old oracle, Follow thy genius, holds

Spontaneity. good in every walk of life. Everything, then, goes to show that genius is that force of the soul which works at its own seemingly capricious will and season, and without conscious effort; that its utterances declare what is learned by spiritual and involuntary discovery : —

> " Vainly, O burning Poets !
> Ye wait for his inspiration,
> Even as kings of old
> Stood by Apollo's gates.
> *Hasten back*, he will say, *hasten back*
> *To your provinces far away !*
> *There, at my own good time,*
> *Will I send my answer to you.*"

Yes, the spontaneity of conception, which alone gives worth to poetry, is a kind of revelation — the imagery of

Revelation through Insight. what genius perceives by Insight. This sense has little to do with reason and induction; it is the inward light of the Quaker, the *a priori* guess of the scientist, the prophetic vision of the poet, the mystic, the seer. If it be direct vision, it should be incontrovertible. In occult tradition the higher angels, types of absolute spirit, were thought to know all things by this pure illumination : —

> " There, on bright hovering wings that tire
> Never, they rest them mute,
> Nor of far journeys have desire,
> Nor of the deathless fruit ;
> For in and through each angel soul
> All waves of life and knowledge roll,
> Even as to nadir streams the fire
> Of their torches resolute."

While this is a bit of Preraphaelite mosaic, it is not too much to say of the essentially poetic soul that at times it becomes, in Henry More's language, —

> " One orb of sense, all eye, all airy ear ; "

that it seems to have bathed, like Ayesha, in central and eternal flame ; or, after some preëxistence, to have undergone the lustration to which, in the sixth Æneid, we find the beclouded spirits subjected : —

> "Donec longa dies, perfecto temporis orbe,
> Concretam exemit labem, purumque relinquit
> Aetherium sensum atque aurai simplicis ignem."[1]

At such times its conclusions are as much more infallible than those worked out by logic as is the off-hand pistol-shot of the expert, whose weapon has become a part of his hand, than the sight taken along the barrel. It makes the leopard's leap, without reflection and without miss. I think it was Leigh Hunt who pointed out that feeling rarely makes the blunders which thought makes. Applied to life, we know that woman's intuition is often wiser than man's wit.

The clearness of the poet's or artist's vision is so much beyond his skill to reproduce it, and so increases with each advance, that he never quite contents himself with his work. Hence the ceaseless unrest and dissatisfaction of the best workman. His ideal is constantly out of reach, — a " lithe, perpetual escape." *The artist's noble discontent.*

From the poet's inadequate attempts at expression countless myths and faulty statements have originated. Still, he keeps in the van of discovery, and has been prophetic in almost every kind of knowledge, — evolution not excepted, — and from time immemorial in affairs that constitute history. This gave rise, from the first, to a belief in the direct inspiration of genius. Insight derives, indeed, the force of inspiration from the sense that a mandate of utterance is laid upon it. To the ancients this seemed the audible command of deity. "The word of the *Inspiration.*

---

[1] " Till Time's great cycle of long years complete
Clears the fixed taint, and leaves the ethereal sense
Pure, a bright flame of unmixed heavenly air."
Cranch's Translation.

Lord came unto me, saying, — "Thus saith the Lord unto me," — "So the spirit lifted me up and took me away, and I went in bitterness, in the heat of my spirit, but the hand of the Lord was strong upon me," — such were the avowals of one of the greatest poets of all time. The vision of Ezekiel and the compulsion to declare it have been the inspiration The prophetic of the prophetic bard, of the impassioned lyric gift. poet, almost to our own day. His time has passed. We cannot have, we do not need, another Ezekiel, another Dante or Milton. Hugo, the last Vates, was the most self-conscious, and his own deity. A vision of the wisdom and beauty of art has inspired much of the superior poetry of recent times. A few prophetic utterances have been heard, evoked in some struggle of humanity, some battle for liberty of belief or nationality or conduct. Yet I doubt not that, whenever a great cause is in progress, — before its culminating triumph, rather than after, — it will have its impassioned and heroic minstrelsy. The occasion will seek out and inspire its poet.

But he must believe in his prophecy, and as something greater than himself, though indomitably believing in him-Indispensa- self as the one appointed to declare it. Re-bility of Faith. flecting upon the lack of originality, of power, of what we may consider tokens of inspiration, in so much of our most beautiful latter-day song, I suspect that it is not due alone to the diversion of effort in many new fields of action and expression, but also to a general doubt of the force and import of this chief art of expression, — even to the modern poet's own distrust in its significance. The higher his gift and training, the more he seems affected by the pleasant cynicism which renders him afraid, above all, of taking himself and his craft "too seriously." This phrase itself is the kind of chaff which he most dreads to incur. Now, I have just spoken of the wisdom of recogniz-ing one's limitations, but if one has proved that he has a rare poetic gift, I think that he scarcely can take it and himself too seriously. The poets of our language and time who have gained the most distinction — such as Tennyson, Browning, Longfellow, Arnold, Emerson — have taken themselves very seriously indeed; have refused to go after strange gods, and have done little but to make poetry or to consider matters demanding the higher exercise of thought and ideality. Doubtless poets are born nowadays as heretofore, though nature out of her " fifty seeds " may elect to bring not even " one to bear." But some who exhibit the most command of their art, and in truth a genuine faculty, are very shy of venturing beyond the grace and humor and tenderness of holiday song.

I think that such a condition might be expected to exist during the unsettled stage of conviction now affecting our purpose and imagination. There is no lack of desire for a motive, but an honest lack of **Cynicism.** motive, — a questioning whether anything is worth while, — a vague envy, perhaps, of the superb optimism of our scientific brethren, to whom the material world is unveiling its splendors as never before, and to whom, as they progress so steadfastly, everything seems worth while.

I remember an impressive lyric, perhaps the finest thing by a certain American writer. Its title, " What is the Use? " was also the burden of his song. He took his own refrain so much to heart that, although he still lives according to its philosophy, there are only a few of us who pay meet honor to him as a poet.

Distinction ever has been achieved through some form of faith, and even the lesser poets have won their respective measures of success, other things being **Faith of some** equal, in proportion to their amount of trust in **kind the stay** certain convictions as to their art, themselves, **of all true art.** and " the use of it all." The serene forms of faith in deity, justice, nationality, religion, human nature, which have characterized men of the highest rank, are familiar to you. Such faiths have been an instinct with sovereign natures, from the Hebraic sense of a sublime Presence to the polemic belief of Bunyan and Milton. Homer cheerfully recognizes the high gods as the inspirers and regulators of all human action. Dante's faith in the ultimate union of perfect beauty and perfect holiness was intense, and his conviction in the doom of the ignoble was so absolute that he felt himself commissioned to pronounce and execute it. Shakespeare made no question of the divinity that doth hedge a king; he believed in institutions, in sovereignty, in the English race. His tranquil acceptance of the existing order of things had no later parallel until the century of Goethe and Emerson and Browning. Byron and Shelley invoked political and religious liberty, and believed in their own crusade against Philistia. Hugo and his band were leaders in a lifelong cause; they carried a banner with "Death to tradition" upon it. The underlying motive of all strenuous and enthusiastic movement, in art or poetry, is faith. Gautier and Musset concerned themselves with beauty and romantic passion; Clough and Arnold, with philosophy and feeling: all were poets and knights-errant according to their respective tempers and nationalities. And so we might go on indefinitely, without invalidating the statement that some kind of faith, with its resulting purpose, has engendered all poetry that is noteworthy for beauty or power. True art, of every class, thrives in an affirmative and motive-breeding atmosphere. It is not the product of cynicism, pessimism, or hopeless doubt. I do not mean "the honest doubt" which Tennyson sets above "half the creeds." The insatiate quest for light is nobler than a satisfied possession of the light we have. The scientific unsettlement of tradition is building up a faith that we are obtaining a new revelation, or, at least, opening our eyes to a continuous one.

But without surmising what stimulants to imaginative expression may be afforded hereafter, let me

A crowning masterpiece of faith.

refer to a single illustration of the creative faith of the poet. For centuries all that was great in the art and poetry of Christendom grew out of that faith.

What seems to me its most poetic, as well as most enduring, written product, is not, as you might suppose, the masterpiece of a single mind, — the " Divina Commedia," for
instance, — but the outcome of centuries, the expression of
many human souls, even of various peoples and races.
Upon its literary and constructive side, I regard the venerable Liturgy of the historic Christian Church   The Church
as one of the few world-poems, the poems uni-   Liturgy.
versal. I care not which of its rituals you follow, the
Oriental, the Alexandrian, the Latin, or the Anglican. The
latter, that of an Episcopal Prayer-Book, is a version familiar to you of what seems to me the most wonderful symphonic idealization of human faith, — certainly the most
inclusive, blending in harmonic succession all the cries
and longings and laudations of the universal human heart
invoking a paternal Creator.

I am not considering here this Liturgy as divine, though
much of it is derived from what multitudes accept for revelation. I have in mind its human quality ; the mystic tide
of human hope, imagination, prayer, sorrows,   Its universal
and passionate expression, upon which it bears   quality.
the worshipper along, and wherewith it has sustained men's
souls with conceptions of deity and immortality, throughout
hundreds, yes, thousands, of undoubting years. The Orient
and Occident have enriched it with their finest and strongest utterances, have worked it over and over, have stricken
from it what was against the consistency of its import and
beauty. It has been a growth, an exhalation,
an apocalyptic cloud arisen " with the prayers   A growth.
of the saints " from climes of the Hebrew, the Greek, the
Roman, the Goth, to spread in time over half the world.
It is the voice of human brotherhood, the   The voice
blended voice of rich and poor, old and young,   of human
the wise and the simple, the statesman and the   brotherhood.
clown ; the brotherhood of an age which, knowing little,
comprehending little, could have no refuge save trust in
the oracles through which a just and merciful Protector, a

pervading Spirit, a living Mediator and Consoler, had been
revealed.   This being its nature, and as the crowning masterpiece of faith, you find that in various and constructive
beauty — as a work of poetic art — it is unparalleled.   It is
Its symphonic lyrical from first to last with perfect and melo-
perfection.   dious forms of human speech.   Its chants and
anthems, its songs of praise and hope and sorrow, have
allied to themselves impressive music from the originative
and immemorial past, and the enthralling strains of its
inheritors.   Its prayers are not only for all sorts and conditions of men, but for every stress of life which mankind
must feel in common — in the household, or isolated, or in
tribal and national effort, and in calamity and repentance
and thanksgiving.   Its wisdom is forever old and perpetually new ; its calendar celebrates all seasons of the rolling
year ; its narrative is of the simplest, the most pathetic,
the most rapturous, and most ennobling life the world has
known.   There is no malefactor so wretched, no just man
so perfect, as not to find his hope, his consolation, his lesson,
in this poem of poems.   I have called it lyrical ; it is dramatic in structure and effect ; it is an epic of the age of
Without a   faith ; but in fact, as a piece of inclusive litera-
parallel.   ture, it has no counterpart, and can have no
successor.   Time and again some organization for worship
and instruction, building its foundations upon reason rather
than on faith, has tried to form some ritual of which it felt
the need.   But such a poem of earth and heaven is not to
be made deliberately.   The sincere agnostic must be content with his not inglorious isolation ; he must barter the
rapture and beauty and hope of such a liturgy for *his* faith
in something different, something compensatory, perchance
a future and still more world-wide brotherhood of men.

Until this new faith, or some fresh interpretation of past
belief, becomes vital in action, becomes more
Tenebræ.   operative, the highest flight of poetry will be
timidly essayed.   The songs of those who are crying, " They

have taken away my Lord, and I know not where they have laid him!" will be little else than tenebræ — cries out of the darkness, impassioned, it may be, but hardly forceful or creative.   I have spoken of Arnold and   Arnold and Clough, the conspicuously honest, noble, intel-   Clough. lectual poets of the transition period.   Just as far as their faith extended, their verse rests firmly in art and beauty, love, and nobility of purpose.   But much of it comes from troubled hearts; its limits are indicated by a spirit of unrest — limits which Arnold was too sure and fine a self-critic not to perceive; so that, after he had reached them, — which was not until he had given us enduring verse, and shown how elevated was his gift, — he ceased to sing, and set himself resolutely to face the causes of his unrest, and to hasten, through his prose investigations, the movement toward some new dawn of knowledge-brightened faith.

A few verses from his "Dover Beach" are in the key of several of his most touching lyrics, — in the varying meas-ure so peculiarly his own, — utterances of a   The troubled feeling which in the end seems to have led him   heart. to forego his career as a poet: "The sea of faith," he plains, —

> "Was once, too, at the full, and round earth's shore
> Lay like the folds of a bright girdle furl'd.
> But now I only hear
> Its melancholy, long, withdrawing roar,
> Retreating, to the breath
> Of the night-wind, down the vast edges drear
> And naked shingles of the world.
>
> "Ah, love, let us be true
> To one another! for the world, which seems
> To lie before us like a land of dreams,
> So various, so beautiful, so new,
> Hath really neither joy, nor love, nor light,
> Nor certitude, nor peace, nor help for pain;
> And we are here as on a darkling plain
> Swept with confused alarms of struggle and flight,
> Where ignorant armies clash by night."

Doubtless Arnold's reserve intensified this sadness. Clough equally felt the perturbed spirit of his time ; but he had a refuge in a bracing zest for life and nature, which so often made the world seem good to him, and not designed for naught.

In time our poets will acquire, with the new learning and the more humane and critical theology, the health and optimism in which a noteworthy art must origi-
The new day.   nate if at all.   As for the new learning —

> " Say, has the iris of the murmuring shell
>   A charm the less because we know full well
>   Sweet Nature's trick ?   Is Music's dying fall
>   Less finely blent with strains antiphonal
>   Because within a harp's quick vibratings
>   We count the tremor of the spirit's wings ?
>   There is a path by Science yet untrod
>   Where with closed eyes we walk to find out God.
>   Still, still, the unattained ideal lures,
>   The spell evades, the splendor yet endures ;
>   False sang the poet, — there is no good in rest,
>   And Truth still leads us to a deeper quest."

For one, I believe that the best age of imaginative production is not past ; that poetry is to retain, as of old, its literary import, and from time to time to prove itself a force in national life ; that the Concord optimist and poet was sane in declaring that " the arts, as we know them, are but initial," that " sooner or later that which is now life shall be poetry, and every fair and manly trait shall add a richer strain to the song."

And now, after all that has been said in our consideration of the nature of poetry, and although this has been
Thoughts in conclusion.   restricted closely to its primal elements, I am sensible of having merely touched upon an inexhaustible theme ; that my comments have been only " words along the way."   Meanwhile the press teems with criticism, our time is alert with debate in countless private and public assemblies respecting almost every verse of all

renowned poets, ancient or contemporary; texts and editions, even if relatively less in number compared with the varied mass of publications, are multiplied as never before, and readers — say what you may — are tenfold as many as in the prime of the elder American minstrels. The study of poetry has stimulated other literary researches. Yet the best thing that I or any one can say to you under these conditions is that a breath of true poetry is worth a breeze of comment; that one must in the end make his own acquaintance with its examples and form his judgment of them. Read the best; not the imitations of imitations. Each of you will find that with which he himself is most in touch, and therewith a motive and a legend — *petere altiora*. The poet's verse is more than all the learned scholia upon it. He makes it by direct warrant; he produces, and we stand by and often too complacently measure his productions. In no wise can I forget that we are regarding even the lowliest poets from our still lower station: we are like earth-dwellers viewing, comparing, mapping out the stars. Whatsoever their shortcomings, their gift is their own; they bring music and delight and inspiration. A singer may fail in this or that, but when he dies the charm of his distinctive voice is gone forever.

WILLIAM DEAN HOWELLS

1837 –

THE ART OF THE NOVELIST

[*From " Criticism and Fiction," 1891. Copyright: Harper &
Brothers*]

I

IN General Grant's confession of novel-reading there is a
sort of inference that he had wasted his time, or else the
guilty conscience of the novelist in me imagines such an
inference.   But however this may be, there is certainly no
question concerning the intention of a correspondent who
once wrote to me after reading some rather bragging claims
I had made for fiction as a mental and moral means.
" I have very grave doubts," he said, " as to the whole list
of magnificent things that you seem to think novels have
done for the race, and can witness in myself many evil
things which they have done for me.   Whatever in my
mental make-up is wild and visionary, whatever is untrue,
whatever is injurious, I can trace to the perusal of some
work of fiction.   Worse than that, they beget such high-
strung and supersensitive ideas of life that plain industry
and plodding perseverance are despised, and matter-of-fact
poverty, or every-day, commonplace distress, meets with
no sympathy, if indeed noticed at all, by one who has wept
over the impossibly accumulated sufferings of some gaudy
hero or heroine."

I am not sure that I had the controversy with this correspondent that he seemed to suppose ; but novels are now
so fully accepted by every one pretending to cultivated taste
— and they really form the whole intellectual life of such
immense numbers of people, without question of their in-

fluence, good or bad, upon the mind — that it is refreshing to have them frankly denounced, and to be invited to revise one's ideas and feelings in regard to them.   A little honesty, or a great deal of honesty, in this quest will do the novel, as we hope yet to have it, and as we have already begun to have it, no harm ; and for my own part I will confess that I believe fiction in the past to have been largely injurious, as I believe the stage play to be still almost wholly injurious, through its falsehood, its folly, its wantonness, and its aimlessness.   It may be safely assumed that most of the novel-reading which people fancy an intellectual pastime is the emptiest dissipation, hardly more related to thought or the wholesome exercise of the mental faculties than opium-eating; in either case the brain is drugged, and left weaker and crazier for the debauch.   If this may be called the negative result of the fiction habit, the positive injury that most novels work is by no means so easily to be measured in the case of young men whose character they help so much to form or deform, and the women of all ages whom they keep so much in ignorance of the world they misrepresent.   Grown men have little harm from them, but in the other cases, which are the vast majority, they hurt because they are not true — not because they are malevolent, but because they are idle lies about human nature and the social fabric, which it behooves us to know and to understand, that we may deal justly with ourselves and with one another.   One need not go so far as our correspondent, and trace to the fiction habit "whatever is wild and visionary, whatever is untrue, whatever is injurious," in one's life ; bad as the fiction habit is it is probably not responsible for the whole sum of evil in its victims, and I believe that if the reader will use care in choosing from this fungus-growth with which the fields of literature teem every day, he may nourish himself as with the true mushroom, at no risk from the poisonous species.

The tests are very plain and simple, and they are perfectly infallible.   If a novel flatters the passions, and exalts them above the principles, it is poisonous; it may not kill, but it will certainly injure; and this test will alone exclude an entire class of fiction, of which eminent examples will occur to all. Then the whole spawn of so-called unmoral romances, which imagine a world where the sins of sense are unvisited by the penalties following, swift or slow, but inexorably sure, in the real world, are deadly poison : these do kill. The novels that merely tickle our prejudices and lull our judgment, or that coddle our sensibilities or pamper our gross appetite for the marvellous are not so fatal, but they are innutritious, and clog the soul with unwholesome vapors of all kinds. No doubt they too help to weaken the moral fibre, and make their readers indifferent to " plodding perseverance and plain industry," and to " matter-of-fact poverty and commonplace distress."

Without taking them too seriously, it still must be owned that the " gaudy hero and heroine" are to blame for a great deal of harm in the world. That heroine long taught by example, if not precept, that Love, or the passion or fancy she mistook for it, was the chief interest of a life, which is really concerned with a great many other things; that it was lasting in the way she knew it; that it was worthy of every sacrifice, and was altogether a finer thing than prudence, obedience, reason; that love alone was glorious and beautiful, and these were mean and ugly in comparison with it. More lately she has begun to idolize and illustrate Duty, and she is hardly less mischievous in this new role, opposing duty, as she did love, to prudence, obedience, and reason. The stock hero, whom, if we met him, we could not fail to see was a most deplorable person, has undoubtedly imposed himself upon the victims of the fiction habit as admirable. With him, too, love was and is the great affair, whether in its old romantic phrase of chivalrous achievement or manifold suffering for love's sake, or its more recent development of the " virile," the bullying, and the brutal, or its still more recent agonies of self-sacrifice, as idle and useless as the moral experiences of the insane asylums. With his vain posturings and his ridiculous splendor he is really a painted barbarian, the prey of his passions and his delusions, full of obsolete ideals, and the motives and ethics of a savage, which the guilty author of his being does his best — or his worst — in spite of his own light and knowledge, to foist upon the reader as something generous and noble. I am not merely bringing this charge against that sort of fiction which is beneath literature and outside of it, " the shoreless lakes of ditch-water," whose miasms fill the air below the empyrean where the great ones sit; but I am accusing the work of some of the most famous, who have, in this instance or in that, sinned against the truth, which can alone exalt and purify men. I do not say that they have constantly done so, or even commonly done so; but that they have done so at all marks them as of the past, to be read with the due historical allowance for their epoch and their conditions. For I believe that, while inferior writers will and must continue to imitate them in their foibles and their errors, no one hereafter will be able to achieve greatness who is false to humanity, either in its facts or its duties. The light of civilization has already broken even upon the novel, and no conscientious man can now set about painting an image of life without perpetual question of the verity of his work, and without feeling bound to distinguish so clearly that no reader of his may be misled, between what is right and what is wrong, what is noble and what is base, what is health and what is perdition, in the actions and the characters he portrays.

The fiction that aims merely to entertain — the fiction that is to serious fiction as the opera-bouffe, the ballet, and the pantomime are to the true drama — need not feel the burden of this obligation so deeply; but even such fiction will not be gay or trivial to any reader's hurt, and criticism will hold it to account if it passes from painting to teaching folly.

More and more not only the criticism which prints its opinions, but the infinitely vaster and powerfuler criticism

which thinks and feels them merely, will make this demand.
I confess that I do not care to judge any work of the
imagination without first of all applying this test to it. We
must ask ourselves before we ask anything else, Is it true? —
true to the motives, the impulses, the principles that shape
the life of actual men and women? This truth, which
necessarily includes the highest morality and the highest
artistry — this truth given, the book cannot be wicked and
cannot be weak ; and without it all graces of style and feats
of invention and cunning of construction are so many
superfluities of naughtiness. It is well for the truth to
have all these, and shine in them, but for falsehood they
are merely meretricious, the bedizenment of the wanton ;
they atone for nothing, they count for nothing. But in
fact they come naturally of truth, and grace it without
solicitation ; they are added unto it. In the whole range
of fiction we know of no true picture of life — that is, of
human nature — which is not also a masterpeice of literature, full of divine and natural beauty. It may have no
touch or tint of this special civilization or of that ; it had
better have this local color well ascertained ; but the truth
is deeper and finer than aspects, and if the book is true to
what men and women know of one another's souls it will be
true enough, and it will be great and beautiful. It is the
conception of literature as something apart from life, super-
finely aloof, which makes it really unimportant to the great
mass of mankind, without a message or a meaning for them ;
and it is the notion that a novel may be false in its portrayal
of causes and effects that makes literary art contemptible
even to those whom it amuses, that forbids them to regard
the novelist as a serious or right-minded person. If they
do not in some moment of indignation cry out against all
novels, as my correspondent does, they remain besotted
in the fume of the delusions purveyed to them, with no
higher feeling for the author than such maudlin affection as
the habitué of an opium-joint perhaps knows for the attend-
ant who fills his pipe with the drug.

Or, as in the case of another correspondent who writes that in his youth he " read a great many novels, but always regarded it as an amusement, like horse-racing and card-playing," for which he had no time when he entered upon the serious business of life, it renders them merely contemptuous. His view of the matter may be commended to the brotherhood and sisterhood of novelists as full of wholesome if bitter suggestion; and we urge them not to dismiss it with high literary scorn as that of some Bœotian dull to the beauty of art. Refuse it as we may, it is still the feeling of the vast majority of people for whom life is earnest, and who find only a distorted and misleading likeness of it in our books. We may fold ourselves in our scholars' gowns, and close the doors of our studies, and affect to depise this rude voice; but we cannot shut it out. It comes to us from wherever men are at work, from wherever they are truly living, and accuses us of unfaithfulness, of triviality, of mere stage-play; and none of us can escape conviction except he prove himself worthy of his time — a time in which the great masters have brought literature back to life, and filled its ebbing veins with the red tides of reality. We cannot all equal them; we need not copy them; but we can all go to the sources of their inspiration and their power; and to draw from these no one need go far — no one need really go out of himself.

Fifty years ago, Carlyle, in whom the truth was always alive, but in whom it was then unperverted by suffering, by celebrity, and by despair, wrote in his study of Diderot: " Were it not reasonable to prophesy that this exceeding great multitude of novel-writers and such like must, in a new generation, gradually do one of two things: either retire into the nurseries, and work for children, minors, and semi-fatuous persons of both sexes, or else, what were far better, sweep their novel-fabric into the dust-cart, and betake themselves with such faculty as they have to understand and record what is true, of which surely there is, and will forever be, a whole infinitude unknown to us of infinite importance to us? Poetry, it will more and more come to be understood, is nothing but higher knowledge ; and the only genuine Romance (for grown persons), Reality."

If, after half a century, fiction still mainly works for " children, minors, and semi-fatuous persons of both sexes," it is nevertheless one of the hopefulest signs of the world's progress that it has begun to work for " grown persons," and if not exactly in the way that Carlyle might have solely intended in urging its writers to compile memoirs instead of building the " novel-fabric," still it has, in the highest and widest sense, already made Reality its Romance. I cannot judge it, I do not even care for it, except as it has done this ; and I can hardly conceive of a literary self-respect in these days compatible with the old trade of make-believe, with the production of the kind of fiction which is too much honored by classification with card-playing and horse-racing. But let fiction cease to lie about life ; let it portray men and women as they are, actuated by the motives and the passions in the measure we all know ; let it leave off painting dolls and working them by springs and wires ; let it show the different interests in their true proportions ; let it forbear to preach pride and revenge, folly and insanity, egotism and prejudice, but frankly own these for what they are, in whatever figures and occasions they appear ; let it not put on fine literary airs ; let it speak the dialect, the language, that most Americans know — the language of unaffected people everywhere — and there can be no doubt of an unlimited future, not only of delightfulness but of usefulness, for it.

II

THIS is what I say in my severer moods, but at other times I know that, of course, no one is going to hold all fiction to such strict account. There is a great deal of it which may be very well left to amuse us, if it can, when we are sick or when we are silly, and I am not inclined to depise it in the performance of this office. Or, if people find pleasure in having their blood curdled for the sake of having it un-curdled again at the end of the book, I would not interfere with their amusement, though I do not desire it. There is a certain demand in primitive natures for the kind of fiction that does this, and the author of it is usually very proud of it. The kind of novels he likes, and likes to write, are in-tended to take his reader's mind, or what that reader would probably call his mind, off himself; they make one forget life and all its cares and duties; they are not in the least like the novels which make you think of these, and shame you into at least wishing to be a helpfuler and wholesomer creature than you are. No sordid details of verity here, if you please; no wretched being humbly and weakly struggling to do right and to be true, suffering for his follies and his sins, tasting joy only through the mortification of self, and in the help of others; nothing of all this, but a great, whirl-ing splendor of peril and achievement, a wild scene of heroic adventure and of emotional ground and lofty tum-bling, with a stage " picture " at the fall of the curtain, and all the good characters in a row, their left hands pressed upon their hearts, and kissing their right hands to the audience, in the good old way that has always charmed and always will charm, Heaven bless it !

In a world which loves the spectacular drama and the practically bloodless sports of the modern amphitheatre the author of this sort of fiction has his place, and we must not seek to destroy him because he fancies it the first place. In fact, it is a condition of his doing well the kind of work he does that he should think it important, that he should believe in himself; and I would not take away this faith of his, even if I could. As I say, he has his place. The world often likes to forget itself, and he brings on his heroes, his goblins, his feats, his hair-breadth escapes, his imminent deadly breaches, and the poor, foolish, childish old world renews the excitements of its nonage. Perhaps this is a work of beneficence ; and perhaps our brave con-jurer in his cabalistic robe is a philanthropist in disguise.

Within the last four or five years there has been throughout the whole English-speaking world what Mr. Grant Allen happily calls the " recrudescence " of taste in fiction. The effect is less noticeable in America than in England, where effete Philistinism, conscious of the dry-rot of its conventionality, is casting about for cure in anything that is wild and strange and unlike itself. But the recrudescence has been evident enough here, too; and a writer in one of our periodicals has put into convenient shape some common errors concerning popularity as a test of merit in a book. He seems to think, for instance, that the love of the marvellous and impossible in fiction, which is shown not only by "the unthinking multitude clamoring about the book counters" for fiction of that sort, but by the "literary elect" also, is proof of some principle in human nature which ought to be respected as well as tolerated. He seems to believe that the ebullition of this passion forms a sufficient answer to those who say that art should represent life, and that the art which misrepresents life is feeble art and false art. But it appears to me that a little carefuler reasoning from a little closer inspection of the facts would not have brought him to these conclusions. In the first place, I doubt very much whether the "literary elect" have been fascinated in great numbers by the fiction in question; but if I supposed them to have really fallen under that spell, I should still be able to account for their fondness and that of the "unthinking multitude" upon the same grounds, without honoring either very much. It is the habit of hasty casuists to regard civilization as inclusive of all the members of a civilized community; but this is a palpable error. Many persons in every civilized community live in a state of more or less evident savagery with respect to their habits, their morals, and their propensities; and they are held in check only by the law. Many more yet are savage in their tastes, as they show by the decoration of their houses and persons, and by their choice of books and pictures; and these are left to the restraints of public opinion. In fact, no man can be said to be thoroughly civilized or always civilized; the most refined, the most enlightened person has his moods, his moments of barbarism, in which the best, or even the second best, shall not please him. At these times the lettered and the unlettered are alike primitive and their gratifications are of the same simple sort; the highly cultivated person may then like melodrama, impossible fiction, and the trapeze as sincerely and thoroughly as a boy of thirteen or a barbarian of any age.

I do not blame him for these moods; I find something instructive and interesting in them; but if they lastingly established themselves in him, I could not help deploring the state of that person. No one can really think that the "literary elect," who are said to have joined the "unthinking multitude" in clamoring about the book counters for the romances of no-man's land, take the same kind of pleasure in them as they do in a novel of Tolstoï, Tourguéneff, George Eliot, Thackeray, Balzac, Manzoni, Hawthorne, Henry James, Thomas Hardy, Palacio Valdés, or even Walter Scott. They have joined the "unthinking multitude," perhaps because they are tired of thinking, and expect to find relaxation in feeling — feeling crudely, grossly, merely. For once in a way there is no great harm in this; perhaps no harm at all. It is perfectly natural; let them have their innocent debauch. But let us distinguish, for our own sake and guidance, between the different kinds of things that please the same kind of people; between the things that please them habitually and those that please them occasionally; between the pleasures that edify them and those that amuse them. Otherwise we shall be in danger of becoming permanently part of the "unthinking multitude," and of remaining puerile, primitive, savage. We shall be so in moods and at moments; but let us not fancy that those are high moods or fortunate moments. If they are harmless, that is the most that can be said for them. They are lapses from which we can perhaps go forward more vigorously; but even this is not certain.

My own philosophy of the matter, however, would not bring me to prohibition of such literary amusements as the writer quoted seems to find significant of a growing indifference to truth and sanity in fiction. Once more, I say, these amusements have their place, as the circus has, and the burlesque and negro minstrelsy, and the ballet, and prestidigitation. No one of these is to be despised in its place; but we had better understand that it is not the highest place, and that it is hardly an intellectual delight. The lapse of all the "literary elect" in the world could not dignify unreality; and their present mood, if it exists, is of no more weight against that beauty in literature which comes from truth alone, and never can come from anything else, than the permanent state of the "unthinking multitude."

Yet even as regards the "unthinking multitude," I believe I am not able to take the attitude of the writer I have quoted. I am afraid that I respect them more than he would like to have me, though I cannot always respect their taste, any more than that of the "literary elect." I respect them for their good sense in most practical matters; for their laborious, honest lives; for their kindness, their good-will; for that aspiration towards something better than themselves which seems to stir, however dumbly, in every human breast not abandoned to literary pride or other forms of self-righteousness. I find every man interesting, whether he thinks or unthinks, whether he is savage or civilized; for this reason I cannot thank the novelist who teaches us not to know but to unknow our kind. Yet I should by no means hold him to such strict account as Emerson, who felt the absence of the best motive, even in the greatest of the masters, when he said of Shakespeare that, after all, he was only master of the revels. The judgment is so severe, even with the praise which precedes it, that one winces under it; and if one is still young, with the world gay before him, and life full of joyous promise, one is apt to ask, defiantly, Well, what is better than being such a master of the revels as Shakespeare was? Let each judge for himself. To the heart again of serious youth uncontaminate and exigent of ideal good, it must always be a grief that the great masters seem so often to have been willing to amuse the leisure and vacancy of meaner men, and leave their mission to the soul but partially fufilled. This, perhaps, was what Emerson had in mind ; and if he had it in mind of Shakespeare, who gave us, with his histories and comedies and problems, such a searching homily as " Macbeth," one feels that he scarcely recognized the limitations of the dramatist's art. Few consciences, at times, seem so enlightened as that of this personally unknown person, so withdrawn into his work, and so lost to the intensest curiosity of after-time ; at other times he seems merely Elizabethan in his coarseness, his courtliness, his imperfect sympathy.

TOLSTOY

[*From " My Literary Passions," 1895. Copyright: Harper &
Brothers*]

I COME now, though not quite in the order of time, to
the noblest of all these enthusiasms, namely, my devotion for the writings of Lyof Tolstoy. I should wish to
speak of him with his own incomparable truth, yet I do not
know how to give a notion of his influence without the
effect of exaggeration. As much as one merely human
being can help another I believe that he has helped me;
he has not influenced me in æsthetics only, but in ethics,
too, so that I can never again see life in the way I saw it
before I knew him. Tolstoy awakens in his reader the will
to be a man; not effectively, not spectacularly, but simply,
really. He leads you back to the only true ideal, away
from that false standard of the gentleman, to the Man
who sought not to be distinguished from other men,
but identified with them, to that Presence in which the
finest gentleman shows his alloy of vanity, and the greatest
genius shrinks to the measure of his miserable egotism. I
learned from Tolstoy to try character and motive by no
other test, and though I am perpetually false to that sublime
ideal myself, still the ideal remains with me, to make me
ashamed that I am not true to it. Tolstoy gave me heart
to hope that the world may yet be made over in the image
of Him who died for it, when all Cæsar's things shall be
finally rendered unto Cæsar, and men shall come into their
own, into the right to labor and the right to enjoy the fruits
of their labor, each one master of himself and servant to
every other. He taught me to see life not as a chase of
a forever impossible personal happiness, but as a field for

endeavor toward the happiness of the whole human family ;
and I can never lose this vision, however I close my eyes,
and strive to see my own interest as the highest good.   He
gave me new criterions, new principles, which, after all, were
those that are taught us in our earliest childhood, before
we have come to the evil wisdom of the world.   As I read
his different ethical books, What to Do, My Confession,
and My Religion, I recognized their truth with a rapture
such as I have known in no other reading, and I rendered
them my allegiance, heart and soul, with whatever sickness
of the one and despair of the other.   They have it yet, and
I believe they will have it while I live.   It is with inexpressible astonishment that I hear them attainted of pessimism,
as if the teaching of a man whose ideal was simple goodness
must mean the prevalence of evil.   The way he showed
me seemed indeed impossible to my will, but to my conscience it was and is the only possible way.   If there is any
point on which he has not convinced my reason it is that of
our ability to walk this narrow way alone.   Even there he
is logical, but as Zola subtly distinguishes in speaking of
Tolstoy's essay on Money, he is not reasonable.   Solitude
enfeebles and palsies, and it is as comrades and brothers
that men must save the world from itself, rather than themselves from the world.   It was so the earliest Christians,
who had all things common, understood the life of Christ,
and I believe that the latest will understand it so.

I have spoken first of the ethical works of Tolstoy,
because they are of the first importance to me, but I think
that his æsthetical works are as perfect.   To my thinking
they transcend in truth, which is the highest beauty, all
other works of fiction that have been written, and I believe
that they do this because they obey the law of the author's own
life.   His conscience is one ethically and one æsthetically ;
with his will to be true to himself he cannot be false to his
knowledge of others.   I thought the last word in literary
art had been said to me by the novels of Tourguenief, but
it seemed like the first, merely, when I began to acquaint

myself with the simpler method of Tolstoy. I came to it
by accident, and without any manner of preoccupation in
The Cossacks, one of his early books, which had been on
my shelves unread for five or six years. I did not know
even Tolstoy's name when I opened it, and it was with a
kind of amaze that I read it, and felt word by word, and
line by line, the truth of a new art in it.

I do not know how it is that the great Russians have the
secret of simplicity. Some say it is because they have not
a long literary past and are not conventionalized by the usage
of many generations of other writers, but this will hardly
account for the brotherly directness of their dealing with
human nature; the absence of experience elsewhere char-
acterizes the artist with crudeness, and simplicity is the last
effect of knowledge. Tolstoy is, of course, the first of them
in this supreme grace. He has not only Tourguenief's
transparency of style, unclouded by any mist of the personality which we mistakenly value in style, and which
ought no more to be there than the artist's personality should
be in a portrait; but he has a method which not only seems
without artifice, but is so. I can get at the manner of most
writers, and tell what it is, but I should be baffled to tell
what Tolstoy's manner is; perhaps he has no manner.
This appears to me true of his novels, which, with their
vast variety of character and incident, are alike in their
single endeavor to get the persons living before you, both
in their action and in the peculiarly dramatic interpretation
of their emotion and cogitation. There are plenty of novelists to tell you that their characters felt and thought so
and so, but you have to take it on trust; Tolstoy alone
makes you know how and why it was so with them and not
otherwise. If there is anything in him which can be copied
or burlesqued it is this ability of his to show men inwardly
as well as outwardly; it is the only trait of his which I can
put my hand on.

After the Cossacks I read Anna Karenina with a deepen-
ing sense of the author's unrivaled greatness. I thought

that I saw through his eyes a human affair of that most sorrowful sort as it must appear to the Infinite Compassion ; the book is a sort of revelation of human nature in circumstances that have been so perpetually lied about that we have almost lost the faculty of perceiving the truth concerning an illicit love. When you have once read Anna Karenina you know how fatally miserable and essentially unhappy such a love must be. But the character of Karenin himself is quite as important as the intrigue of Anna and Vronsky. It is wonderful how such a man, cold, Philistine and even mean in certain ways, towers into a sublimity unknown (to me, at least,) in fiction when he forgives, and yet knows that he cannot forgive with dignity. There is something crucial, and something triumphant, not beyond the power, but hitherto beyond the imagination of men in this effect, which is not solicited, not forced, not in the least romantic, but comes naturally, almost inevitably from the make of man.

The vast prospects, the far-reaching perspectives of War and Peace made it as great a surprise for me in the historical novel as Anna Karenina had been in the study of contemporary life ; and its people and interests did not seem more remote, since they are of a civilization always as strange and of a humanity always as known.

I read some shorter stories of Tolstoy's before I came to this greatest work of his : I read Scenes of the Siege of Sebastopol, which is so much of the same quality as War and Peace ; and I read Policoushka and most of his short stories with a sense of my unity with their people such as I had never felt with the people of other fiction.

His didactic stories, like all stories of the sort, dwindle into allegories ; perhaps they do their work the better for this, with the simple intelligences they address ; but I think that where Tolstoy becomes impatient of his office of artist, and prefers to be directly a teacher, he robs himself of more than half his strength with those he can move only through the realization of themselves in others. The simple pathos,

and the apparent indirectness of such a tale as that of Policoushka, the peasant conscript, is of vastly more value to
the world at large than all his parables; and The Death of
Ivan Ilyitch, the Philistine worldling, will turn the hearts of
many more from the love of the world than such pale fables
of the early Christian life as Work while ye have the Light.
A man's gifts are not given him for nothing, and the man
who has the great gift of dramatic fiction has no right to
cast it away or to let it rust out in disuse.

Terrible as the Kreutzer Sonata was, it had a moral effect
dramatically which it lost altogether when the author descended to exegesis, and applied to marriage the lesson of
one evil marriage. In fine, Tolstoy is certainly not to be
held up as infallible. He is very distinctly fallible, but I
think his life is not less instructive because in certain things
it seems a failure. There was but one life ever lived upon
the earth which was without failure, and that was Christ's,
whose erring and stumbling follower Tolstoy is. There is
no other example, no other ideal, and the chief use of
Tolstoy is to enforce this fact in our age, after nineteen
centuries of hopeless endeavor to substitute ceremony for
character, and the creed for the life. I recognize the truth
of this without pretending to have been changed in anything
but my point of view of it. What I feel sure is that I can
never look at life in the mean and sordid way that I did
before I read Tolstoy.

Artistically, he has shown me a greatness that he can
never teach me. I am long past the age when I could
wish to form myself upon another writer, and I do not think
I could now insensibly take on the likeness of another; but
his work has been a revelation and a delight to me, such
as I am sure I can never know again. I do not believe
that in the whole course of my reading, and not even in
the early moment of my literary enthusiasms, I have known
such utter satisfaction in any writer, and this supreme joy
has come to me at a time of life when new friendships, not
to say new passions, are rare and reluctant. It is as if the

best wine at this high feast where I have sat so long had been kept for the last, and I need not deny a miracle in it in order to attest my skill in judging vintages. In fact, I prefer to believe that my life has been full of miracles, and that the good has always come to me at the right time, so that I could profit most by it. I believe if I had not turned the corner of my fiftieth year, when I first knew Tolstoy, I should not have been able to know him as fully as I did. He has been to me that final consciousness, which he speaks of so wisely in his essay on Life. I came in it to the knowledge of myself in ways I had not dreamt of before, and began at least to discern my relations to the race, without which we are each nothing. The supreme art in literature had its highest effect in making me set art forever below humanity, and it is with the wish to offer the greatest homage to his heart and mind, which any man can pay another, that I close this record with the name of Lyof Tolstoy.

SIDNEY LANIER

1842 – 1881

THE ENGLISH NOVEL

[*From " The English Novel: A Study in the Development of Personality*," 1883. *Copyright: Charles Scribner's Sons*]

IF you should be wandering meditatively along the bank of some tiny brook, a brook so narrow that you can leap across it without effort, so quiet in its singing that its loudest tinkle cannot be heard in the next field, carrying upon its bosom no craft that would draw more water than the curving leaf of a wild-rose floating down stream, too small in volume to dream of a mill-wheel and turning nothing more practical than maybe a piece of violet-petal in a little eddy off somewhere, — if, I say, you should be strolling alongside such a brook and should see it suddenly expand, without the least intermediate stage, into a mighty river, turning a thousand great wheels for man's profit as it swept on to the sea, and offering broad highway and favorable currents to a thousand craft freighted with the most precious cargoes of human aspiration : you would behold the aptest physical semblance of that spiritual phenomenon which we witnessed at our last meeting, when in tracing the quiet and mentally-wayward course of demure Marian Evans among the suave pastorals of her native Warwickshire, we came suddenly upon the year 1857 when her first venture in fiction — *The Scenes of Clerical Life* — appeared in *Blackwood's Magazine* and magically enlarged the stream of her influence from the diameter of a small circle of literary people in London to the width of all England.

At this point it seems interesting now to pause a moment, to look about and see exactly what network English fiction had done since its beginning, oniy about a century before, to note more particularly what were the precise gains to humanity which Thackeray and Dickens had poured in just at this time of 1857, and thus to differentiate a clear view of the actual contribution which George Eliot was now beginning to make to English life and thought.

It is not a pleasant task, however instructive, to leave off looking at a rose and cast one's contemplation down to the unsavory muck in which its roots are imbedded. This, however, is what one must do when one passes from the many-petalled rose of George Eliot's fiction to the beginning of the English novel.

This beginning was as curious as it was unlooked-for by the people engaged in it. In the year 1740 a book in two volumes called *Pamela : or Virtue Rewarded*, was printed, in which Samuel Richardson took what seems to have been the first revolutionary departure from the wild and complex romances — such as Sir Philip Sidney's *Arcadia* — which had formed the nearest approach to the modern novel until then. At this time Richardson was fifty years old, and probably the last man in England who would have been selected as likely to write an epoch-making book of any description. He had worked most of his life as a printer, but by the time referred to had gotten so far towards the literary life as to be employed by booksellers to arrange indexes and to write prefaces and dedications. It so happened that on a certain occasion he was asked by two booksellers to write a volume of letters on different subjects which might serve as models to uneducated persons — a sort of Every Man His Own Letter Writer, or the like.

The letters, in order to be more useful, were to be upon such subjects as the rustic world might likely desire to correspond about. Richardson thinks it over; and presently writes to inquire, "Will it be any harm, in a piece you want to be written so low, if we should instruct them how they should think and act in common cases, as well as indite?" This seemed a capital idea and in the course of time, after some experiments and after recalling an actual story he had once heard which gave him a sort of basis, he takes for his heroine a simple servant-girl, daughter of Goodman Andrews, a humbly born English farmer, rather sardonically names her Pamela after the Lady Pamela in Sir Philip Sidney's *Arcadia*, carries her pure through a series of incredibly villainous plots against her by the master of the house where she is at service, who has taken advantage of the recent death of his wife, Pamela's mistress, to carry these on, and finally makes the master marry her in a fit of highly spasmodic goodness, after a long course of the most infamous but unsuccessful villainy, calls the book *Pamela: or Virtue Rewarded*, prints it, and in a very short time wins a great host of admiring readers, insomuch that since the first two volumes ended with the marriage, he adds two more showing the married life of Pamela and her squire.

The whole novel, like all of Richardson's, is written in the form of letters passing between the characters. It is related, apropos of his genius in letter-writing, that in his boyhood he was the love-letter-writer-in-chief for three of the young ladies of his town, and that he maintained this embarrassing position for a long time without suspicion from either of the three. Richardson himself announces the moral purpose of his book, saying that he thinks it might "introduce a new species of writing that might possibly turn young people into a course of reading different from the pomp and parade of romance-writing, and . . . promote the cause of religion and virtue;" and in the preface to the continuation before-mentioned he remarks as follows: "The two former volumes of *Pamela* met with a success greatly exceeding the most sanguine expectations; and the editor hopes" (Richardson calls himself the editor of the letters) "that the letters which compose these will be found equally written to nature; avoiding all romantic flights, improbable surprises, and irrational machinery; and that the passions are touched where requisite; and rules equally new and practicable inculcated

throughout the whole for the general conduct of life." I
have given these somewhat tedious quotations from Richardson's own words to show first that the English novel starts
out with a perfectly clear and conscious moral mission, and
secondly to contrast this pleasing moral announcement of
Richardson's with what I can only call the silly and hideous
realization of it which meets us when we come actually to
read this wonderful first English novel — *Pamela*.

I have already given the substance of the first two
volumes in which the rich squire, Mr. B. (as he is called
throughout the novel) finally marries and takes home the
girl who had been the servant of his wife and against
whom, ever since that lady's death, he had been plotting
with an elaborate baseness which has never before been,
and I sincerely hope will never hereafter be described.
By this action Mr. B. has in the opinion of Richardson,
of his wife, the servant-girl and the whole contemporary
world, saturated himself with such a flame of saintliness
as to have burnt out every particle of any little misde-
meanor he may have been guilty of in his previous existence; and I need only read you an occasional line from
the first four letters of the third volume in order to show
the marvelous sentimentality, the untruth towards nature,
and the purely commercial view of virtue and of religion
which make up this intolerable book. At the opening of
Volume III we find that Goodman Andrews, the father
of the bride, and his wife have been provided with a
comfortable farm on the estate of Mr. B., and the second
letter is from Andrews to his daughter, the happy bride,
Pamela. After rhapsodizing for several pages Andrews
reaches this climax — and it is worth while observing that
though only a rude farmer of the eighteenth century,
whose daughter was a servant maid, he writes in the most
approved epistolary style of the period:

"When here in this happy dwelling and this well-stocked
farm, in these rich meadows and well-cropped acres, we look

around us and whichever way we turn our heads see blessings
upon blessings and plenty upon plenty: see barns well stored,
poultry increasing, the kine lowing and crowding about us, and
all fruitful; and are bid to call all these our own. And then
think that all is the reward of our child's virtue! O, my dear
daughter, who can bear these things! Excuse me! I must
break off a little! For my eyes are as full as my heart; and
I will retire to bless God, and your honored husband."

Here there is a break in the page, by which the honest
farmer is supposed to represent the period of time occupied
by him in retiring, and dividing his blessing, as one hopes,
impartially, between the Creator and Pamela's honored
husband, — and the farmer resumes his writing:

"So — my dear child — I now again take up my pen. But
reading what I had written, in order to carry on the thread,
I can hardly forbear again being in like sort affected. — "

And here we have a full stop and a dash, during which
it is only fair to suppose that the honest Andrews manages
to weep and bless up to something like a state of repose.
Presently Pamela writes:

"My dear father and mother; I have shown your letter to
my beloved. . . . ' Dear good souls,' said he, 'how does everything they say and everything they write manifest the worthi-
ness of their hearts! Tell them . . . let them find out another
couple as worthy as themselves and I will do as much for
them. Indeed I would not place them,' continued the dear
obliger, 'in the same county, because I would wish two counties
to be blessed for their sakes.' . . . I could only fly to his
generous bosom . . . and with my eyes swimming in tears of
grateful joy . . . bless God and bless him with my whole
heart; for speak I could not! but almost choaked with my joy,
sobbed to him my grateful acknowledgements. . . . ''T is too
much, too much,' said I, in broken accents: 'O, sir, bless me
more gradually and more cautiously — for I cannot bear it!'
And indeed my heart went flutter, flutter, flutter, at his dear
breast as if it wanted to break its too narrow prison to mingle
still more intimately with his own."

And a few lines further on we have this purely commercial view of religion:

"And if our prayers shall be heard," continues Pamela, "and we shall have the pleasure to think that his" (her husband's) "advances in piety are owing not a little to them; . . . then indeed may we take the pride to think we have repaid his goodness to us and that we have satisfied the debt which nothing less can discharge."

Or again, in the same letter she exclaims anew:

"See, O see, my excellent parents, how we are crowned with blessings upon blessings until we are the talk of all who know us; you for your honesty, I for my humility and virtue;" so that now I have "nothing to do but to reap all the rewards which this life can afford; and if I walk humbly and improve my blessèd opportunities, will heighten and perfect all, in a still more joyful futurity."

Perhaps a more downright creed, not only of worldliness, but of "other-worldliness," was never more explicitly avowed.

Now — to put the whole moral effect of this book into a nutshell — Richardson had gravely announced it as a warning to young servant-girls: but why might he not as well have announced it as an encouragement to old villains? The virtue of Pamela, it is true, is duly rewarded: but Mr. B., with all his villainy, certainly fares better than Pamela: for he not only receives to himself a paragon of a wife, but the sole operation of his previous villainy towards her is to make his neighbors extol him to the skies as a saint, when he turns from it; so that, considering the enormous surplus of Mr. B.'s rewards as against Pamela's, instead of the title *Pamela: or Virtue Rewarded*, ought not the book to have been called *Mr. B.: or Villainy Rewarded?*

It was expressly to ridicule some points of Richardson's *Pamela* that the second English novel was written. This

was Henry Fielding's *Joseph Andrews*, which appeared in
1742. It may be that the high birth of Fielding — his
father was great-grandson of the Earl of Denbigh, and
a lieutenant-general in the army — had something to do
with his opposition to Richardson, who was the son of a
joiner; at any rate, he puts forth a set of exactly opposite
characters to those in Pamela, takes a footman for his
virtuous hero, and the footman's mistress for his villainous
heroine, names the footman Joseph Andrews, (explaining
that he was the brother of Richardson's Pamela who you
remember was the daughter of Goodman Andrews) makes
principal figures of two parsons (Parson Adams and Parson
Trulliber, the former of whom is set up as a model of
clerical behavior, and the latter the reverse) and with
these main materials, together with an important pedler,
he gives us the book still called by many the greatest
English novel, originally entitled *The Adventures of Joseph
Andrews and His Friend Abraham Adams*.

I will not, because I cannot, here cite any of the vital
portions of *Joseph Andrews* which produce the real moral
effect of the book upon a reader. I can only say that it is
not different in essence from the moral effect of Richardson's
book just described, though the tone is more clownish.
But for particular purposes of comparison with Dickens and
George Eliot hereafter let me recall to you in the briefest
way two of the funny scenes. To show that these are fair
samples of the humorous atmosphere of the book I may
mention that they are both among the number which were
selected by Thackeray, who was a keen lover of Fielding
generally, and of his *Joseph Andrews* particularly, for his
own illustrations upon his own copy of this book.

In the first scene Joseph Andrews is riding along the
road upon a very unreliable horse who has already given
him a lame leg by a fall, attended by his friend Parson
Adams. They arrive at an inn, dismount, and ask for
lodging; the landlord is surly and presently behaves un-
civilly to Joseph Andrews; whereupon Parson Adams, in

defence of his lame friend, knocks the landlord sprawling upon the floor of his own inn; the landlord, however, quickly receives reinforcements and his wife, seizing a pan of hog's blood which stands on the dresser, discharges it with powerful effect into the good parson's face. While the parson is in this condition, enters Mrs. Slipshod — a veritable Grendel's mother —

"Terrible termagant, mindful of mischief,"

and attacks the landlady, with fearsome results of uprooted hair and defaced feature. In scene second, Parson Adams being in need of a trifling loan goes to see his counter-parson Trulliber, who was noted, among other things, for his fat hogs. Unfortunately Parson Adams meets Mrs. Trulliber first, and is mistakenly introduced by her to her husband as "a man come for some of his hogs." Trulliber immediately begins to brag of the fatness of his swine and drags Parson Adams to his sty insisting upon examination in proof of his praise. Parson Adams complies; they reach the sty and by way of beginning his examination Parson Adams lays hold of the tail of a very high-fed, capricious hog; the beast suddenly springs forward and throws Parson Adams headlong into the deep mire. Trulliber bursts into laughter and contemptuously cries: "Why, dost not know how to handle a hog?"

It is impossible for lack of space to linger over further characteristics of these writers. In 1748 appears Richardson's *Clarissa Harlowe* in eight volumes, which from your present lecturer's point of view is quite sufficiently described as a patient analysis of the most intolerable crime in all history or fiction, watered with an amount of tears and sensibility as much greater than that in Pamela as the cube of eight volumes is greater than the cube of four volumes.

In 1753 Richardson's third and last novel, *Sir Charles Grandison*, appeared; a work differing in motive, but not in moral tone, from the other two, though certainly less hideous than *Clarissa Harlowe*.

Returning to bring up Fielding's novels, in 1743 appeared his *History of the Life of the late Mr. Jonathan Wild the Great,* in which the hero Jonathan Wild was a taker of thieves, or detective, who ended his own career by being hanged; the book being written professedly as " an exposition of the motives that actuate the unprincipled great, in every walk and sphere of life, and which are common alike to the thief or murderer on the small scale and to the mighty villain and reckless conqueror who invades the rights or destroys the liberties of nations." In 1749 Fielding prints his *Tom Jones,* which some consider his greatest book. The glory of *Tom Jones* is Squire Allworthy, whom we are invited to regard as the most miraculous product of the divine creation so far in the shape of man; but to your present lecturer's way of thinking the kind of virtue represented by Squire Allworthy is completely summed in the following sentence of the work introducing him in the midst of nature. It is a May morning, and Squire Allworthy is pacing the terrace in front of his mansion before sunrise; " when," says Fielding, " in the full blaze of his majesty up rose the sun, than which one object alone in this lower creation could be more glorious, and that Mr. Allworthy himself presented — a human being replete with benevolence meditating in what manner he might render himself most acceptable to his Creator by doing most good to his creatures : " that is, in plain commercial terms, how he might obtain the largest possible amount upon the letter of credit which he found himself forced to buy against the inevitable journey into those foreign parts lying beyond the waters of death.

Out of Fielding's numerous other writings, dramatic and periodical, it is perhaps necessary to mention farther only his *Amelia,* belonging to the year 1751, in which he praised his first wife and satirized the jails of his time.

We must now hastily pass to the third so-called classic

writer in English fiction, Tobias Smollett, who, after being educated as a surgeon, and having experiences of life as surgeon's mate on a ship of the line in the expedition to Carthagena, spent some time in the West Indies, returned to London, wrote some satires, an opera, &c., and presently when he was still only twenty-seven years old captivated England with his first novel, *Roderick Random*, which appeared in 1748, the same year with *Clarissa Harlowe*. In 1751 came Smollett's *Peregrine Pickle*, famous for its bright fun and the caricature it contains of Akenside — *Pleasures of Imagination* Akenside — who is represented as the host in a very absurd entertainment after the ancient fashion. In 1752 Smollett's *Adventures of Ferdinand Count Fathom* gave the world a new and very complete study in human depravity. In 1769, appeared his *Adventures of an Atom*: a theme which one might suppose it difficult to make indecorous and which was really a political satire ; but the unfortunate liberty of locating his atom as an organic particle in various parts of various successive human bodies gave Smollett a field for indecency which he cultivated to its utmost yield. A few months before his death in 1771 appeared his *Expedition of Humphrey Clinker*, certainly his best novel. It is worth while noticing that in *Humphrey Clinker* the veritable British poorly-educated and poorspelling woman begins to express herself in the actual dialect of the species, and in the letters of Mrs. Winifred Jenkins to her fellow maid-servant Mrs. Mary Jones at Brambleton Hall, during a journey made by the family to the North, we have some very worthy and strongly-marked originals not only of Mrs. Malaprop and Mrs. Partington, but of the immortal Sairey Gamp and of scores of other descendants in Thackeray and Dickens, here and there.

I can quote but a few lines from the last letter of Mrs. Winifred Jenkins concluding the *Expedition of Humphrey Clinker*, which by the way is told entirely through letters from one character to another, like Richardson's.

" To Mrs. Mary Jones at Brambleton Hall.

    " Mrs. Jones, —

        " Providence has bin pleased to make great halteration in the pasture of our affairs. We were yesterday three kiple chined by the grease of God in the holy bands of matter-money."

(The novel winds up with a general marriage of pretty much all parties concerned, mistress, maid, master and man); "and I now subscribe myself Loyd, at your sarvice." Here she of course describes the wedding. " As for Madam Lashmiheygo, you nose her picklearities — her head to be sure was fantastical; and her spouse had wrapped her with a long . . . clock from the land of the selvedges. . . . Your humble servant had on a plain pea-green tabby sack, with my runnela cap, ruff toupee, and side-curls. They said I was the very moral of Lady Rick-manstone but not so pale — that may well be, for her ladyship is my elder by seven good years or more. Now, Mrs. Mary, our satiety is to suppurate; and we are coming home " — which irresistibly reminds us of the later Mrs. Malaprop's famous explanation in *The Rivals:* — " I was putrefied with astonish-ment." — " Present my compliments to Mrs. Gwillim, and I hope she and I will live upon dissent terms of civility. Being by God's blessing removed to a higher spear you'll excuse my being familiar with the lower sarvints of the family, but as I trust you will behave respectful and keep a proper distance you may always depend on the good will and protection of

                      " Yours,

                              " W. LOYD."

To these three — Richardson, Fielding and Smollett — I have now only to add the name of Laurence Sterne, whose *Tristram Shandy* appeared in 1759, in order to complete a group of novel writers whose moral outcome is much the same and who are still reputed in all current manuals as the classic founders of English fiction. I need give no characterization of Sterne's book, which is prob-ably the best known of all. Every one recalls the Chinese puzzle of humor in *Tristram Shandy*, which pops something grotesque or indecent at us in every crook. As to its morality, I know good people who love the book; but to me, when you sum it all up, its teaching is that a man may spend his life in low, brutish, inane pursuits and may have a good many little private sins on his conscience, — but will nevertheless be perfectly sure of heaven if he can have retained the ability to weep a maudlin tear over a tale of distress; or, in short, that a somewhat irritable state of the lachrymal glands will be cheerfully accepted by the Deity as a substitute for saving grace or a life of self-sacrifice. As I have said, these four writers still maintain their position as the classic novelists and their moral influence is still copiously extolled; but I cannot help believing that much of this praise is simply well-meaning ignorance. I protest that I can read none of these books without feeling as if my soul had been in the rain, draggled, muddy, miserable. In other words, they play upon life as upon a violin without a bridge, in the deliberate endeavor to get the most depressing tones possible from the instrument. This is done under pretext of showing us vice.

In fine, and this is the characterization I shall use in contrasting this group with that much sweeter group led by George Eliot, the distinctive feature of these first novelists is to show men with microscopic detail how bad men may be. I shall presently illustrate with the George Eliot group how much larger the mission of the novel is than this: meantime, I cannot leave this matter without recording in the plainest terms that — for far deeper reasons than those which Roger Bacon gave for sweeping away the works of Aristotle — if I had my way with these classic books I would blot them from the face of the earth. One who studies the tortuous behaviors of men in history soon ceases to wonder at any human inconsistency; but, so far as I can marvel, I do daily that we regulate by law the sale of gunpowder, the storage of nitro-glycerine, the administration of poison — all of which can hurt but our bodies — but are absolutely careless of these things — so-called classic books, which wind their infinite insidiousnesses about the souls of our young children and either strangle them or cover them with unremovable slime under our very eyes, working in a security of fame and so-called classicism that is more effectual for this purpose than the security of the dark. Of this terror it is the sweetest souls who know most.

In the beginning of *Aurora Leigh*, Mrs. Browning speaks this matter so well that I must clinch my opinion with her words. Aurora Leigh says, recalling her own youthful experience :

> " Sublimest danger, over which none weeps,
> When any young wayfaring soul goes forth
> Alone, unconscious of the perilous road,
> The day-sun dazzling in his limpid eyes,
> To thrust his own way, he an alien, through
> The world of books! Ah, you! — you think it fine,
> You clap hands — 'A fair day!' — you cheer him on
> As if the worst, could happen, were to rest
> Too long beside a fountain. Yet behold,
> Behold! — the world of books is still the world ;
> And worldlings in it are less merciful
> And more puissant. For the wicked there
> Are winged like angels. Every knife that strikes
> Is edged from elemental fire to assail
> A spiritual life ; the beautiful seems right
> By force of beauty, and the feeble wrong
> Because of weakness.   .   .   .   .
>   . . . In the book-world, true,
> There 's no lack, neither, of God's saints and kings,
> .   .   .   .
> True, many a prophet teaches in the roads ;   .   .
> .   .   .   .   .   .
> But stay — who judges ?   .   .   .   .
>   . . . The child there ? Would you leave
> That child to wander in a battle-field
> And push his innocent smile against the guns ;
> Or even in a catacomb — his torch
> Grown ragged in the fluttering air, and all
> The dark a-mutter round him ? not a child."

But to return to our sketch of English fiction, it is now delightful to find a snowdrop springing from this muck of the classics. In the year 1766 appeared Goldsmith's *Vicar of Wakefield*.

One likes to recall the impression which the purity of this charming book made upon the German Goethe. Fifty years after Goethe had read it — or rather after Herder read to him a translation of the *Vicar of Wakefield* while he was a law-student at Strasburg — the old poet mentions in one of his letters to Zelter the strong and healthy influence of this story upon him, just at the critical point of his mental development; and yesterday while reading the just published *Reminiscences of Thomas Carlyle* I found a pleasant pendant to this testimony of Goethe's in favor of Goldsmith's novel in an entry of the rugged old man in which he describes the far outlook and new wisdom which he managed to conquer from Goethe's *Wilhelm Meister*, after many repulsions.

"Schiller done, I began *Wilhelm Meister*, a task I liked perhaps rather better, too scanty as my knowledge of the element, and even of the language, still was. Two years before I had at length, after some repulsion, got into the heart of *Wilhelm Meister*, and eagerly read it through; my sally out, after finishing, along the vacant streets of Edinburgh, a windless, Scotch-misty morning, is still vivid to me. 'Grand, serenely, harmoniously built together, far-seeing, wise and true. Where, for many years, or in my whole life before, have I read such a book?' Which I was now, really in part as a kind of duty, conscientiously translating for my countrymen, if they would read it — as a select few of them have ever since kept doing."

Of the difference between the moral effect of Goldsmith's *Vicar of Wakefield* and the classical works just mentioned I need not waste your time in speaking. No great work in the English novel appears until we reach Scott whose *Waverley* astonished the world in 1814; and during the intervening period from this book to the *Vicar of Wakefield* perhaps there are no works notable enough to be mentioned in so rapid a sketch as this unless it be the society novels of Miss Burney, *Evelina* and *Cecilia*, the dark and romantic stories of Mrs. Radcliffe, the *Caleb Williams* of William Godwin — with which he believed he was making an epoch because it was a novel without love as a motive — Miss Edgeworth's moral tales and the quiet and elegant narratives of Jane Austen.

But I cannot help mentioning here a book which occurs during this period, and which attaches itself by the oddest imaginable ties to what was said, in a previous lecture, of the novel as the true meeting-ground where the poetic imagination and the scientific imagination come together and incorporate themselves. Now, to make the true novel — the work which takes all the miscellaneous products of scientific observation and carries them up into a higher plane and incarnates them into the characters (as we call them) of a book, and makes them living flesh and blood like ourselves — to effect this, there must be a true incorporation and merger of the scientific and poetic faculties in one : it is not sufficient if they work side by side like two horses abreast, they must work like a man and wife with one soul ; or, to change the figure, their union must not be mechanical, it must be chemical, producing a thing better than either alone ; or, to change the figure again, the union must be like that which Browning has noticed as existing among the ingredients of a musical chord, when, as he says, out of three tones, one makes not a fourth, but a star.

Now the book I mean shows us the scientific faculty and the poetic faculty — and no weak faculties either — working along together, not merged, not chemically united, not lighting up matters like a star, — with the result, as seems to me, of producing the very funniest earnest book in our language. It is *The Loves of the Plants*, by Dr. Erasmus Darwin, grandfather, I believe, to our own grave and patient Charles Darwin. *The Loves of the Plants* is practically a series of little novels in which the heroes and heroines belong to the vegetable world. Linnæus had announced the sexuality of plants, and had made this idea a principle of classification, the one-stamen class, *Monan-dria*, two-stamen class, *Diandria*, etc., etc. All this the diligent and truly loving Doctor framed into poetry, and poetry which so far as technical execution goes is quite as good as the very best of the Pope school which it follows. Here are a few specimens of the poem :

> " Descend, ye hovering Sylphs ! aërial Quires ;
> And sweep with little hands your silver lyres ;
> With fairy footsteps print your grassy rings,
> Ye Gnomes ! accordant to the tinkling strings :
> While in soft notes I tune to oaten reed
> Gay hopes, and amorous sorrows of the mead ; —
> From giant Oaks, that wave their branches dark,
> To the dwarf Moss that clings upon their bark,
> What Beaux and Beauties crowd the gaudy groves,
> And woo and win their vegetable Loves."

> " First the tall Canna lifts his curled brow
> Erect to heaven, and plights his nuptial vow;
> The virtuous pair, in milder regions born,
> Dread the rude blast of Autumn's icy morn ;
> Round the chill fair he folds his crimson vest,
> And clasps the timorous beauty to his breast."

Here, however, a serious case presents itself ; in *Canna* there was one stamen to one pistil, and this was comfortable ; but in the next flower he happened to reach — the *Genista* or Wild Broom — there were ten stamens to one pistil, that is, ten lovers to one lady ; but the intrepid Doctor carries it through, all the same, managing the whole point simply by airy swiftness of treatment :

> " Sweet blooms Genista [1] in the myrtle shade,
> And ten fond brothers woo the haughty maid."

But sometimes our botanist comes within a mere ace of beautiful poetry, as for example :

[1] Genista, or *Planta Genista*, origin of " Plantagenet," from the original name-giver's habit of wearing a tuft of his native heath or broom in his bonnet.

" When o'er the cultured lawns and dreary wastes,
Retiring Autumn flings her howling blasts,
Bends in tumultuous waves the struggling woods,
And showers their leafy honors on the floods;
In withering heaps collects the flowery spoil;
And each chill insect sinks beneath the soil:
Quick flies fair Tulipa the loud alarms,
And folds her infant closer in her arms;
In some lone cave, secure pavilion, lies,
And waits the courtship of serener skies."

This book has what it calls Interludes between the parts, in which the Bookseller and the Poet discuss various points arising in it; and its oddity is all the more increased when one finds here a number of the most just, incisive, right-minded and large views not only upon the mechanism of poetry, but upon its essence and its relations to other arts.[1]

Nor need I dwell upon Scott's novels which stretch from 1814 to 1831, which we have all known from our child-

---

[1] Carlyle's opinion of the book is given with a comical grimness in his Reminiscences *à propos* of the younger Erasmus Darwin, who used much to visit the Carlyles after they settled in London:

"Erasmus Darwin, a most diverse kind of mortal, came to seek us out very soon ('had heard of Carlyle in Germany,' etc.), and continues ever since to be a quiet house-friend, honestly attached; though his visits latterly have been rarer and rarer, health so poor, I so occupied, etc., etc. He had something of original and sarcastically ingenious in him; one of the sincerest, naturally truest, and most modest of men; elder brother of Charles Darwin (the famed Darwin on Species of these days), to whom I rather prefer him for intellect, had not his health quite doomed him to silence and patient idleness — grandsons, both, of the first famed Erasmus ('Botanic Garden,' etc.), who also seems to have gone upon 'species' questions, '*omnia ex conchis*' (all from oysters) being a dictum of his (even a stamp he sealed with still extant), as this present Erasmus once told me, many long years before this of Darwin on Species came up among us! Wonderful to me, as indicating the capricious stupidity of mankind: never could read a page of it, or waste the least thought upon it."

hood as among the most hale and strengthening waters in which the young soul ever bathed. They discuss no moral problems, they place us in no relation towards our fellow that can be called moral at all, they belong to that part of us which is youthful, undebating, wholly unmoral — though not immoral, — they are simply always young, always healthy, always miraculous. And I can only give now a hasty additional flavor of these Scott days by reminding you of the bare names of Thomas Hope, Lockhart, Theodore Hook, Mrs. Trollope, Mrs. Gore and Miss Mitford. It seems always comfortable in a confusion of this kind to have some easily-remembered formula which may present us a considerable number of important facts in portable shape. Now the special group of writers which I wish to contrast with the classic group, consisting of Dickens, Thackeray, Tennyson, Mrs. Browning, Charlotte Brontë and George Eliot, are at work between 1837 and 1857, and for the purpose of giving you a convenient skeleton or set of vertebræ containing some main facts affecting the English novel of the nineteenth century I have arranged this simple table which proceeds by steps of ten years up to the period mentioned.

For example: since these all end in seven; beginning with the year 1807 it seems easy to remember that that is the date of Charles and Mary Lamb's *Tales from Shakspere;* skipping ten years to 1817, in this year *Blackwood's Magazine* is established, a momentous event in fiction generally and particularly as to George Eliot's; advancing ten years, in 1827 Bulwer's *Pelham* appears and also the very stimulating *Specimens of German Romance* which Thomas Carlyle edited; in 1837 the adorable *Pickwick* strolls into fiction; in 1847 Thackeray prints *Vanity Fair*, Charlotte Brontë gives us *Jane Eyre*, and Tennyson *The Princess;* and finally in 1857, as we have seen, George Eliot's *Scenes of Clerical Life* are printed, while so closely upon it in the previous year as to be fairly considered contemporary comes Mrs. Browning's *Aurora Leigh*.

I do not know any more vivid way of bringing before you the precise work which English fiction is doing at the time George Eliot sets in than by asking you to run your eye along the last four dates here given, 1827, 1837, 1847, 1857. Here, in 1827, advances a well-dressed man, bows a fine bow, and falls to preaching his gospel: "My friends, under whatever circumstances a man may be placed, he has it always in his power to be a gentleman;" and Bulwer's gentleman is always given as a very manful and Christian being. I am well aware of the modern tendency to belittle Bulwer, as a slight creature; but with the fresh recollection of his books as they fell upon my own boyhood, I cannot recall a single one which did not leave as a last residuum the picture in some sort of the chivalrous gentleman impressed upon my heart. I cheerfully admit that he sometimes came dangerously near snobbery, and that he was uncivil and undignified and many other bad things in the *New Timon* and the Tennyson quarrel; and I concede that it must be difficult for us, — you and me, who are so superior and who have no faults of our own — to look upon these failings with patience; and yet I cannot help remembering that every novel of Bulwer's is skillfully written and entertaining, and that there is not an ignoble thought or impure stimulus in the whole range of his works.

But, advancing, here in 1837 comes on a preacher who takes up the slums and raggedest miseries of London and plumps them boldly down in the parlors of high life and, like the boy in the fairy tale whose fiddle compelled every hearer to dance in spite of himself, presently has a great train of people following him, ready to do his bidding in earnestly reforming the prisons, the schools, the workhouses, and the like, what time the entire train are roaring with the genialest of laughter at the comical and grotesque figures which this preacher Dickens has fished up out of the London mud.

But again: here in 1847 we have Thackeray exposing shame and high vulgarity and minute wickedness, while

Charlotte Brontë and Tennyson, with the widest difference in method, are for the first time expounding the doctrine of co-equal sovereignty as between man and woman, and bringing up the historic conception of the personality of woman to a plane in all respects level with, though properly differentiated from, that of man. It is curious to see the depth of Charlotte Brontë's adoration for Thackeray, the intense, high-pitched woman for the somewhat slack and, as I always think, somewhat low-pitched satirist; and perhaps the essential utterance of Thackeray, as well as the fervent tone which I beg you to observe is now being acquired by the English novel, the awful consciousness of its power and its mission, may be very sufficiently gathered from some of Charlotte Brontë's words about Thackeray which occur in the Preface to the second edition of her *Jane Eyre*.

" There is a man in our own days whose words are not framed to tickle delicate ears; who, to my thinking, comes before the great ones of society much as the son of Imlah came before the throned kings of Judah and Israel; and who speaks truth as deep, with a power as prophet-like and as vital — a mien as dauntless and as daring. Is the satirist of *Vanity Fair* admired in high places? I cannot tell; but I think if some of those amongst whom he hurls the Greek-fire of his sarcasm, and over whom he flashes the levin-brand of his denunciation, were to take his warnings in time, they or their seed might yet escape a fatal Ramoth-Gilead.

" Why have I alluded to this man? I have alluded to him, reader, because I think I see in him an intellect profounder and more unique than his contemporaries have yet recognized; because I regard him as the first social regenerator of the day — as the very master of that working corps who would restore to rectitude the warped system of things."

Into this field of beneficent activity which the novel has created, comes in 1857 George Eliot: comes with no more noise than that of a snow-flake falling on snow, yet — as I have said and as I wish now to show with some detail — comes as an epoch-maker, both by virtue of the peculiar mission she undertakes and of the method in which she carries it out.

What then is that peculiar mission?

In the very first of these stories, *Amos Barton*, she announces it quite explicitly, though it cannot be supposed at all consciously. Before quoting the passage, in order that you may at once take the full significance of it, let me remind you of a certain old and grievous situation as between genius and the commonplace person. For a long time every most pious thinker must have found immediately in his path a certain obstructive odium upon the Supreme Being (I speak with the greatest reverence) in the matter of the huge and apparently unjustifiable partiality of His spiritual gifts as between man and man.

We have a genius (say) once in a hundred years: but this hundred years represents three generations of the whole world; that is to say, here are three thousand million commonplace people to one genius.

At once, with all the force of this really inconceivable numerical majority, the cry arises, How monstrous! Here are three thousand millions of people to eat, sleep, die, and rot into oblivion, and but one man is to have such faculty as may conquer death, win fame, and live beyond the worms!

No one feels this inequality so keenly as the great genius himself. I find in Shakspere, in Beethoven, in others, often an outcrop of feeling which shows that the genius cringes under this load of favoritism, as if he should cry in his lonesome moments, *Dear Lord, why hast thou provided so much for me, and so little for yonder multitude?* In plain fact, it seems as if there was never such a problem as this: what shall we do about these three thousand millions of common men as against the one uncommon man, to save the goodness of God from seeming like the blind caprice of a Roman Emperor?

It is precisely here that George Eliot comes to the rescue, and though she does not solve the problem — no one ex-

pects to do that — at any rate she seems to me to make
it tolerable, and to take it out of that class of questions
which one shuts back for fear of nightmare and insanity.
Emerson has treated this matter, partially, and from a sort
of side-light. "But," he exclaims in the end of his essay
on *The Uses of Great Men*, "*great men:* — the word is
injurious. Is there caste? Is there fate? What becomes
of the promise to virtue? . . . Why are the masses, from
the dawn of history down, food for knives and powder?
The idea dignifies a few leaders, . . . and they make
war and death sacred; but what for the wretches whom
they hire and kill? The cheapness of man is everyday's
tragedy." And more to this purport. But nothing could
be more unsatisfactory than Emerson's solution of the
problem. He unhesitatingly announces on one page that
the wrong is to be righted by giving every man a chance
in the future, in (say) different worlds; every man is
to have his turn at being a genius: until "there are no
common men." But two pages farther on this elaborate
scheme of redress is completely swept away by the announcement that after all the individual is nothing, the
quality is what abides, and so falls away in that most
marvelous delusion of his — the strange wise man! — that
personality is to die away into the first cause.

On the other hand, if you will permit me to quote a few
pathetic words which I find in Carlyle's *Reminiscences*, in
the nature of a sigh and aspiration and breathed blessing
all in one upon his wife and her ministrations to him during
that singular period of his life when he suddenly left London
and buried himself in his wild Scotch farm of Craigenputtoch, I shall be able to show you how Carlyle, most unconsciously, dreams toward a far more satisfactory end of this
matter than Emerson's, and then how George Eliot actually
brings Carlyle's dream to definite form and at least partial
fulfilment in the very beginning of her work. Carlyle is
speaking of the rugged trials and apparent impossibilities
of living at Craigenputtoch when he and his Jeanie went

there, and how bravely and quietly she faced and overcame the poverty, the ugliness, the almost squalor, which was their condition for a long time. " Poverty and mean obstruction continued," he says, " to preside over it, but were transformed by human valor of various sorts into a kind of victory and royalty. Something of high and great dwelt in it, though nothing could be smaller and lower than many of the details. How blessed might poor mortals be in the straitest circumstances, if only their wisdom and fidelity to Heaven and to one another were *adequately* great ! It looks to me now like a kind of humble russet-coated *epic*, that seven years' settlement at Craigenputtoch, very poor in this world's goods, but not without an intrinsic dignity greater and more important than then appeared ; thanks very mainly to her, and her faculties and magnanimities, without whom it had not been possible."

And now, let us hear the words in which George Eliot begins to preach the " russet-coated epic " of every-day life and of commonplace people.

" The Rev. Amos Barton, whose sad fortunes I have undertaken to relate, was, you perceive, in no respect an ideal or exceptional character; and perhaps I am doing a bold thing to bespeak your sympathy on behalf of a man who was so very far from remarkable, — a man whose virtues were not heroic, and who had no undetected crime within his breast ; who had not the slightest mystery hanging about him, but was palpably and unmistakably commonplace; who was not even in love, but had had that complaint favourably many years ago. ' An utterly uninteresting character ! ' I think I hear a lady reader exclaim — Mrs. Farthingale, for example, who prefers the ideal in fiction; to whom tragedy means ermine tippets, adultery, and murder ; and comedy, the adventures of some personage who is quite a ' character.'

" But, my dear madam, it is so very large a majority of your fellow-countrymen that are of this insignificant stamp. At least eighty out of a hundred of your adult male fellow-Britons returned in the last census are neither extraordinarily silly, nor extraordinarily wicked, nor extraordinarily wise; their eyes are neither deep and liquid with sentiment, nor sparkling with sup-

pressed witticisms; they have probably had no hair-breapth
escapes or thrilling adventures; their brains are certainly not
pregnant with genius, and their passions have not manifested
themselves at all after the fashion of a volcano. They are
simply men of complexions more or less muddy, whose conversation is more or less bald and disjointed. Yet these commonplace people — many of them — bear a conscience, and
have felt the sublime prompting to do the painful right; they
have their unspoken sorrows and their sacred joys; their hearts
have perhaps gone out towards their first-born, and they have
mourned over the irreclaimable dead. Nay, is there not a
pathos in their very insignificance, — in our comparison of
their dim and narrow existence with the glorious possibilities
of that human nature which they share?

"Depend upon it, you would gain unspeakably if you would
learn with me to see some of the poetry and the pathos, the
tragedy and the comedy, lying in the experience of a human
soul that looks out through dull gray eyes, and that speaks in
a voice of quite ordinary tone. In that case, I should have no
fear of your not caring to know what farther befell the Rev.
Amos Barton, or of your thinking the homely details I have to
tell at all beneath your attention. As it is, you can, if you please,
decline to pursue my story farther; and you will easily find reading more to your taste, since I learn from the newspapers that
many remarkable novels, full of striking situations, thrilling
incidents, and eloquent writing, have appeared only within the
last season."

Passing on to *Adam Bede*, *The Mill on the Floss*, and
the rest of George Eliot's works in historic order, let us see
with what delicious fun, what play of wit, what ever-abiding
and depth-illuminating humor, what creative genius, what
manifold forms of living flesh and blood, George Eliot
preached the possibility of such moral greatness on the
part of every most commonplace man and woman as completely reduces to a level the apparent inequality in the
matter of genius, and so illustrated the universal "russet-
coated epic."

HENRY JAMES
1843 –

SAINTE-BEUVE [1]

[*Published in " The North American Review," 1880. Revised by the Author for the present publication*]

WHEN, in publishing some years since the small collection of letters which Sainte-Beuve had addressed
to his gracious and appreciative friend the Princess Mathilde,
his last secretary, M. Troubat, announced his intention of
getting together and bringing to the light the general correspondence of the great critic, the thing seemed a capital
piece of literary good news.   After a considerable interval
the editor has redeemed his promise, and we have two
substantial volumes of Sainte-Beuve's letters.   The result
may be said, on the whole, to be very interesting — our pro-
spect of high entertainment was not illusory.   The letters
extend from the year 1822 to the autumn of 1869, the
moment of the writer's death, and are naturally most abundant during the closing years of his career — the second
volume occupying entirely the period from 1865.   The
editor mentions that during the passage of the second
volume through the press a number of letters of whose
existence he had not been aware came into his hands.
These he has reserved for a supplementary volume ; the
reader will have to interpolate them at their proper dates.
I do not longer await the appearance of this volume — it
was promised several months ago — in order to speak of its
predecessors, for these are complete in themselves, and are

[1] Correspondance de C. A. Sainte-Beuve (1822–69).   Paris,
Calmann Lévy, 1878.

so rich in interesting matter that I shall be able to do them but scanty justice.

Sainte-Beuve's letters do nothing but complete a picture which was already a very vivid one. He had already painted his own portrait, painted it in a myriad fine, unerring, cumulative touches; no writer was ever more personal, more certain, in the long run, to infuse into his judgments of people and things those elements out of which an image of himself might be constructed. The whole of the man was in the special work — he was *all* a writer, a critic, an appreciator. He was literary in every pulsation of his being, and he expressed himself totally in his literary life. No character and no career were ever more homogeneous. He had no disturbing, perverting tastes; he suffered no retarding, embarrassing accidents. He lost no time, and he never wasted any. He was not even married; his literary consciousness was never complicated with the sense of an unliterary condition. His mind was never diverted or distracted from its natural exercise — that of looking in literature for illustrations of life, and of looking in life for aids to literature. Therefore it is, as I say, that his work offers a singularly complete image of his character, his tastes, his temper, his idiosyncrasies. It was from himself always that he spoke — from his own personal and intimate point of view. He wrote himself down in his published pages, and what was left for his letters was simply to fill in the details, to supply a few missing touches, a few inflections and shades. As a matter of course he was not an elaborate letter-writer. He had always his pen in his hand, but it had little time for long excursions. His career was an intensely laborious one — his time, attention and interest, his imagination and sympathies were unceasingly mortgaged. The volumes before us contain almost no general letters, pages purely sociable and human. The human and sociable touch is frequent, is perpetual; to use his own inveterate expression, he "slips it in" wherever there is an opening. But his occasions are mostly those of rapid notes dictated by some professional or technical pretext. There is very little overflow of his personal situation, of his movements and adventures, of the incidents of his life. Sainte-Beuve's adventures, indeed, were not numerous, and the incidents in his life were all intellectual, moral, professional incidents — the publication of his works, the changes, the phases, the development of his opinions. He never traveled ; he had no changes of place, of scenery, of society, to chronicle. He once went to Liège, in Flanders, to deliver a course of lectures, and he spent a year at Lausanne for the same purpose ; but, apart from this, his life was spent uninterruptedly in Paris.

Of course, when one makes the remark that a man's work is in a peculiar degree the record of a mind, the history of a series of convictions and feelings, the reflection of a group of idiosyncrasies, one does not of necessity by that fact praise it to the skies. Everything depends on what the mind may have been. It so happened that Sainte-Beuve's was extraordinary, was so rich and fine and flexible, that this personal accent, which sounds everywhere in his writings, acquired a superior value and an exquisite rarity. He had indeed a remarkable combination of qualities, and there is something wondrous in his way of reconciling certain faculties which are usually held to be in the nature of things opposed to each other. He had, to begin with, two passions, which are commonly assumed to exclude each other — the passion for scholarship and the passion for life. He was essentially a creature of books, a *literatus ;* and yet to his intensely bookish and acquisitive mind nothing human, nothing social or mundane was alien. The simplest way to express his particular felicity is to say that, putting aside the poets and novelists, the purely imaginative and inventive authors, he is the student who has brought into the study the largest element of reflected life. No scholar was ever so much of an observer, of a moralist, a psychologist ; and no such regular and beguiled *abonné* to the general spectacle was ever so much of a scholar. He valued life and literature equally for the light they threw upon each other; to his mind one implied the other; he was unable to conceive of them apart. He made use in literature, in an extraordinary manner, of the qualities that are peculiarly social. Some one said of him that he had the organization of a nervous woman and the powers of acquisition of a Benedictine. Sainte-Beuve had nerves assuredly; there is something feminine in his tact, his penetration, his subtlety and pliability, his rapidity of transition, his magical divinations, his sympathies and antipathies, his marvelous art of insinuation, of expressing himself by fine touches and of adding touch to touch. But all this side of the feminine genius was re-enforced by faculties of quite another order — faculties of the masculine stamp; the completeness, the solid sense, the constant reason, the moderation, the copious knowledge, the passion for exactitude and for general considerations. In attempting to appreciate him it is impossible to keep these things apart; they melt into each other like the elements of the atmosphere; there is scarcely a stroke of his pen that does not contain a little of each of them. He had ended by becoming master of a style of which the polished complexity was a complete expression of his nature — a style which always reminds one of some precious stone that has been filed into a hundred facets by the skill of a consummate lapidary. The facets are always all there; the stone revolves and exhibits them in the course of a single paragraph. When I speak of attempting to appreciate him I know it is not an easy matter, and I have no intention of undertaking a task for which his own resources would have been no more than sufficient. He might have drawn himself, intendingly, from head to foot, but no other artist holds in his hand the fine-tipped, flexible brushes with which such a likeness should be pointed and emphasized.

Various attempts, nevertheless, have been made to appraise him, as was eminently natural and inevitable. He spent his life in analyzing and pondering other people, and

it was a matter of course that he also should be put into
the scales. But, as a general thing, on these occasions they
were not held with a very even hand; as too often happens
in France, the result was disfigured by party passion. This
is especially the case with the judgments of hostility, of
which the number, as may well be imagined, is not small.
Sainte-Beuve had wounded too many susceptibilities and
vanities — had taken upon himself functions too thankless
and invidious — to find the critic's couch a bed of roses.
And he not only offended individuals, he offended societies
and "sets," who, as a general thing, never forgave him, and
who took their revenge according to their lights and their
means. The very pivot of his intellectual existence was what
he would have called the liberty of appreciation; it was upon
this he took his stand — it was in the exercise of this privilege
that his career unfolded itself. Of course he did not claim
a monopoly of the privilege, and he would never have
denied that the world was at liberty to appreciate Sainte-
Beuve. The greater wisdom, to my mind, was on his side;
his great qualities — his intense interest in the truth of any
matter, his desire to arrive at the most just and comprehensive perception of it, his delight in the labor involved
in such attempts, and his exquisite skill in presenting the
results of such labor — these things have never been im-
pugned. Into the innumerable hostilities and jealousies
of which he was the object — the resentments more or
less just, the reproaches more or less valid, the calum-
nies more or less impudent — no stranger, fortunately,
need pretend to penetrate. These are matters of detail,
and here the details are altogether too numerous. Sainte-
Beuve's greatest admirers are not obliged to accept him
unconditionally. Like every one else he had the defects of his qualities. He had a very large dose of what
the French call "malice" — an element which was the
counterpart of his subtlety, his feminine fineness of perception. This subtlety served him not only as a magical
clew to valuable results, but it led him sometimes into small

deviations that were like the lapses, slightly unholy, of the tempted. It led him to analyze motives with a minuteness which was often fatal to their apparent purity; it led him to slip in — to *glisser*, as he always says — the grain of corrosive censure with the little parcel of amenities. For feats of this kind his art was instinctive; he strikes the reader as more than feminine — as positively feline. It is beyond question that he has at times the feline scratch. The truth is, that his instrument itself — his art of expression — was almost a premium upon the abuse of innuendo. The knowledge that he could leave the impression without having said the thing must frequently have been an intellectual temptation. Besides, it may be said that his scratch was really, on the whole, defensive, or, at the worst, retributive; it was, to my belief, never wanton or aggressive. We each have our defensive weapon, and I am unable to see why Sainte-Beuve's was not a legitimate one. He had the feline agility and pliancy; nothing was more natural than that he should have had the feline claw. But he apprehended the personality, the moral physiognomy of the people to whom he turned his attention — Victor Cousin, for instance, Lamartine, Villemain, Balzac, Victor Hugo, Chateaubriand — with an extraordinary clearness and sharpness; he took intellectual possession of it and never relaxed his grasp. The image was always there, with all its features, for familiar reference; it illuminated and colored every allusion he had occasion to make to the original. " What will you have? " he would have said; " I am so intensely impressible, and my impressions are so vivid, so permanent. One can go but by one's impressions; those are mine. Heaven knows how the plate has been polished to take them! " He was very apt to remember people's faults in considering their merits. He says in one of his letters that he is more sensitive to certain great faults than to certain great merits. And then, with his passion for detail, for exactitude and completeness, for facts and examples, he thought nothing unimportant. To be vague was the last thing possible to him, and the deformities or misdemeanors of people he had studied remained in his eyes as definite as the numbers of a " sum " in addition or subtraction.

His great justification, however, it seems to me, is, that the cause he upheld was the most important, for it was simply the cause of liberty, in which we are all so much interested. This, in essence, is what I mean by saying that certain of those habits of mind which made many people dislike him were defensive weapons. It was doubtless not always a question of defending his own character, but it was almost always a question of defending his position as a free observer and appreciator. This is the fine thing about him, and the only thing with which, as strangers, happily detached from that imbroglio of rival interests and ambitions in which his lot was cast, we need greatly concern ourselves. In a society that swarmed with camps and coteries, with partisans and advocates, he was more than any one else the independent individual, pinning his faith to no emblazoned standard and selling his vote to no exclusive group. The literary atmosphere in France has always been full of watchwords and catchwords, the emblems and tokens of irreconcilable factions and of what may be called vested literary interests. His instinct, from the beginning of his career, was to mistrust any way of looking at things which should connect the observer with a party pledged to take the point of view most likely to minister to its prosperity. He cared nothing for the prosperity of parties ; he cared only for the ascertainment of the reality and for hitting the nail on the head. He only cared to look freely — to look all round. The part he desired to play was that of the vividly intelligent, brightly enlightened mind, acting in the interest of literature, knowledge, taste, and spending itself on everything human and historic. He was frankly and explicitly a critic ; he attributed the highest importance to the critical function, and he understood it in so large a way that it gives us a lift to agree with him. The critic, in his conception, was not the narrow lawgiver or the rigid censor that he is often assumed to be ; he was the student, the inquirer, the interpreter, the taker of notes, the active, restless commentator, whose constant aim was to arrive at justness of characterization. Sainte-Beuve's own faculty of characterization was of the rarest and most remarkable ; he held it himself in the highest esteem ; his impression was the thing in the world he most valued. There is something admirable in his gravity, consistency and dignity on this point. I know nothing more finely characteristic of him than a phrase which occurs in one of the volumes before me in the course of his correspondence with Madame Christine de Fontanes on the subject of the biographical notice he had undertaken to supply for a new edition of her father's works. The whole correspondence is most interesting and shows him at his best — full of urbanity and tact, but full also of firmness and reason, knowing exactly what he wishes and means and adhering to it absolutely. M. de Fontanes, whose reputation has sensibly faded now, was a critic and poet of eminence under the First Empire and the Restoration ; his daughter was editing a " definitive " collection of his writings, and Sainte-Beuve had sent her his own article to read before insertion. The tone of the article was respectful and sympathetic (it is included at present among his " Portraits Littéraires "), but to certain points in his judgment of her father the Comtesse de Fontanes had taken exception. He offered to withdraw the article altogether, but he refused to alter a word. " Upon anything else in the world I would yield," he says ; "*pas sur les choses de la plume quand une fois je crois avoir* DIT " (not on things of the pen when once I think I have hit it) " . . . That 's my weakness," he adds ; " can you forgive me?" For my own part, I can forgive him easily ; I should have found it hard to forgive him if he had acted otherwise. All Sainte-Beuve is in those few words — all his famous " method," which has been so much talked about, and, one may almost say, all his philosophy. His method was to " hit it " — to " say it," as he says — to express it, to put his

fingers on the point; his philosophy was to accept and make
the best of truths so discriminated. He goes on to give
Madame Christine de Fontanes several examples of what he
means. "I wrote a biographical notice of M. Ampère the
elder, from private documents supplied by the son, my
friend. I didn't read him the notice. He only saw it
printed, and he was content, save with a word that I had
slipped in upon something that I believed to be a weakness
of character in M. Ampère with regard to great people.
He said to me, 'I was pleased with it all, except that word,
which I would have begged you to leave out if I had seen
it beforehand.' It was just for that that I had not sub-
mitted my article to him. *If I had not been free to write
that word I would not have written the notice. . . . .* When
I wrote upon Madame de Staël," he goes on, " Madame
de Broglie [her daughter] sent for me, and, with all that
authority of grace and virtue which was hers, prescribed to
me certain limits; she desired me to communicate my
article in advance; I was unwilling to do so. When she
came to read it she was pleased, except with regard to a
page which nothing in the world would have induced me to
withdraw, for it consisted of my reserves and my insinuations
(with regard to the 'romantic' life at Coppet)." Nothing
could be more characteristic and delightful than this frank
allusion to his insinuations. To "insinuate" was a part of
his manner, and was to his sense a perfectly legitimate way
of dealing with a subject. Granting certain other of the
conditions, he was assuredly right. And indeed there is
nothing intrinsically unlawful in an insinuation; everything
depends on the rest of the tone, and also on the thing in-
sinuated. "From all this," he pursues, after various other
remarks upon the points at issue with Madame de Fontanes, "I conclude that it is impossible that the notice
should go into the edition. On your side is your duty; on
mine is a feeling which I don't know how to name, *mais
qui est ma nature même.*" It was in fact Sainte-Beuve's
" very nature " to trust his perception and to abide by what

he considered his last analysis of a matter. He knew with
what quality of intelligence he had aimed at point — he
knew the light, the taste, the zeal, the experience he had
brought to bear upon it. A certain side of his feeling
about criticism is strikingly expressed in one of the later
letters (in date) of this collection. The page is so
excellent, so full of a sense of the realities of life as distinguished from the shadows, that I quote the greater part
of it. It contains an allusion, by the way, which helps to
understand the little discussion of which I have just partly
given an account. He is writing to M. Ernest Bersot:

"Is it not necessary," he asks, " to break with that false
conventionality, that system of cant, which declares that we
shall judge a writer not only by his intentions, but by
his pretensions? It is time that this should come to an
end. I will take the critics as instances. What! am I
to see nothing of M. de Fontanes but the great master,
polished, noble, elegant, trimmed with fur, religious — not
the quick, impetuous, abrupt, sensual man that he was?
What! La Harpe shall be but a man of taste, eloquent in
his academic chair, and I shall not see him of whom Voltaire used to say, ' *Le petit se fâche!* ' And for the present,
come now — I talk to you without circumlocution — I have
no animosity at heart, and I appreciate those who have
been, in whatever degree, my masters; but here are five-
and-thirty years, and more, that I live before Villemain, the
great talent, the fine mind, so draped and decorated with
generous, liberal, philanthropic, Christian, civilizing sentiments, etc., and in fact the most sordid soul — *le plus
méchant singe qui existe*. What must one do, in definitive
— how must one conclude with respect to him? Must one
go on praising his noble, lofty sentiments, as is done invariably all round him? And, as this is the reverse of the
truth, must one be a dupe and continue to dupe others?
Are men of letters, historians and moralistic preachers nothing more than comedians, whom one has no right to take
outside of the *rôle* that they have arranged for themselves?

Must one see them only on the stage and look at them only while they are there? Or else is it permitted, when the subject is known, to come boldly, though at the same time discreetly, and slip in the scalpel and show the weak point of the breastplate — show the *seam*, as it were, between the talent and the soul; to praise the one, but to mark also the defect of the other, perceptible even in the talent itself and in the effect that it produces in the long run? Will literature lose by this? It is possible; but moral science will gain. That's where we are going, fatally. *There is no longer such a thing as an isolated question of taste.* When I know the man, then only can I explain to myself the talker, and especially that species of talker who is the most artful of all — the one who prides himself on having nothing of the mere talker left. And the great men (you will say), and the respect one owes them, and the reputation that must be so dearly paid for? Very true; every man who competes for praise and celebrity is devoted to every infamy by that very fact. It is the law. Molière is insulted by Bossuet, Goethe by the first rowdy that comes along; only yesterday Renan and Littré by Dupanloup — and insulted in his character, in his morality. What is to be done about it? It isn't by cuddling one's self that one can escape from it. One must *be* something or some one; and in that case one resists — one has one's army — one counts in spite of one's detractors. As soon as you penetrate a little under the veil of society, as in nature, you see nothing but wars, struggles, destructions and recompositions. This Lucretian view of criticism isn't a cheerful one; but, once we attain to it, it seems preferable, even with its high sadness, to the worship of idols."

If it be needful to admit that the harsher side of Sainte-Beuve's temperament comes out in such a passage as I have just quoted, it may be added that these volumes are by no means without testimony to the extreme acuteness with which he could feel irritation and the inimitable neatness and lucidity with which he could express it. The letter to

M. Villemain, of the date of September, 1839, and that to
Victor Cousin, of July, 1843, are highly remarkable in this
respect, and remarkable, too, for the manner in which they
appeal to the sympathy of a reader who is totally unac-
quainted with the merits of the quarrel. The delicate acer-
bity of the tone, the absence of passion, of violence, of
confusion, produce an impression of beauty, and our intellectual relish of the perfection with which he says what he
desires suffices by itself to place us on his side. There are
various examples of his skill in that process known to the
French as telling a person *son fait.* " I only ask of you
one thing," he writes to Madame Louise Colet, who had
pestered him to publish a critical appreciation of her literary productions, " to admire you in silence, without being
obliged to point out to the public just where I cease to admire you." In the letters to the Princess Mathilde there
occurs a very entertaining episode, related by Sainte-Beuve
to his sympathetic correspondent. A lady had sent him
her manuscript commonplace-book to read, with the request
that he would give an opinion upon the literary value of
its contents. Turning it over, Sainte-Beuve encountered a
passage relating to himself and not present to the lady's
mind when she sent him the volume — a passage of a highly
calumnious character, attributing to him the most unattract-
ive qualities and accusing him of gross immorality. He
copies out for the Princess the letter with which he has
returned the manuscript of his imprudent friend and in
which, after administering a rebuke of the most ingeniously
urbane character, he concludes by begging her " to receive
the assurance of an esteem which he shall never again have
occasion to express." The whole letter should be read.
Even in perfectly friendly letters his irrepressible " malice "
crops out — it has here and there even a slightly diaboli-
cal turn. A most interesting letter to Charles Baudelaire,
of the year 1858, is full of this quality, especially in the
closing lines : " . . . It is n't a question of compliments.
I am much more disposed to scold [Baudelaire had just

sent him " Les Fleurs du Mal "], and if I were walking with you on the edge of the sea, along a cliff, without pretending to play the Mentor, I would try and trip you up, my dear friend, and throw you suddenly into the water, so that, as you know how to swim, you should henceforth take your course out there in the sunshine and the tide." The most interesting parts of the contents of these volumes, however, I have found to be the graver and more closely personal ones. In the history of such a mind every autobiographical touch has a high interest. There are a number of autobiographical touches bearing on his material life and illustrating his extreme frugality and the modesty — the more than modesty — of his literary income. " From 1830 to 1840," he says, " I lived in a student's room (in the Cour du Commerce) on a fourth floor, and at the rate of *twenty-three francs* a month, my breakfasts included." In 1840 he was appointed titular librarian at the Bibliothèque Mazarine, and then " I found myself rich, or at my ease, for the first time in my life. I began to study again, I learned Greek ; my work contains indications of this increase of leisure and of my being able to do it as I chose. Then came the Academy, towards 1843 ; I became a member of the committee of the Dictionary, and really I had hard work to spend my income. To do so, I had to buy rare books, for which the taste came to me little by little . . . I have *never* had a debt in my life . . . they attack me there on my strong side. I have my weaknesses, I have told you so : they are those which gave to King Solomon the disgust of everything and the satiety of life. I may have regretted feeling sometimes that they quenched my ardor — but they never perverted my heart."

Of autobiographical touches of the other sort — those that bear upon his character and his opinions — there are a considerable number — a number which, however, would be a good deal larger if the letters written before the year 1860 had been more carefully preserved by his correspondents. I have marked a great many of these passages, but I must content myself with a few extracts. There was an element of philosophic stoicism in Sainte-Beuve, which is indicated in his earliest letters ; the note is struck at intervals throughout the correspondence. "Take care of yourself," he says to one of his friends, in a letter written at the age of twenty-four ; " pass the least time possible in regrets ; resign yourself to having had no youth, no past, no future ; I don't tell you not to suffer from it, not to die of it even, at the end ; but I tell you not to lose your temper over it, nor to let it make you stand still and stamp." This is quite the same man who found himself impelled to write in 1864 : "The more I go on the more indifferent I become ; only, judgments take form within me, and, once established, after being shaken and tested two or three times, they never leave me. I believe, moreover, that I have no animosity. Observe that I have no time for that ; animosities themselves need to be cultivated. Obliged as I am to change so often the direction of my mind and my interest, to fasten and make them sink into writings and authors so different, trying to find in each of these the greatest possible amount of truth, I grow case-hardened to pricks and irritations, and after a little while I don't even know what they are meant for. But, I repeat to you — and it is the misfortune and also a little the honor of the critical spirit — my judgments abide with me." That is the Sainte-Beuve of my predilection — I may almost say of my faith — the Sainte-Beuve whose voice was incapable of the note of vulgarity, whose vision was always touched with light. I see no element of narrowness or obstinacy in the declaration I have just quoted ; I only see the perceptive mind, the ripe intelligence. There is an expression of this ripe intelligence, this faculty of perception resting upon a sense of experience, in a letter of 1863 to a female friend. " We are getting ready for a great battle, in which philosophic minds will be known by true marks. I am one of them, after all. I went in for a little Christian mythology in my day, but that has evaporated. It was like the swan of Leda, a means of get-

ting at the fair and wooing them in a more tender fashion.
Youth has time and makes use of everything. Now I am
old and I have chased away all the clouds. I mortify myself less, and I see *plus juste*. It is a pity that all this can
not last, and that the moment when one is most master of
one's self and one's thoughts should be that at which they
are nearest faltering and finishing." I don't know at what
period Sainte-Beuve disentangled himself from the "Christian mythology," but already in 1845 he makes a striking
allusion to what he deems to be the collapse of his power
to feel at the seat of feeling. "Your letter touched me,
honored me ; but I always find myself without words before
your praise, feeling so little worthy of it, passed as I have
into the state of a pure critical intelligence, and assisting as
I do with a melancholy eye at the death of my heart. I
judge myself, and I rest calm, cold, indifferent. I am dead,
and I see myself dead — but without emotion or confusion.
Whence comes this strange state? Alas ! there are causes
old and deep. Here I am talking to you suddenly as to a
confessor; but I know you are so friendly, so *charitable* —
and it is this, this last point, which is everything, and which
the world calls the heart, that is dead in me. The intellect
shines over the graveyard like a dead moon." This is
strongly stated ; apparently Sainte-Beuve is speaking of a
certain special function of the heart which, after forty, is
supposed to have seen its best days. Of a certain intellectual cordiality, the power of tender, of sympathetic understanding, he gave full proof during the remainder of his
long career. If his heart was dead its ghost at least very
restlessly walked. Moreover, the heart can hardly be said
to die. In some cases it has never existed, and in these it
is not likely to spring into being. But when it has once
existed the imagination, in spite of what surgeons call the
removal, does some of the work. The house may be closed,
but the garden still goes on.

It was to be expected that the letters of a great critic
should contain a great deal of good criticism, and in this

respect these volumes will not be found disappointing. They contain a great variety of fragmentary judgments and of characteristic revelations and sidelights. With his great breadth of view, his general intelligence and his love of seeing "juste," Sainte-Beuve was nevertheless a man of strong predispositions, of vigorous natural preferences. He never repudiated the charge of having strong "bents" of taste. This indeed would have been most absurd ; for one's taste is an effect, more than a cause, of one's preferences ; it is indeed the result of a series of particular tastes. With Sainte-Beuve, as with every one else, it grew more and more flexible with time ; it adapted itself and opened new windows and doors. He achieved in his last years feats that may fairly be called extraordinary in the way of doing justice to writers and works of an intensely "modern" stamp — to Baudelaire and Flaubert, to Feydeau and the brothers Goncourt. There is even in the second of these volumes a letter, on the whole appreciative, to the young writer whose vigorous brain, in later years, was to give birth to the monstrous "Assommoir." But originally Sainte-Beuve's was not a mind that appeared likely, even at a late stage of its evolution, to offer hospitality to M. Émile Zola. He was always a man of his time ; he played his part in the romantic movement ; Joseph Delorme and the novel of "Volupté" are creations eminently characteristic of that fermentation of opinion, that newer, younger genius which produced the great modern works of French literature. Sainte-Beuve, in other words, was essentially of the generation of Lamartine and Victor Hugo, of Balzac and George Sand. But he was, if not more weighted, more anchored than some of his companions ; he was incapable of moving in a mass ; he never was a violent radical. He had a high tenderness for tradition, for the old models, for classic ideas. In 1845 he was open to the charge of "reactionary" taste ; it must be remembered that the critics and commentators cannot, in the nature of things, afford to run the risks and make the bold experiments of the poets and producers. "I have *never* liked

the modern drama as Hugo and Dumas have made it, and
I have never recognized in it, the least in the world, the
ideal that I conceive in this respect. . . . I should be
unable to express to you what I feel with regard to the
enormities which have partly defeated our hopes, but there
are points on which I hold my ground, and I flatter myself
that I have never deserted my early convictions. It is all the
same to me that Madame de Girardin should come and tell
me that I am going in for reaction pure and simple, and I
don't give myself the trouble even of heeding it ; but, if you
say it, I permit myself to answer *no*, and to tell you that
you are completely mistaken, which is the result, perhaps,
of your not attaching the same importance as I to purely literary points — points on which I have remained very much
the same." Sainte-Beuve here defends himself against the
charge of having dropped out of the line ; he intimates that
it is he who has adhered to the pure " romantic " tradition,
and that the eccentric movement refers itself to the two
writers he mentions. They were not the only ones of whom
he failed to approve ; it is unfortunately a substantial fact
that he never rendered half justice to Balzac, and that to
George Sand he rendered but half at the most. There is
an interesting passage bearing upon this in a letter of 1866,
written to a critic who had published an appreciative notice
of Sainte-Beuve's long and delightful article upon Gavarni.
" You have indeed put your finger upon the two delicate
points. At bottom, I know, Musset had *passion* and Théo
[Théophile Gautier] did n't have it ; and one warms people
up only by having a flame one's self. And then Balzac, I
know too, with defects that I feel too much (being of quite
another family), had *power*, and Gavarni only had an infinitude of wit, elegance and observation. But Gavarni
had taste and *le trait juste* — things I greatly value. That
being said, I have my private idea, not as an advocate, but
as a critic of conviction, which is, namely, that in our day
there is too much water carried to the river, too much admiration *quand même*, too little real judging. Once the

word genius is pronounced, everything is accepted and pro-
claimed. Musset's worst verses are quoted as proverbs;
they are admired on trust. So for the great novelist. It
would seem that there had been no observer but he; that
Eugène Sue, Frédéric Soulié — all those big fellows — have
ceased to exist, have been absorbed by him. But it is,
above all, when it is a question of the great men of the
past, that I am unable to accept the high figure at which
they put his genius. This is the bottom of my thought,
and it doubtless judges me myself. . . ." And it is here
that he goes on to add the remark I have quoted, to the
effect that he is more sensitive to certain great defects than
to a certain order of qualities. He had, in his latter years,
an occasional caprice or slight perversity of judgment; he
took two or three very incongruous literary fancies. Such
was the high relish which, for a certain period, he professed for the few first productions of M. Ernest Feydeau, and such the serious attention that he appears to have
bestowed upon the literary activity of Charles Baudelaire.
Both of these writers had their merits, but one would have
said that Sainte-Beuve, who discriminated so closely, would
not have found his account in them. He writes to M. Feydeau, in 1860, on the occasion of this gentleman having
put the finishing touches to a novel on a peculiarly repulsive theme, which was a very light literary matter into the
bargain: "It will be very nice of you to tell me when
'Sylvie' will be worthy in your eyes to make her début in
my faubourg; I shall be all eyes, all ears, to receive her."

But he paid so many tributes of a different kind that it is
out of place to do more than touch upon that one. Here
is quite another note. "If you knew English," he writes to
a clerical friend who had sent him some poetic attempts,
"you would have a treasure-house upon which you could
draw. They have a poetic literature very superior to ours
— and, above all, more healthy, more full. Wordsworth
is not translated; one does n't translate those things; one
goes and drinks them at the fount. Let me enjoin upon

you to learn English. . . . In a year or two you would be
master of it, and you would have a private poetic treasure
for your own use. Be a poet — I was only a little rivulet
from those beautiful poetic lakes, with all their gentleness
and melancholy." What I have found most interesting in
these pages is the mark of the expert, as I may call it —
the definiteness and clearness, the ripe sagacity, of the
writer's critical sense. When it is a case of giving advice,
of praising or of blaming, of replying to a question or an
appeal, there is something delightful in our impression of
the perfect competence. He always knows so well the
weak point, always touches in passing upon the remedy.
"The day on which you shall be willing to sacrifice a little
to that French taste which you know so well, to our need of
a frame and a border, you will have the value of all your
essential qualities." He writes that to his distinguished
fellow critic M. Schérer, whose culture he deemed a little
too Germanic; and it would have been impossible to give
him in a single sentence better practical advice. There is
an admirable letter to M. Taine, on the appearance of the
latter's rather infelicitous attempt at satire — the volume of
impressions of M. Graindorge. This letter should be read
by every one who has read the book — it is impossible to
express more felicitously the feeling of discomfort produced
by seeing a superior man make a great mistake. I have
spoken of Sainte-Beuve's letter to Émile Zola; it is full of
exquisite good sense (the writer's great quality), and the
closing lines are worth quoting as an illustration of the
definite and practical character of the critical reflections
that he offered his correspondents. The allusion is to M.
Zola's first novel, "Thérèse Raquin." "You have done a
bold act; you have, in your work, braved both the public
and the critics. Don't be surprised at certain indignations —
the battle has begun; your name has been sounded. Such
struggles terminate, when an author of talent is so minded,
by another work equally bold, but a little less on the stretch,
in which the public and the critics fancy they see a con-

cession to their own sense ; and the affair is wound up by
one of those treaties of peace which consecrate one more
reputation." It must be added that this was not the advice
that M. Émile Zola took. He has never, that I know of,
signed a treaty of peace ; and, though his reputation is great,
it can hardly be said to have been " consecrated." But
I must make no more quotations ; I must do no more than
recommend these two volumes to all those readers for whom
our author may have been at any time a valued companion.
They will find a complete reflection of the man and the
writer — the materials for a living image. They will find
too a large confirmation of their confidence. Sainte-Beuve's
was a mind of a thousand sides, and it is possible sometimes
to meet it at a disconcerting or displeasing angle. But. as
regards the whole value I should never for an instant hesi-
tate. If it is a question of taking the critic or leaving him
— of being on his " side " or not — I take him, definitively,
and on the added evidence of these letters, as the very
genius of observation, discretion and taste.